# MISTY

## DIGGING DEEP IN VOLLEYBALL AND LIFE

### MISTY MAY-TREANOR

#### WITH JILL LIEBER STEEG

Scribner

New York   London   Toronto   Sydney

SCRIBNER

A Division of Simon & Schuster, Inc.
1230 Avenue of the Americas
New York, NY 10020

First Scribner hardcover edition June 2010

SCRIBNER and design are registered trademarks of The Gale Group, Inc.,
used under license by Simon & Schuster, Inc., the publisher of this work.

For information about special discounts for bulk purchases,
please contact Simon & Schuster Special Sales at 1-866-506-1949
or business@simonandschuster.com.

The Simon & Schuster Speakers Bureau can bring authors to your live event.
For more information or to book an event contact the Simon & Schuster Speakers
Bureau at 1-866-248-3049 or visit our website at www.simonspeakers.com.

Designed by Carla Jayne Jones

Manufactured in the United States of America

1   3   5   7   9   10   8   6   4   2

Library of Congress Cataloging-in-Publication Data

May-Treanor, Misty.
Misty : digging deep in volleyball and life / Misty May-Treanor with Jill Lieber Steeg.
p. cm.
1. Volleyball players—United States—Biography. 2. Volleyball for
women—United States. I. Steeg, Jill Lieber. II. Title.
V1015.26.M39 2010
796.325092—dc22 2009052452

ISBN 978-1-4391-4854-9
ISBN 978-1-4391-5577-6 (ebook)

All insert photos are courtesy of the author unless marked otherwise.

To Mom, whom I miss dearly every day. I would give back both of my Olympic gold medals just to be able to tell you I love you one more time.
*Misty May-Treanor*

To Jim, the love of my life. You are my heart and soul, my rock, my shoulder, my dream.
*Jill Lieber Steeg*

# CONTENTS

# Contents

# Dreams Do Come True

A ll my life, I've dreamed in gold.

When I was a tyke, scampering through the sand, a jump serve away from my parents' pizza stand at Muscle Beach in Santa Monica, California.

When I was eight years old, playing in my first beach volleyball tournament, at Will Rogers State Beach in Pacific Palisades, with Dad as my partner.

When I was the outside hitter for Newport Harbor High School, and we won two California Interscholastic Federation (CIF) state championships.

When I was the setter for Long Beach State, and we captured the 1998 Division I NCAA Women's Volleyball Championship.

When I was twenty-seven and considered the best defensive beach volleyball player in the world, and my partner Kerri Walsh and I steamrolled through seven straight matches without losing a single game to win the 2004 Olympic gold medal in Athens, Greece.

And yes, even when I was strutting my stuff in fancy costumes, theatrical makeup, and ultra-high heels as a contestant on ABC's *Dancing with the Stars*.

Yet, when I served the ball and Kerri blasted it by China's Tian Jia and Wang Jie to give us our second Olympic gold medal, on August 21, 2008, in Beijing, China, the crowning moment wasn't bathed in gold.

Instead, it was an absolute blur of colors, from the pastel pink, green, and blue plastic ponchos draped over the twelve-thousand-plus fans packed into Chaoyang Park for the monsoon-drenched gold medal match, to the fluorescent orange T-shirts and bright yellow baseball caps and beach umbrellas designating the two dozen or so family members and friends, who'd lovingly dubbed themselves "Misty's Misfits" as they traipsed across the globe over the years cheering me on. And, of course, the red, white, and blue of hundreds of American flags.

As the ball hit the beach for match point, my knees buckled from all the emotion, and I slid down onto my butt in my sopping wet, white bikini. I clenched my fists and let out a scream. "WOOOOO!" Kerri grabbed me from behind, and we rolled around on the sand, squeezing each other so tightly I'm surprised we didn't pass out due to a severe lack of oxygen. Kerri pulled me to my feet, and then I jumped onto her, wrapping my legs around her waist. I thrust my arms into the air and let out another scream. "We did it! Can you believe it? We did it!" I yelled.

We'd shared a once-in-a-lifetime experience over the past eight years, and we'd be forever joined. Sisters. Friends. Teammates. Business partners. Trailblazers. We composed ourselves, ran to the other side of the court, and shook hands with the Chinese team, and then we shook hands with the referees and volunteers.

After those few minutes of decorum, it was a full-on Beijing Olympics gold medal celebration. I began clapping to "Celebration," by Kool & the Gang, which was blaring over the loudspeakers, and I turned to scope out the crowd, hoping to find my loved ones. Instantly, everything shifted into super slow motion. I saw a sea of colors but couldn't make out people's faces. It was a complete jumble, and it reminded me of the way a TV screen looks when the reception gets scrambled.

I began running around the stadium, searching for anybody I knew, jumping up off the sand, squealing with happiness, shaking hands and slapping high fives. Somebody handed me an American flag the size of a large beach towel. Someone else gave me a small American flag on a stick. Suddenly, I turned into a two-fisted, bikini-clad Lady Liberty, madly waving both of them as if it were the Fourth of July. Except, instead of a crown, my head was wrapped in a red sweatband. I noticed the Beach Girls, the beach volleyball dance team who'd entertained the crowds in their skimpy bikinis throughout the Games during breaks in the action, and I began gyrating my hips and shaking my booty, mimicking their sexy moves. "WOOOOO!" I screamed again.

My heart was pumping so hard I thought it was going to fly right out of my chest, and my adrenaline was surging so quickly my skin tingled from head to toe. At that time, I weighed between 150 and 155 pounds, but I remember thinking, "I feel so incredibly light." Out of the blue, a thought shot through my brain, "Didn't the Olympics start yesterday?" We'd been competing almost two weeks, but the time had flown by, and now our happy ending was unfolding just as I'd imagined. However, I admit I was somewhat dumbfounded it had actually turned out that way. In fact, part of me kept waiting for someone to shake me and say, "Wake up, Misty! It's only a dream!"

Despite the iconic, first-name-only status we'd achieved in our sport over the past four years, it was truly unbelievable to me that we'd managed to become the first beach volleyball team ever to win back-to-back Olympic gold medals. From the outside, it may have looked easy, but having lived, breathed, eaten, and slept volleyball since the day I was born, I knew what we'd pulled off in Beijing was no small feat.

When I finally was able to bring my eyes into focus, I started scanning the crowd, looking for Misty's Misfits. My lovable crew had grown as the Olympics had ground on, with friends flying in from the United States for the semifinals and finals. Even President George

W. Bush had jumped on the Misty and Kerri bandwagon, visiting us at practice the day before our opening match and bumping the ball with me on the beach. Why, he'd even slapped the large tattoo on my lower back for good luck, and it had affectionately become known throughout the U.S. Olympic contingent as "the Bush slap." He'd tried calling us the night before our gold medal match, but we were already in bed.

Tickets to the beach volleyball events at the Beijing Olympics had been hard to come by. They'd gone on sale in early May and had sold out in thirty-six hours, so Dad and I were still trying to get tickets for family and friends after we got to China. As a result, Misty's Misfits weren't sitting together. They were spread out all over Chaoyang Park. When I finally caught my breath, the faces of those people who'd had an impact on my life became crystal clear throughout the stadium. None of them were random: I'd purposely invited them all to Beijing to share in what I suspected might be the final leg of my volleyball journey. One by one, I spotted each of them, ran over to their side of the stadium, shot them a smile, mouthed them a "thank you," and blew them a kiss or engulfed them in a big, rain-and-sweat soaked hug.

I spotted Dad, who was standing courtside, wearing a shocking pink poncho. He was, and still is, the best volleyball coach I've ever had. He's technically phenomenal, very demanding, and never without an opinion. I couldn't have won two Olympic gold medals without him.

I spotted Kerri's parents, Tim and Marge, and the rest of Team Walsh. In 2000, Tim and Marge, along with Dad and Mom, had come up with the idea to pair Kerri and me on the beach. Tim and Marge had the same core family values as Dad and Mom. They'd poured their hearts and souls into their children, doing everything in their power to help make our dream of Olympic gold come true.

I spotted Troy Tanner, our coach, who'd joined our team in 2007, after Kerri and I had reached a critical crossroads in our partnership and friendship. We'd struggled on the court, and rumors swirled about us playing with different partners. Troy had broken down our game and taken us back to the basics. He'd refined our skills, recharged our batteries, rekindled our relationship, and rebuilt us into a powerhouse.

I spotted Debbie Green, the Long Beach State assistant coach who'd taught me how to set and what it took to be a world-class athlete. A silver medalist on the 1984 U.S. Olympic indoor volleyball team, Debbie had believed in me even when I didn't believe in myself. She'd flown in to surprise me for the semifinals, but she'd sent a present to me in Beijing before her arrival—a gold necklace with a volleyball icon and five Olympic rings that she'd worn at the '84 Los Angeles Games. It had become my instant good luck charm.

I spotted Eileen Clancy McClintock, who'd met my parents at Muscle Beach when she was eleven and later became Dad's longtime partner in Southern California tournaments. Together, they were the most successful mixed doubles team of all time. She'd lived through my parents' long bouts with alcoholism and their subsequent battles for sobriety. She'd supported Mom during her two-year fight against cancer. My relationship with Eileen was deep, too, dating back to the days when I was a baby, crawling around on Muscle Beach. She'd become my "second mother" after Mom passed away.

I spotted Jim Steele and his partner Gail Gaydos, longtime family friends who'd lived in Long Beach and also had watched me grow up. I considered them my second set of parents. They'd celebrated holidays with our family, attended our birthday parties, weddings, funerals, Olympic send-offs and homecomings, you name it. Jim had shuttled me to and from the airport countless times, and he'd taken care of my house and my two beloved boxers, Gruden and Boogie, as I'd chased my Olympic dream around the world and my husband, Matt Treanor, had chased his major league baseball dream across the country.

I spotted some of Mom's closest friends from the beach and two of her former volleyball teammates, Sandra Golden, who'd played on her Mavericks team that won the 2001 Huntsman World Senior

Games Championship in St. George, Utah, and Sandy Malpee, who'd been responsible for the bright yellow beach umbrellas Misty's Misfits were sitting under.

I spotted Sandra Beckman, who'd shot photos for my wedding to Matt in 2004. Seeing her reminded me of how happy I was that day—it felt exactly like how I was feeling now—and I was disappointed that Matt, a catcher for the Florida Marlins, couldn't join me in Beijing. Because our professional athletic seasons overlapped, he'd seen me play in person only a handful of times over the past five years, but we'd zealously supported each other, both ascending to the top of our sports very quickly after we'd gotten together.

I spotted my family members, Matt's brother Markell, my half brother Scott May, and my aunt Bonnie Wong, Dad's sister from Seattle. I'd watched Aunt Bonnie, a middle school principal, raise her three kids as a single parent after her husband had died on a volleyball court. She'd accomplished everything she'd ever set out to do, including traveling the world, and she was someone I'd always looked up to.

I spotted Gordon and Billie Pi'ianaia, Dad's lifelong friends from Honolulu, Hawaii. Adventurers, educators, and community leaders, they'd opened their arms to hundreds of people, including Dad, Mom, and me. We had become a vital part of their family, and they had become a vital part of ours. They'd taught me the Hawaiian word *hanai,* which means "to take in," a sentiment my parents and I have always embraced.

I spotted Loren Woll, who'd worked at MGM's film lab with Dad. He'd never had any children of his own, and he'd "adopted" me as a niece. So, I called him "Uncle Loren." He'd do anything and everything for me, and his voice always stood out above the crowd at indoor volleyball tournaments, when he'd razz me with "Look at the butt on number five!"

I spotted my girlfriends Christine Phillips, my club volleyball teammate; Kristy Warino, owner of Tracy's Bar and Grill, my favorite haunt in Long Beach; and Anya Tronson, a personal trainer who'd helped whip me into the best shape of my life for Beijing.

As I spotted face after face, and thought about what each had meant to me over the years, it was as if the credits to the movie of my life were rolling by on a screen. The night before, I'd started replaying my journey through volleyball and life, scrolling through the contacts list on my cell phone, then calling or texting "Thank you!" to everybody who'd played an important role, telling each I couldn't have made it this far without his or her love and support. I'd gotten in touch with everybody, except for my two dogs.

Then, it was time to thank Mom, my heart, my soul, my compass, and my angel coach. I'd felt her influencing my matches, particularly those in Athens and Beijing. The past six years, Dad and I, as well as some of her best friends, had spread her ashes in all of her favorite spots on earth, and so far, we'd taken her to Honolulu, Hawaii; Utah's Zion National Park; and Athens, Greece. Earlier in the Olympics, she went along on a sightseeing trip with Misty's Misfits (and me) to the Great Wall of China.

In 2004, at the Athens Olympics, I'd sprinkled her ashes from one of her antinausea prescription pill bottles onto the court after the semifinals and finals. It was not a religious experience. In fact, it never occurred to me to say any special prayers. It was all about Mom being a major part of our celebration, about throwing her into the air as if we were raising a glass of champagne to toast her for all the life lessons she'd taught me. It was all about making sure she joined in on our Olympic gold medal fun.

I'd always had a great time with the ritual. "She's knocking on the lid of the container," I'd kid as I pulled her ashes out of my duffel bag. "She's saying, 'Let me outta here! It's time to celebrate!'"

I'd always joked with Dad about the exact makeup of her ashes. "I don't know which part of her I sprinkled onto the court, maybe her little finger, maybe her big toe," I'd tease after throwing them onto the sand.

In 2008, at the Beijing Olympics, because of the torrential downpour that had inundated our gold medal match, the volunteers had built a wooden platform to surround the medals podium and keep the dignitaries bestowing the medals from having to maneuver on the soggy sand. I was so excited, so wound up, and so in the moment that I just tossed Mom into the air, not paying any attention to the direction in which I was throwing her ashes from a film canister. Lo and behold, they ended up strewn across the wooden platform.

Oops.

It cracked me up, and I knew Mom would've gotten a big chuckle out of it, too. These days, I say that Mom embarked on her own journey that day, dreaming of gold wherever that darned wooden platform has gone since then.

I've never been one to cry, but I'd started getting choked up a few hours before the gold medal match, on the bus ride to the venue. Deep down, I knew what we were about to do. I understood the enormity of the moment. I also knew that I was going to step away from the sport afterward; for how long, I wasn't sure. I'd told myself to save the tears for later, and then, as luck would have it, after Kerri and I'd won the gold medal, I was so excited that I couldn't cry.

Filled with joy, I ran over to Dad and handed him the empty film canister that held Mom's ashes. "Mom and I love you very much," he whispered in my ear. "We're so proud of you."

And with that, I dissolved into tears in his arms.

---

# 2

# DAD

M y father was born on November 7, 1941, in Honolulu, Hawaii, and raised in a two-bedroom house on Pualani Way, one of the last two dirt streets at the end of Waikiki Beach. His father, Robert, Sr., was an electrician for the Navy, and his mother, Mele, was a medical file clerk at Tripler Army Medical Center. While it might sound like an insignificant fraction, Dad is quite proud of the fact that he is "three-eighths Hawaiian." His father was "half" Hawaiian, his mother "one-quarter." Growing up, Dad often jokes, he was "too white to be Hawaiian and too Hawaiian to be white." When he moved to Northern California in 1959, his friends at El Camino High School in Sacramento questioned his heritage, saying, "Butch, you don't look Hawaiian." Dad always replied, "You're right. I'm from Oklahoma." This was typical of his quirky sense of humor, which I've inherited.

Although Dad is widely considered a Southern California beach volleyball guru—he's arguably one of the best coed doubles players ever—he sure took an interesting route to becoming a legend. As a kid, volleyball was barely in his vocabulary. He spent all of his free time on Waikiki surfing, swimming, skin diving, or fishing. Deep down, he wanted to be a football star, but physically, he was an extremely late bloomer. As a junior in high school in Honolulu, Dad was one of the smallest players on the team. He stood six feet tall, but weighed just

131 pounds. Back in those days, Dad says, he looked like E.T., the alien movie creature, with an oversized head on a pencil-thin neck and torso.

Truth be told, Dad stumbled onto beach volleyball. In 1951, at the age of ten, he began working as a shoeshine boy, setting up his box at the banyan trees beside the bus stop at Kuhio Beach Park on the Diamond Head end of Waikiki. Behind a nearby pavilion, there was an asphalt volleyball court where many of Oahu's best players congregated. Some played in shoes, some in bare feet. Dad was mesmerized by how high they could jump, how hard they could spike the ball, and how esteemed they were in the eyes of others. Being such a beanpole, whenever he asked to play, Dad always got the brush-off. "Stand aside, kid," they'd say time and again.

That is, until one afternoon, five years later. Dad, then fifteen, had just finished surfing and was walking back up Waikiki toward his family's house. He spotted a group of locals and tourists playing volleyball on the sand in front of Kaiser's Hawaiian Village resort. Arthur Lyman, one of Hawaii's leading musicians, was on the locals' team, and he noticed Dad looking longingly at the court. When Dad asked if he could play, he heard a resounding, emphatic no. Except from Lyman. "Just put the kid in the corner," he insisted.

From that moment on, Sundays at 3:00 P.M., Dad played with the Kaiser volleyball crew. To be accepted, on and off the court, was very important to him. They'd pass around buckets of beer, but Dad only took a couple of sips, mind you. As a rookie, he hung back on the sidelines before the start of the games, waiting for the tourists to form their teams. The rule was rookies never could play with the best local players, but they could participate as fill-ins on the tourists' teams. The thought of being part of the inner circle of volleyball in Honolulu was enticing to Dad. He'd heard that Honolulu's Outrigger Canoe Club, one of the most prestigious private clubs in the world, located near Waikiki in Kapiolani Park, had, by far, the best volleyball players in town. In fact, he was told, they even played on their own private courts. An entrée to the Outrigger and a shot at legendary status in volleyball became Dad's ultimate goals.

As luck would have it, Dad had stumbled upon some of the best coaches in the sport. He learned the nuances of volleyball from Neil Eldredge, a member of the Air Force, who played volleyball several months of the year for the military. Eldredge, who stood five feet five, partnered with Gordon Mew, who was six feet five, and together they beat the best players at Kaiser's Hawaiian Village. Eldredge was passionate about volleyball, and very patient, and he spent hours tutoring Dad.

Most important, Eldredge suggested Dad train with legendary volleyball coach Col. Edward B. (Burt) DeGroot, who was inducted into the Volleyball Hall of Fame in 1990. DeGroot, also an outstanding track coach, introduced drills to improve jumping, explosiveness, quickness, and flexibility, something nobody else was doing in volleyball circles at the time. With DeGroot's input, Dad's game started to take off.

In 1957, at sixteen, after a year of playing with the Kaiser crew, Dad met the man who later would change his life: Robert Franklin (Bob) Nikkel. A jovial, cigar-smoking gentleman from Northern California, Nikkel called himself "the largest smallest lumber broker in the world." He later became a member of the board of regents at the University of the Pacific in Stockton, California. Nikkel loved playing six-man volleyball on the beach. He also had a passion for the Olympics—he'd attended the 1956 Summer Olympics in Melbourne, Australia—and he'd regale Dad with stories about the athletes and the competitions. Nikkel took a strong interest in Dad, both athletically and academically. Soon, Dad looked on Nikkel as his "second father," and Nikkel was indeed a great role model for Dad. Nikkel promised Dad a job in a Northern California lumber mill after his high school graduation, along with a spot in classes at the University of the Pacific.

"I'll send you a plane ticket," Nikkel told Dad.

On May 29, 1959, at seventeen, Dad took Nikkel up on his offer. Dad lied to his mother, telling her he'd gotten his high school diploma, even though he hadn't (he still needed to pass algebra), sold his surfboards, and off he went to the Mainland. He ended up in Loyalton, California, a little town in Sierra County, where he worked as a laborer for the Feather River Lumber Company, making $1.17 an hour. At the end of the summer, he moved to Sacramento to live with Nikkel. (Nikkel's wife, Phyllis, and their two children were living in Rome, Italy, site of the 1960 Olympics. He'd relocated his family to the Olympic city, a year before the Games, to soak up the ambiance.) Dad enrolled in high school in Sacramento, repeated his senior year, and graduated at eighteen.

Nikkel continually stoked Dad's fire for sports. Everything was a contest to him. He pitted Dad in races against his two nephews. One was an 800-meter runner, the other was a miler. In order to better compete with them, Dad suggested they run a two-mile race, a mile out and back, barefoot. The hot asphalt blistered the bottoms of their feet, and Dad caught them at the turn. Nikkel was livid because it put his nephews out of commission for a while. But Dad had won, which was all that mattered, of course.

Nikkel also regularly talked up the Olympics to him.

"Great athletes go to the Olympics," Nikkel would say. "Do you want to go to the Olympics?"

"Of course," Dad replied.

"Earn it," Nikkel challenged him.

But which sport? Dad figured he was too slow for track and didn't know enough about field events. When it came to swimming, he was a sinker. What about crew? He'd paddled in Hawaii, so maybe that might be his ticket. But he'd also watched members of the University of California–Berkeley crew train and couldn't believe their size and physique. They were absolutely fit, incredibly cut. He weighed only 140 pounds, soaking wet. Wrestling, perhaps? Growing up in Waikiki, professional wrestlers Sky High Lee, Stan Kowalski, and Lord Blears had lived two doors from his family. The first time he tried wrestling, though, he got tied up in a knot and pinned in thirty-seven seconds by a seventy-year-old veterinarian with arthritis. Afterward, Dad says, he was so tired his toenails needed oxygen.

So, what, then? Dad concocted a crazy plan to improve his five-and-a-half-minute mile time. He had his pal Huey, who wasn't even old enough to drive, get behind the wheel of Nikkel's Jeep and motor it at a steady pace of seventeen miles per hour along the levee at the

American River. Dad hung on to the back for about half a mile, then he let go and tried to keep up his foot speed for several more minutes. But, of course, he never could. After three weeks of this wacky training, Dad wasn't getting any faster. So, he gave up.

The day he graduated from high school, Dad moved back to Loyalton to work in the lumber mill. Then, one day, while attending a local rodeo, he noticed the bull-riding competition had a twelve-hundred-dollar purse. "What does it take to enter?" Dad asked. "Just pay twenty-five dollars and hang on," was the reply. He finished fourth, winning $158, and thought he'd struck it rich. Instantly, bull riding became Dad's new passion. It was exciting to him because it was so dangerous. Young and naïve, he thought he was bulletproof. Nikkel knew better. He wasn't at all happy about Dad's attempt at rodeo stardom—he worried about Dad's health and safety—and he did everything he could to discourage and distract him.

And that included securing tickets to the 1960 Winter Olympics in Squaw Valley, California, and asking Dad to go along. Dad recalls watching U.S. figure skater Carol Heiss win the Olympic gold medal, with first-place votes from all nine judges. He also saw the U.S. ice hockey team defeat the Soviet Union in a thrilling, down-to-the-wire, 3–2 victory. (A day later, the U.S. went on to win its first gold medal in ice hockey, defeating Czechoslovakia, 9–4.) Both of these events were held in Blyth Arena, open-air on its south side, enabling a view of the mountains.

One afternoon, after eight and a half hours of watching figure skating and ice hockey, Dad, frozen to the bone, walked into the back of the Olympic Village Inn, home to more than 750 athletes. He ate, warmed up, and talked with athletes from around the globe.

"Where are you from?" somebody asked.

"Sacramento," Dad replied.

"What country is that?" someone else wanted to know.

"What event are you in?" another piped up.

"Nothing. We're here to watch all of them, or as many as we can," Dad said.

That's when he found out he wasn't supposed to be in the Olympic Village.

Those four days at the 1960 Olympics had a profound impact on Dad's life. He felt a strong connection to the athletes. He described his experience as "a walking *Sports Illustrated* magazine." From that moment on, Dad desperately wanted to be an Olympian. But although his heart was in it, his mind certainly wasn't there yet.

For the next few years, Dad bounced around a lot, from state to state, job to job, college to college. He put much more energy into being a free spirit and following his wanderlust than he did into chasing his Olympic dreams. A rascal and a rebel, he got himself into quite a few crazy situations. After multiple brushes with prejudice at Magic Valley Christian College in Albion, Idaho, he became so outraged by the rigid atmosphere that he dangled the two prized goats of the school's president, by their horns, from a telephone pole. After illegally hitchhiking on Dallas highways, he was thrown into the back of a Texas Highway Patrol squad car and handcuffed to a prostitute named Rose. After consuming a quart of whiskey and a dozen beers and passing out in the basement of a Reno restaurant, he woke up long after closing, pushed open the front door, and set off the security alarms. The next thing he knew, the place was swarming with dozens of cops. Dad says he saw more guns that night than he has ever seen at Wal-Mart.

Dad was young. He had no ties, no obligations. He was so unpretentious, so unmotivated by material things, that he only needed money for the bare necessities. And even then, he didn't need much. In fact, for several months, when work in Loyalton was difficult to come by, Dad lived in an abandoned shack with holes in the windows and roof. To stay warm, he'd sleep in the sawmill beside the steam-operated machinery. Eventually, Ralph Johnson, a well-respected logger, and his wife, Dixie, "adopted" Dad, luring him to their ranch with promises of a warm bedroom and plenty of home-cooked meals.

It took a horrific rodeo injury in summer 1961 to shock Dad into reality. He was thrown under a bull, and the animal stepped on the inside of his leg, pinching off an artery. He retreated to San Francisco, where his parents now lived. His foot was so swollen that he couldn't put on a sock, much less a slipper. It was about the size of his thigh, Dad says. His body temperature soared to 104 degrees. His mother begged him to have a doctor check it. Finally, Dad relented. The doctor advised Dad to keep his foot elevated and prescribed some medicine. A few days later, the swelling subsided. When he went back to see the doctor, Dad learned how incredibly lucky he was that his leg hadn't had to be amputated. Then the doctor joked, "Why don't you take up a noncontact sport, like girls' volleyball?"

Volleyball.

A lightbulb went off in Dad's head. Great memories came flooding back. However, Dad resisted taking up volleyball again because his tough-guy friends in the logging industry and on the rodeo circuit thought it was a "sissy sport."

And then, several months later, in the winter of 1961, after another failed stint in Loyalton, Dad moved back to San Francisco again. Soon after, he followed the doctor's orders: He began playing volleyball at the Embarcadero YMCA, through the coaxing of some Hawaiian friends he'd made. It was the first time he'd played organized indoor volleyball, and he really threw himself into it. Mondays, Wednesdays, and Fridays, he played at lunchtime with local businessmen. Tuesday evenings, he participated in group practices, and Thursday evenings, he played in organized games. Saturdays and Sundays, he trained or latched on to pickup games.

As he honed his skills and got into better shape, Dad followed some of his volleyball buddies to San Francisco's legendary Olympic Club. Dad recalls waiting outside for the kitchen workers to throw away food scraps, then sneaking into the Olympic Club through a side door to play volleyball. While at the Olympic Club, he discovered that DeGroot, one of his early mentors, had retired from the Air Force and had coached the club's volleyball team. In 1962, Dad bumped into DeGroot at a volleyball tournament at the Naval Air Station in Alameda, California.

"Do you remember me?" Dad asked.

"Sure, I do," DeGroot said.

"What do I have to do to become a member of the Olympic Club?" Dad asked.

"Practice," DeGroot said.

DeGroot wasn't being a smart aleck, he was just being honest. The Olympic Club team was one of the nation's elite. But Dad figured it would take more than practice to make that team. He'd spent all of his life on the outside looking in, and to be accepted at such a lofty club would take money, social stature, a college education, and athletic prowess. At that point, he had no claim to fame. He'd recently spun his wheels for a semester at California State University–Fresno, majoring in agriculture so he could try out for the school's rodeo team. He'd also been playing for the Fresno YMCA volleyball team.

Then, DeGroot went one better.

"Why don't you move to Santa Monica?" DeGroot asked.

He explained to Dad that he was now coaching at Santa Monica City College, where he'd won the national college championship in 1961. So, in August 1963, Dad set off for Southern California. He stayed at DeGroot's house the first night he arrived in Santa Monica. He registered at Santa Monica City College the following day and joined the volleyball team in informal fall practices. The season started in spring 1964.

"I'd like you to meet somebody who has just arrived from New York," DeGroot said to Dad before the first practice.

Then, DeGroot introduced Dad to Ernie Suwara, a talented East Coast volleyball player. In July, Ernie had hitchhiked his way across the country, estimating he'd taken about eighty different rides, to train under DeGroot and to play for a Southern California volleyball team. Dad and Ernie became fast friends—today, Dad considers him a brother—and they lived together in an apartment on the last block in Santa Monica before you got to Venice Beach.

Dad was instantly smitten by the Southern California lifestyle, its beach culture, and the idolization of local volleyball stars. He played in his first Southern California beach volleyball tournament, in the spring of 1964, at Muscle Beach, with Ernie as his partner. They finished third in the single-A class.

Dad felt the lure of the beach. It was different from Waikiki. There was so much more sand and so many more beach volleyball courts. Plus, this was the early 1960s, and this was Southern California, where surfers were big shots. The world was captivated by the Beach Boys, Jan & Dean, surfin' safaris, and little deuce coupes. And now, great Southern California volleyball players were being elevated into gods, too. Dad ate it up—all of it.

In one season under DeGroot at Santa Monica City College, Dad was transformed from a solid recreational player into an aspiring Olympian. DeGroot told Dad that by understanding the fundamentals of the game and implementing them flawlessly, he could raise his level of play. DeGroot was right on. Finally, with focus, fine tuning, and excellent coaching, Dad became one of the best volleyball players in the country.

Even though he was serious about volleyball, Dad wasn't beyond letting a little fun get in the way of his game. One time, he had been out too late the night before, and he showed up hungover for a tournament at Santa Monica City College. DeGroot could smell whiskey on his breath—it also didn't help matters, Dad says, that his eyes were orange—and he was benched. Until the finals, when DeGroot inserted him so Santa Monica City College could win the tournament.

However, it was another incident that really ticked off DeGroot. As Dad tells the story, he and Ernie, and some of the rest of their teammates, had "goofed around" in a tournament at UCLA, losing to the Bruins. If they'd won, they'd have automatically qualified to play in the United States Volleyball Association (USVBA) national college championship tournament. Although they were one of the best teams in the nation, DeGroot said he wasn't going to take "an embarrassment" to nationals.

"I'm going to let the student body decide if you should go," DeGroot said.

The Santa Monica City College student body voted to send them.

"You guys are so damn lucky," DeGroot told the team after the votes were tallied.

Off they went to the USVBA national college championship tournament, which was held at the U.S. Air Force Academy, north of Colorado Springs, Colorado. Before the tournament started, Dad and his teammates stumbled upon a noncommissioned officers' club. Leave it to college kids to sniff out "fifteen-cent beer night." DeGroot sniffed it out, too. Dad had just sat down at a table overflowing with beer bottles when DeGroot walked up.

"Damn it, whose beers are these?" DeGroot asked.

Since Dad was the only one old enough to be drinking legally, he said the beers were his.

"Let me talk to you," DeGroot said, pulling Dad off to the side.

DeGroot's face quickly turned a bright shade of red.

"How could you do this?" he asked Dad.

"I thought I was buying beers for guys from the Air Force," Dad said.

"If we don't win this thing . . ." DeGroot started to say.

"Don't worry, Coach," Dad interrupted. "We'll win it!"

And with that, Dad says, Santa Monica City College absolutely annihilated everybody on the way to winning the 1964 USVBA national college championship. Being a member of that championship team was Dad's entrée to big-time volleyball. Al Scates, the UCLA coach, offered Dad a scholarship. "If you get your grades up and graduate from Santa Monica, I'll give you a scholarship to UCLA," Scates told him, adding that Dad would have eighteen months to accomplish this.

"I want to play football at UCLA," Dad said.

"You're coming to play volleyball," Scates said.

So Dad turned Scates down. Looking back, Dad says this is one of the many dumb mistakes he has made in his life. Finally, he'd found himself as a volleyball player, and yet he thought he wanted to do something else. What was he thinking?

Because Dad had been named a 1964 USVBA College All-American and was playing for the Hollywood YMCA's Comets, he was one of twenty-four people chosen to try out for the 1964 Olympics. The Trials were composed of players from the top five teams— Hollywood YMCA Stars, Long Beach Century Club, Hollywood YMCA Comets, Stockton YMCA, and Honolulu YMCA—plus an all-star team from the USVBA national collegiate championships. The participants played a round-robin series of matches to permit the U.S. Olympic volleyball committee to select twelve players plus six alternates. As it turned out, Dad was named the first alternate on the 1964 U.S. Olympic team, which finished ninth in Tokyo.

After the Olympics, Dad moved back up to San Francisco and became a "contributing member" of the Olympic Club, playing on the club's rugby and volleyball teams from 1965 to 1968. Sports turned out to be the most stable element of his life. In March 1966, he married his first wife, Linda Stutsman, then just seventeen. They'd met when she'd worked at Hot Dog on a Stick, a food shack at Muscle Beach. Five months after their marriage, Linda gave birth to a son, Brack, but their union didn't last, and they divorced in November 1967.

When the marriage fell apart, Dad moved back to Southern California. He played volleyball for the Westside Jewish Community Center team in West Los Angeles. His Westside Jewish Community Center B team ended up third at USVBA nationals in 1968. Westside's A team finished first. Dad, a member of the B team, was selected as one of twenty-four men to try out for the 1968 U.S. Olympic team.

Dad quit his job in the composing room at the *Los Angeles Herald-Examiner* to chase his Olympic dream. The selection process was extensive. There was a ten-day camp at California State University–Northridge, as well as a four-week camp in Lake Tahoe, California. Known for having quite a temper, Dad made a fatal mistake during tryouts. He got into a disagreement with two-time Olympian Mike Bright and punched him. Dad says Mike was worried about his wife, Patti, making the 1968 U.S. Olympic women's indoor volleyball team because she wasn't having great practices. So, Dad says, Mike was sulking and not playing hard.

"Come on, Mike, pick it up!" Dad hollered.

"We're already on the team!" Mike shot back. "Screw these guys!"

"What did you say?" Dad replied, then popped him.

In an instant, Dad says, he went from a solid member of the 1968 U.S. Olympic team to last on the list.

Dad also got caught up in behind-the-scenes politics. Head coach Jim Coleman told Dad that he wanted his close friend Jim Vineyard to make the team. In addition, Coleman told him that because he had shown no social skills or discipline, he was more than likely not going to be chosen for the team. However, Coleman was going to let the eleven members of the Olympic team choose the twelfth player. It came down to Dad and Coleman's friend Vineyard, and the players chose Dad. Afterward, Dad recalls, Coleman shook hands with everybody but Dad.

"You're on the team, but it doesn't mean you're going to play," Coleman told Dad.

The U.S. opened with a match against the Soviet Union, the world's best team, and as instructed by Coleman, Dad worked out, alone, in a side room for two hours. The U.S. went on to post what is still considered one of the greatest Olympic upsets in U.S. volleyball history, a 3–2 victory over the Soviets, the eventual gold medalists.

Throughout the Games, Dad says, Coleman continually told him to practice by himself. "Just because you made the team, doesn't mean I have to play you," Coleman said.

Meanwhile, the U.S. went on to lose to Czechoslovakia, 3–1, then beat Brazil, 3–0. After that, it was a downward spiral. The U.S. lost to Bulgaria, 3–2, Poland, 3–0, East Germany, 3–0, and Japan, 3–0. Eventually, the U.S. scored two victories, defeating Mexico, 3–1, and Belgium, 3–0, to finish seventh.

Angry and frustrated, Dad challenged Coleman's decision to play Wink Davenport in the Bulgaria match. After that loss, he went to Coleman's room to ask to be sent home. In the heat of the discussion, Dad closed his fist and said, "Jim, when I open this, what do you see?"

"Nothing," Coleman replied.

"That's exactly what you know about volleyball," Dad snapped.

Soon after, Dad started throwing Coleman's clothes out the window of his room in the Olympic Village. As Coleman was watching his clothes trickle to the ground, Dad grabbed him by the waist and dangled his head and arms over the side of the building.

"I ought to throw your ass out of here!" Dad said.

At that moment, U.S. Olympic men's basketball coach Hank Iba and assistant U.S. Olympic men's volleyball coach John Lowell burst into the room.

"If you ever want to play volleyball again, Butch, you can't do this!" Lowell said.

Dad shouted some expletives and yanked Coleman back into the room.

"Pack your bag, you're leaving!" Coleman said. "You're off the team."

"I was never on the team," Dad said. "I quit my job seven weeks ago, and I could've stayed home."

Lowell tried to defuse the situation.

"Butch, leave the room," Lowell said. "I want to talk to Jim."

Lowell came to Dad's room later that evening.

"You're still on the team," he told Dad. "I want you to suit up tomorrow."

Looking back, Dad says he doesn't condone his actions, but explains that he was despondent over the behind-the-scenes politics of the 1968 U.S. Olympic team. Dad hadn't wanted his Olympic experience to be in vain. He'd just wanted to play volleyball.

The next day, in a losing match against Poland, the U.S. already had burned through its time-outs when Bright threw up his hands and walked off the court. Dad was the only person left on the bench who legally could enter the game without the U.S. forfeiting. Coleman refused to talk to him, so Lowell sent him in. On the first play, Dad open-hand dinked the ball, and Edward Skorek, the best hitter in the world, spiked his dink, shattering the little finger on Dad's right hand.

"If I don't look at it, it won't hurt," Dad told himself.

Because the U.S. was out of substitutions, Dad asked the team manager to throw him some adhesive tape, so he could stabilize the floppy finger. He pulled his finger back into place as best he could, taped it up, served, and finished out the game.

Dad wound up playing in all four remaining matches, and he played well. After the final match, back at the Olympic Village, Coleman went room to room, shaking the players' hands and thanking them for their efforts. All except for Dad. Although he was still upset about his blowup with Coleman, Dad felt satisfied with his performance and most of the rest of his Olympic experience.

Now, Dad realizes that, as a young man, he wasn't mature enough to handle his emotions. His blowups at the 1968 Olympics represented many of his greatest shortcomings. If he'd been able to recognize this before getting to Mexico City, he says, perhaps he would've been a better person and athlete. If he'd been able to take a more level-headed approach to challenging situations, perhaps he would've been a better husband, father, teammate, student, and friend.

Sadly, Dad is still haunted by a lot of regrets from his Mexico City Olympics experience, his two failed marriages to Linda (he remarried her in 1969, she gave birth to another son, Scott, and they divorced in 1970), and his lack of participation as a father to their two children. If he could go back in time, if he could undo his mistakes, he certainly would. In a split second. However, there's no way he can take any of it back, Dad says, so he just makes sure he's a better person today than he was yesterday.

Several years after the 1968 Olympics, Dad was given an opportunity to resolve some of the hard feelings with Coleman. They ran into each other at a Santa Monica restaurant. Figuring Coleman might be resistant to speaking with him, Dad put his foot behind Coleman's chair, so he couldn't pull it back. Then Dad took a deep breath and cleared his throat.

"Jim, I want to apologize for what I did in 1968," Dad said, looking Coleman in the eye. "I was immature, and I'm sorry."

Dad can't remember if Coleman responded, but he does recall Coleman shook his hand, albeit lightly. And with that, Dad walked out of the restaurant, still feeling uneasy about the 1968 Olympics. But he understood it was time to move on.

# 3

# MUSCLE BEACH

My parents' beach volleyball journey began in Santa Monica, on Muscle Beach, a world-renowned spot with a handful of courts just south of the Santa Monica Pier. Originally, it was called "The Playground." Through the years, Muscle Beach was noted for all sorts of activities, including exhibitions of strength and agility by bodybuilders, gymnastics and acrobatics competitions, adagio training, and bathing beauty contests.

Jack LaLanne, the godfather of fitness, helped put Muscle Beach on the map. He trained there, as did other famous musclemen, including Vic Tanny, a pioneer in the creation of the modern health club; Joe Gold, the founder of Gold's Gym and World Gym; and California governor and actor Arnold Schwarzenegger.

Muscle Beach attracted all sorts of interesting people, not the least of whom was my father.

In the years leading up to the 1968 Olympics, Dad had spent more and more time playing beach volleyball, as a way of improving his skills, speed, strength, and overall fitness. As time went on, he grew into one of the best coed beach players in Southern California. In the Santa Monica beach volleyball culture, all you had to do was play in, and win, the right tournaments, and everybody who was anybody knew who you were, all the way to Hollywood.

Dad's second-favorite sandy stomping ground was Sorrento Beach, the handful of courts north of the Santa Monica Pier along Palisades Beach Road on Santa Monica's "Gold Coast." Those who lived along Beach Road were fabulously wealthy. In the early days, it was home to four of the five men who created Hollywood—Irving Thalberg and his wife, Oscar-winning actress Norma Shearer; oilman J. Paul Getty; comedian Harold Lloyd; and leading man Douglas Fairbanks and his wife, silent-screen star Mary Pickford. The locals dubbed the stretch "Rolls Royce Row." It was such a desirable spot that, in 1928, newspaper magnate William Randolph Hearst commissioned Julia Morgan, architect of Hearst Castle in San Simeon, California, to build a beachfront estate for his mistress, actress Marion Davies. Morgan created a three-story, 118-room Georgian mansion, with thirty-four bedrooms and fifty-five bathrooms. The estate also had three guest houses, two swimming pools, tennis courts, and dog kennels.

And don't get the idea that, over the years, the rest of the neighbors were slouches. That glitzy Who's Who included actress Mae West; Academy Award–winning producer, writer, actor, and studio executive Darryl F. Zanuck; movie mogul Samuel Goldwyn; Warner Bros. founder Harry Warner; hotel mogul Barron Hilton; and actor Peter Lawford and then-wife Patricia Kennedy, sister to President John F. Kennedy. When President Kennedy visited Los Angeles, he officially checked into the Hilton in Beverly Hills, but he spent a lot of time on Sorrento Beach. So, during that era, the Gold Coast went by another nickname: "the Western Branch of the White House."

Dad was drawn to the Gold Coast's glamour and excitement. He liked rubbing shoulders with the "in crowd." He still tells stories about seeing men who were "guests" of West, filing in and out of her house. When he noticed security guards in suits and sunglasses patrolling Lawford's house, he figured Jack or Bobby Kennedy was on the premises. He recalls playing beach volleyball with actors Doug McClure,

Tony Dow, and Tom Selleck, and Hall of Fame baseball pitcher Jim Palmer. Why, in the early 1960s, the Santa Monica beach volleyball scene was so much the rage that JFK and Marilyn Monroe turned up as spectators at games, and the Beatles participated in a local tournament, then gave a concert at Sorrento Beach.

Dad embraced the Santa Monica beach culture, and everything that went with it. After all his years of searching, trying to find himself, he finally hit on a place where he felt as if he belonged. He appreciated the fact that he could spend his days shirtless, wearing nothing more than shorts and flip-flops. And he especially got a kick out of all the colorful beach bums, folks who ran the gamut, as he likes to say, "from Yale to jail."

Dad still remembers the first time he laid eyes on the woman who later would become my mother. Or should I say, laid eyes on her beautiful legs? It was April 19, 1970. He was in his car, driving through Palos Verdes, on his way to 1968 U.S. Olympic teammate Wink Davenport's wedding reception, when a tan, blonde, athletic Southern California girl ran across the street. He just couldn't help himself.

"If I had her legs, I could jump over volleyball nets," he exclaimed.

Naturally, his wife at the time, Linda, wasn't pleased by his comment.

Several months later, Dad saw those gorgeous legs again. He was playing volleyball at Muscle Beach, and the other side of his court opened up. So he checked the sign-up sheet, then yelled to the next two people in line to play, "Okay, B. and D.! It's your turn!" Up sprang Barbara (B.) Grubb and her friend Darlene (D.) Roberts. Instantly, Dad recognized Barbara's legs.

"Do you play?" Dad asked the two young women.

"Not really," Darlene said, shrugging her shoulders.

Ever the coach, Dad was happy to teach them the game. He says what impressed him the most about Barbara—other than her legs—was her reflexes. She wasn't quick, but she could do things with one hand that a lot of players had a hard time doing with two. Also, she was equally talented moving to her right or to her left.

There was a reason she was so athletically gifted. She and her two older siblings, Betty Ann and Edward, were part of a talented Southern California tennis family. In 1968, Betty Ann, then eighteen, was ranked first in the nation in the 18-and-under age group by the U.S. Tennis Association, while Mom, then seventeen, was ranked fifteenth. Edward, at the time, was playing tennis for UCLA, where one of his teammates was Arthur Ashe.

In 1969 and 1970, Betty Ann went to Wimbledon, playing singles, doubles (with Stephanie Grant both years), and mixed doubles (Tom Karp, '69; Stephen Warboys, '70). In '70, Mom went along on the trip. She always told the story that they'd left Wimbledon in a hurry because Betty Ann suddenly announced she was going to marry Guy Hansen, a pitcher from UCLA who was drafted by the Kansas City Royals in 1969. She had to leave England immediately, if not sooner, Betty Ann told Mom. It was now or never, if she wanted to marry Guy. They were married on July 17, 1970.

Well, Mom never made it back to Wimbledon, as a spectator or a qualifier. Meanwhile, Betty Ann, who eventually divorced Hansen and married tennis teacher Ken Stuart, reached the U.S. Open doubles final with Renée Richards in 1977. Betty Ann's third husband was Australian tennis pro Phil Dent. Their son (and my cousin) Taylor Dent has had four Association of Tennis Professionals (ATP) tournament victories in his career. My aunt played Wimbledon twice more, as Betty Ann Stuart in 1979 in singles, doubles (Ilana Kloss), and mixed doubles (Ross Case), and as Betty Ann Dent in 1980 in singles, doubles (Kloss), and mixed doubles (Phil Dent).

Dad recognized Barbara and Darlene, also a tennis player, were great athletes, even though he and his partner Sy Rubin, who was in his seventies, easily beat B. and D. in that first game. At that time, though, they just didn't know the nuances of volleyball. However, if they stuck out an arm, everything went up. They resembled human pinball machines.

Neither Dad nor Sy could resist gloating after their victory.

"You ladies gave us a good match," Sy chuckled.

Mom and Darlene needled them right back.

"Let's see you two move around a tennis court," Darlene said.

"I don't like tennis," Sy said.

So Mom hatched a plan.

"Butch, I'll play you in a set of tennis," she said. "I'll spot you forty points for each of the six games."

"How can you go wrong with that?" Dad said.

And then, Mom set some more parameters for their singles match. If she won, he had to teach her as much as he could about volleyball. If he won, he could never talk to her about tennis. Later that day, in less than twenty minutes, she deflated his ego—he never won a point.

After their day of volleyball and tennis, Dad and Mom joined the players from Muscle Beach at Sydney's, a bar on the promenade. Dad's cronies laughed at him because he'd gotten demolished on the tennis court. Dad asked Mom how old she was. She lied, saying she was twenty-one. Actually, she was nineteen, a sophomore at UCLA and a member of the women's tennis team. At the time, Dad was twenty-eight and working at the MGM film lab. They dated for a year before Mom admitted she was under age. When she was refused entrée to a bar, she blurted out, "I need to get an ID." He was shocked.

Soon after meeting Dad, she decided to withdraw from UCLA. She was beginning to feel burned out by big-time tennis, and she really wanted to pursue her new passion, volleyball. In spring 1970, she enrolled at Santa Monica College, formerly Santa Monica City College, where she played on the tennis team and participated in coed volleyball. In fall 1972, while getting ready to transfer to California State University–Northridge, she asked Dad if they'd ever get married. Trying to push off the decision, he replied, "If you graduate from college, we'll get married." Now, Mom, who was a great student, had a goal to shoot for.

Sure enough, two years later, on June 7, 1974, Dad's promise came home to roost. He was playing volleyball at Muscle Beach when he heard Mom's piercing whistle.

"Can I talk to you?" she yelled.

"After the game," Dad shouted back.

Mom insisted. "No, now!" she said. Then, she opened an envelope and pulled out her college diploma. She had a bachelor's in physical education. She waved it proudly in the air. "Remember, you said we'd get married when I got my degree?" she asked.

Dad gulped. "No, when you get your master's degree," he said.

"That's not what you promised," she said. "Let's go get the marriage license."

Off they went, Dad decked out in his clam diggers, tank top, and flip-flops; Mom wearing a smile from ear to ear. They walked from Muscle Beach to the Santa Monica Courthouse, where they learned wedding ceremonies were no longer performed. But, they were told, they could apply for a marriage license.

"I didn't bring any money," Dad said, still trying to squirm out of his promise.

"Well, I just happen to have eighteen dollars," Mom said.

As they walked through the courthouse, they bumped into one of Dad's volleyball friends, sheriff Paul Piet, a bailiff and a courthouse security guard. When they explained they'd come to get married, but had been told it was impossible, Paul offered to see if his friend Judge Edward Rafeedie might make an exception.

"That's not necessary," Dad said.

Paul disappeared into the judge's chambers, came out half a minute later, and announced, "He'd be happy to do it."

"But we don't have a best man," Dad argued.

"Don't worry, I'll stand up for you," Paul said.

Dad thought he was going to faint. As he always jokes, "In twenty-two minutes, we'd gone from a whistle to a wedding."

And it took less than that for Mom's father, Kenneth Grubb, a Santa Monica city clerk, to appear in the back of the courtroom and witness the ceremony. The news of their impending marriage had shot through the halls of nearby city hall like a rocket. My grandfather was in tears.

"Is your father happy?" Dad asked Mom.

"No, he's pissed!" Mom said.

After the ceremony, Dad went back to Muscle Beach to finish his game, and Mom went along with him to tell everybody her good fortune.

"Where'd you go?" his cronies asked.

"We got married," Dad replied.

"No, you didn't," his buddies said, knowing Dad was pretty adept at spinning yarns.

Mom interrupted. "Yes, we did," she said. "And you're going to give me a ring, right?"

To be honest, my grandparents never got over my parents' marriage. They'd hoped Mom would pursue a career in professional tennis, traveling the world, winning tournaments, and making tons of money, and they'd also dreamed of her marrying well. Instead, Mom later went to California State University–Los Angeles and worked toward a master's in adapted physical education. Dad, meanwhile, was completely consumed with beach volleyball, spending practically every spare moment at the beach. He also did a little surfing, played some rugby, and raced motorcycles in the desert. In my grandparents' minds, Dad was a beach bum with no professional future. However, what they never understood was that all Mom wanted in life was someone to love her completely, and that's what she'd found with my father.

Two days after their wedding, Mom and Dad had their "reception"—a beer bash at Ye Olde King's Head, a British-style pub in Santa Monica. Of course, the bar was packed wall-to-wall with their friends from Muscle Beach. Later that summer, they took over a food stand, Tee's, next to the Sand & Sea Club, as a favor to the owner. Mom had been playing a lot of paddle tennis at the private club, and she and Dad accepted the challenge of turning Tee's into a moneymaker. They downsized the menu from more than a dozen items to six. Hot dogs. Hamburgers. Cheeseburgers. Grilled cheese sandwiches. Egg and tuna salad sandwiches. Dad says their cheeseburgers earned the reputation of being the best on the beach. Later, he introduced Schwarz's sausages from San Francisco—kielbasa and cheese dogs. Their endeavor was a smashing success. The following spring Dad and Mom turned back Tee's to Doug Badt, the club's lease holder.

Six months after that, Dad and Mom scraped up seventeen thousand dollars to take over Victorio's, a New York–style pizza stand on Ocean Park Walk, at the foot of the Santa Monica Pier, a few steps from Muscle Beach. Dad cobbled together money from his credit union, his mother, and his friend Henry Conners, buying the business and the three-year lease. It was a turnkey operation. They opened two weeks before Memorial Day, in 1976, and they made only $7.50 for the day. Dad was irate, cursing at the top of his lungs. Mom said, sheepishly, "You think maybe tomorrow might be better?" The second day, they made $22.00. Over Memorial Day weekend, they averaged $125 an hour each day, and once school let out for the summer, things at the concession stand really turned around.

For three years, Dad and Mom ran Victorio's, opening it from Memorial Day weekend through Labor Day weekend. In the off-season, they opened only on nice weekends—the temperature had to be at least seventy degrees. When their lease was up in 1979, they didn't renew because, Dad says, the landlord wanted half the profits. Dad estimates they pulled in an average of two thousand dollars a week during the summer season, but, he says, they hired so many of their friends, his coworkers at MGM, down-on-their-luck folks who needed jobs, or kids who wanted money for college that they had very little profit left for themselves. Still, it was the perfect way for Dad and Mom to be grounded at Muscle Beach. Even today, Dad says, he's proud of the fact that Victorio's allowed them to be "true Muscle Beachers."

## 4

# GROWING UP

Three years after my parents married, I came along, quite fittingly, in the middle of the summer, at the height of beach volleyball season. I was born at Kaiser Permanente Medical Center in Los Angeles, on July 30, 1977, and, as luck would have it, Dad missed my grand entrance. He'd spent seven and a half hours with Mom, propping her up on pillows, holding her hands, rubbing her feet, coaching her to breathe. Finally, he'd given up.

"B., nothing's changed," he said, in frustration.

Dad was antsy to get back to Muscle Beach to open up the pizza stand. His Saturday help had bailed on him. Mom could sense his anxiety, so she gave him the green light. Sure enough, no sooner had he unlocked the door to the pizza stand than my grandmother, Betty Grubb, phoned to say my head was crowning. Dad raced back to the hospital, armed with a big tub full of balls for the son he was hoping to have—a volleyball, a basketball, a football, a baseball, a softball, a rugby ball, golf balls, and tennis balls.

His dreams were dashed when he swung open the door to Mom's hospital room.

"It's a girl!" my grandmother screamed.

Dad was a bit disappointed. He wound up ditching the balls in a hospital elevator. He hurried to the nursery, took one look at me, and gasped.

"My God, she looks like a werewolf!" Dad exclaimed.

Granted, I did have long dark hair all over my face. He asked the nurse if she'd please double-check my wristband. She told Dad, yes, indeed, it read GIRL MAY.

"Don't worry, the hair will come off in a few days," the nurse reassured him.

Then my grandmother gave Dad another jolt.

"Since you weren't present for the birth, Butch, I get to name the baby," she said. "It's customary for the maternal grandmother to do so."

Dad hadn't heard of such a custom. "Well, what are you planning to call her?" he said.

"Desiree," my grandmother replied.

"Over my dead body," Dad said.

"Okay, what do you want to call her?" my grandmother asked.

Having been born and raised in Hawaii, Dad had hoped to give me a beautiful, exotic Hawaiian name. He stepped away from the nursery and placed a long-distance call to his cousin-in-law Mina Dods, who lived in Honolulu. First, he asked Mina for permission to name me after her daughter, Misty, then fourteen years old. She'd always been a favorite of Dad and Mom's. Then, Dad asked Mina to create a Hawaiian version of the name Misty. So Mina asked Dad to look out the hospital window, just as she had done when her daughter was born, and describe the day's weather. It had started with an early morning mist, a bit overcast and gray, he told Mina, but later in the day, the sun had come out and burned off the haze, with the skies turning a glorious shade of blue.

Instantly, Mina came up with the perfect Hawaiian name for me: Kehaunani. Nani, in Hawaiian, means beautiful. Kehau translates to mist, misty, or dew. Beautiful Mist. Mina had captured my birthday, as well as the sentiment my father was looking for.

Dad marched to the nurses' station to provide the official Hawaiian name for my birth certificate. The nurse, witnessing the baby-naming war between my father and my grandmother, seemed a bit on edge. She'd already written Desiree May on my birth certificate. Dad took one look at it and said, "No, take that off." Then, he proudly pronounced my Hawaiian name for her. She pulled out a new birth certificate and proceeded to type my name as she'd heard it: Kekakanani.

Fortunately, Dad asked the nurse to read my name back to him.

"Kekakanani," the nurse dutifully replied.

Dad panicked. "Kaka?!" he shrieked, envisioning the horrible name cemented in stone by the State of California. "Scratch that!"

The nurse protested. "What do you mean, scratch that?" she said.

"Scratch that, right now!" Dad demanded. "Number one, it's spelled wrong. Number two, just type this: Misty, M-I-S-T-Y, Elizabeth May."

With that, my poor grandmother left the hospital and went home. If either of them had asked me, and I could have answered, I would have told them I was thrilled with the outcome. Misty was a much better choice.

You know the saying, "Life is a beach?" Well, I'm convinced it was coined for me. From the moment I took my first breath, my life has been about the beach. The sand was, and always has been, my playground. Or more accurately, when I was a baby, my playpen.

A week after I was born, Mom and Dad introduced me to Muscle Beach. From that day on, they passed me back and forth to each other, taking turns holding me as the activities unfolded. When Dad played beach volleyball, Mom held me. When she worked the pizza stand, Dad held me. If they both were tied up, playing games or making pizzas, their Muscle Beach buddies kept me tightly in their mitts. Other times, tucked into my stroller and parked on the side of the courts, I'd be lulled to sleep by the sounds of the Pacific Ocean crashing against the sand and the batting of volleyballs back and forth across the nets.

When I became old enough to crawl, my parents would set me down in the sand, and I'd scoot around on my hands and knees like a mini sand crab. Alice Chambers Sanchez, a volleyball teammate of Mom's, recalls seeing me crawling around on the sand and actually eating it. And what did I wear on the beach in those days? Absolutely nothing.

And I was exposed to the indoor game, too. When my parents were coaching indoor volleyball at Santa Monica College, I got dragged along. Mom was the head women's coach from fall 1977 through spring 1982, and Dad was her unpaid assistant. Plenty of times the college players snatched me up in their arms, threw me into a netted volleyball bag, and hung me from the hooks on the side of the gymnasium wall to keep me out of their way. Other times, they duct taped my body to the court to stop me from running around the gym.

It should come as no surprise, then, that my first word wasn't Mama or Dada. It was ball. Not volleyball. Just ball.

When I started walking, Mom became a lot more worried about my whereabouts. You know how they say an apple doesn't fall too far from the tree? Well, I clearly was Butch and Barbara May's daughter. As their energetic, self-sufficient, curious, only child, I was very adept at finding ways to entertain myself.

"Stay right here, Dad's only going to play a couple of points," he'd say.

Off he'd go to play volleyball, and wouldn't give me a second thought. I'd shag balls for him and his buddies for a while, then I'd get caught up in playing with my little friends. Later, Mom would show up at the courts, and wouldn't be able to find me, and she'd holler, "Butch, where is Misty?" Dad would nonchalantly shrug his shoulders, as if to say, "Not to worry, B., I've got it under control." Then, he'd quickly scan the beach, trying to locate me. Finally, he'd point and yell, "There she is, B.!" pretending to have known where I was all along.

Oftentimes, they'd find me performing acrobatics in the grassy area near the courts. I used to love to play on the jungle gym equipment, especially the rings, the seesaw, and the trampoline. When I got older, I'd ask Mom for a little money, and off I'd scamper with my friend Carol Luber, up onto Santa Monica Pier to play the games or ride the bumper cars. Sometimes, we'd pedal our bikes to Venice and back.

In my early childhood years, I was always around beach volleyball, but I really wasn't into it. Weekday afternoons, I did my homework sitting in the sand, while Dad played games after working at MGM. He'd work the early shift, from 4:00 A.M. to 12:30 P.M., in order to get his daily beach volleyball fix. Mom, meanwhile, coached volleyball or gave tennis lessons for the Beverly Hills and Culver City parks and recreation departments. Weekends, we'd fill a cooler with sandwiches and drinks and drive down to Muscle Beach a little after 8:00 A.M. The minute we hit the sand, Dad would run from court to court, writing his name on the sign-up sheets. Because Dad was such a beach volleyball rat, we'd be at Muscle Beach all day, sometimes as late as 7:30 or 8:00 P.M., depending on the time of year and the hours of daylight.

In those days, though, I was completely wrapped up in my own little world, oblivious to the fact that some of the best beach volleyball players in history were performing at my feet. There were legends like Kathy Gregory, the matriarch of women's beach volleyball, who reigned supreme in the 1960s and 1970s, and there were up-and-coming stars like Karch Kiraly, now the most celebrated American male beach volleyball player ever, and the only person to have won Olympic gold medals in both the indoor (1984 and 1988) and beach (1996) versions of the sport.

As a child, I had no idea how good anybody was, not even Karch. It was, "That's Karch." Or, since I couldn't pronounce his first name, "That's Krotch." Sometimes, I even referred to him as "Scotch Tape." To me, he was just an old guy—seventeen years older, in fact. He was not some famous volleyball stud. Rather, he was my all-time favorite "babysitter," the big brother Dad asked to look after me on the beach when Krotch, er, Karch wasn't playing. For instance, after graduating from UCLA and making the commitment to the U.S. national team, Karch ended up "babysitting" me during a mixed doubles tournament in San Diego. Dad, who'd teamed up that weekend with his successful, longtime doubles partner Eileen Clancy McClintock, recalls being in the throes of a match against NBA Hall of Famer Bill Walton, when suddenly, out of the corner of his eye, he noticed Bill's son Luke sitting on my chest.

"Bill, would you ask that big galoot to get off of Misty?" Dad said. Although I was three years older than Luke, who now plays for the NBA's Los Angeles Lakers, he already was a lot bigger than I.

Up until a couple years ago, I must admit, I didn't have the guts to talk to Karch. Because, at some point, he'd gone from "That's just Krotch" to "That's Karch Kiraly!" When I finally got a clue about his talent, I began idolizing him. I began wanting to be just like him. I studied how he trained, how he played, how he conducted himself. I still do. Karch was, and still is, The Legend, the gold standard. When I finally realized how important he was to the sport, I told myself that one day, if I ever got good enough, I'd chase Karch's legend. I'd try to rewrite history for women's volleyball. I'd try to create a legacy as golden as his. I'd try to become the female Karch Kiraly. While I've never surpassed his accomplishments in the sport—on one level, I know men and women can't, and shouldn't, be compared—until the day I die, I'll keep on chasing Karch because he's the best there ever was.

You know, the more I think about it, the more I realize that I have never, ever ranked the players at Muscle Beach by their talent, especially back when I was growing up. I always have just embraced them as people. It was their personalities that always resonated with me. And the kookier, the better. At times, all the crazy characters at Muscle Beach gave it a circuslike atmosphere.

There was a boxer named "Two-Way Tony," who played volleyball by day, but dressed up as a woman by night, going by the name "Judy." There was "Byron Buns," a pint-sized muscleman with a pronounced butt. There was "Daddy Gordon," an elderly gent from Arkansas, who pranced around in his teeny, tiny Speedo and a ten-gallon cowboy hat. He was a chick magnet, thanks to his little Chihuahua named Tina. All the ladies fussed over him, cooing, "Oh, Daddy Gordon, what a cute little dog." And, oh yes, there was Miss Nude America.

But my all-time favorite Muscle Beach character was Wilt Chamberlain, the legendary NBA Hall of Famer who got hooked on volleyball in his midthirties to rehabilitate from a knee injury. At seven foot one and 275 pounds, Wilt towered over everybody in the sand. Dad later joined him on Wilt's Big Dippers, a four-man team that traveled the country playing six-man teams. It was volleyball's version of the Harlem Globetrotters.

Dad always jokes that Wilt's most challenging games on the beach occurred when he was trying to pick up bikini-clad women. Wilt had a routine. He'd spot a woman he wanted to meet, then he'd turn to Dad and say, "There's a beautiful girl. Go tell her that somebody tall, dark, and handsome wants to meet her." Dad would always reply, "Well, Wilt, two out of three isn't bad."

When I was growing up, Muscle Beach was unique, in that friendships came before volleyball, thanks to Dad and Mom. Everybody knew everybody. It was a place where strong, emotional connections meant more than tough, competitive games. Back then, I don't think the Muscle Beach regulars even considered beach volleyball a sport. It was a way of life. In those days, if you won an amateur tournament, you got a cooler or a case of beer. Basically, you got bragging rights. There was such a strong emotional connection with Muscle Beach, it got to the point where people raced to get there every weekend, just to see, and be with, one another. It had a strong pull, like a Pacific Ocean undertow.

From the outside looking in, the Muscle Beach group might have been an odd mix of people—beach rats, families, athletes, actors, business executives, millionaires, bodybuilders, and sun-worshippers—all enamored of the Santa Monica beach lifestyle. But they were all very nice to me. That had a lot to do with my parents, who were very down-to-earth people. They treated everybody the same, with dignity and respect, whether that person lived in a mansion or in a car. It was one of the most important life lessons my parents ever taught me. Being so open to others, accepting them for who they are, my parents had an incredible wisdom about people. Especially Dad. All of the colorful characters became a meaningful part of our Muscle Beach family, and Dad and I still maintain those relationships today.

Although it always felt as if we were rushing to Muscle Beach, because Dad's heart was beating so fast at the anticipation of playing volleyball, we really didn't have to. It took us all of two minutes by car to get there. We lived in a small, two-bedroom apartment on Eleventh Street, between Olympic and Arizona, several blocks from the Santa Monica Pier. Frankly, we should've just pitched a tent at the Pier for the amount of time we spent there. Now that I'm older, I realize I was destined to play beach volleyball, there was just no way around it.

When I was two and a half, Dad, Mom, and their Muscle Beach cronies would bump the ball to me. Dad says he used it to distract me. People would ask him to play a game, and he'd give in, without any arm-twisting, saying, "Okay, but just one game."

"Just ones?" I'd ask, holding up one finger.

"Yes, just ones," Dad would promise.

Later on, as I grew older and got wise to his little white lies, Dad realized I could count. Throughout the games, I'd ask, "What's the score?" Dad would say, "10–6" or "12–4" or "13–8."

Several points later, depending on what the scenario was, I knew the game was over, and I'd start pleading with Dad.

"Now it's time to play with me!" I'd beg.

Dad always tried to hoodwink me by saying, "Oh, not that game, this game."

Without even realizing it, I was absorbing volleyball by osmosis, just by being around it, every single waking minute. Even if my parents and I weren't physically at the beach, volleyball was still the major focus of our conversations. From the time I was four, Dad had me bumping, passing, and setting balloons in our living room. He would also cut up old volleyballs, pull out the bladders, blow them up, and we would bat them back and forth over the coffee table.

"Don't break anything!" Mom would yell from the kitchen, as she was cooking dinner.

At some point, there'd be a loud crash, and she'd holler, "What was that?"

In unison, Dad and I would innocently reply, "Nothing."


You might be surprised to learn that dancing was my first organized activity. When I was five, Mom enrolled me in dance classes at the Santa Monica Dance Studio. Over the next six years, I participated in tap, ballet, jazz, and even baton twirling. I was the kind of little girl who loved all the frilly outfits that went with each and every style of dancing. (Now, I guess you could say I was destined to become a contestant on ABC's *Dancing with the Stars,* too.)

Mom wanted to expose me to dancing. She knew it was the thing for little girls to do back then, and she believed it would help me in the future, in whatever sport I chose to pursue. Plus, her parents, my grandparents, were ballroom dancing aficionados. They'd travel around, following certain ballroom dance bands, whether they were playing at Disneyland or on cruise ships. I loved watching my grandparents dance. It was spellbinding. I was captivated by my grandmother's long, flowing dresses. I enjoyed putting on her jewelry and strutting around in her high heels. I was a very lucky little girl. By the time I was in the seventh grade, my grandparents had taken me on several cruises, and I'd watched them dance practically all the way around the world.

Mom also understood that dancing would be an important activity for me because it was something I could experience with my peers, since I spent the bulk of my time with my parents or their friends. Don't get me wrong. It was nice being Butch and Barbara May's only child. I got a lot of attention. Although Dad had two sons from his previous marriages, Brack and Scott, who were eleven and eight years older, respectively, I rarely saw them growing up. Not only because they lived in Northern California with their mother, Linda, but also because my parents preferred to keep me isolated from any possible family melodrama.

In my mind, dancing was an important activity because it allowed me to let down my hair; to challenge myself physically and express myself emotionally; to tap into the fun side of my personality (even ham it up at times); and to have something that was mine, and mine alone. Plus it was a blast. There was a side to me that loved performing. When I was little, Dad recalls, every time somebody said the word "Hollywood" to me, I'd beam from ear to ear.

Being raised as Butch and Barbara May's only child helped me develop quite an imagination and a flair for the dramatic. I was the kind of kid who plastered stars all over her ceiling, falling asleep every night making wishes on them. After my family got its first video camera, I put on the entire production of *Cinderella,* with my cats, Spike and Pokey, starring in it with me. The cats played the mice who made the dresses for the ball. I played Cinderella, the Fairy Godmother, the prince, the wicked stepmother, and the two horrible stepsisters. And when the video camera wasn't rolling, I'd draw pictures, paint watercolors, or build forts in my closet. I'd play video games, including Atari. I'd put on skits with my Barbie dolls. I'd cut my own hair. My favorite TV show? On Saturday mornings, I loved to watch the *Gorgeous Ladies of Wrestling* with my friend Liz Martinez. And the weirdest of all? When my parents would leave the apartment, I'd clear out the vegetables from the refrigerator and empty the canned foods from the cabinets, and I'd play grocery store checkout person. I thought it was the greatest job ever. (I'll never forget the first time I stumbled on a self-checkout line at K-Mart. I thought, "Dream come true!")

When I was growing up, we never had a lot of money, so my participation in dance was a bit of a stretch for my family. People have this perception that I grew up with a silver spoon in my mouth. In actuality, it was more like a rusty spoon. My entire life, we lived paycheck to paycheck. I remember watching my mother doing the family's bookkeeping at the kitchen table. She would always lament, "I hope your dad gets paid this week. We need the money."

My dad couldn't understand why dancing required more than one class. You take Ballet I one night, Ballet II another. With every class, there's a recital at the end, and you need a costume for each. "Can't you just wear the same outfit for all these dances?" Dad would ask. He is the kind of guy who wears things until they fall off. "No, because each dance is different," Mom would try to explain. Dad never complained about my dance lessons because he knew he always could work weekends at MGM to make extra cash. However, he never comprehended the expense of all the costumes.

When it came to school clothes, though, I always got hand-me-downs from my cousin. My parents bought the essentials—shoes and underwear—but things from department stores like Macy's or Nordstrom came from Natalie Grubb, Uncle Edward's youngest daughter. I didn't have a fashion sense, and when these clothes arrived, it was like Christmas to me. They were beautiful, expensive, and cutting edge. And it seemed as if they'd only been worn once. Some, in fact, still had tags attached. Because Mom had married Dad, he says, my grandparents didn't give her the financial jump starts they gave Uncle Edward or Aunt Betty Ann. Dad always has felt guilty about holding Mom back. In fact, he still refers to himself as "the black sheep" of the Grubb family. Throughout their marriage, he'd ask Mom, "Do you regret marrying me?" She'd always answer, "No, absolutely not." When I grew taller, Natalie's clothes quit coming because they didn't fit me anymore. Dad says he'll never forget Uncle Edward saying, in jest, "Misty, it's too bad you're so cute, and your parents are so poor."

The struggle to make ends meet was an undertone throughout much of my early childhood. Yet, through sports, we were able to rub elbows with successful and influential people. Not that I, as a child, always was aware of the socioeconomic divide. We were treated as honorary members of the Sand & Sea Club, a private social and athletic club on the beach in Santa Monica with a strong Jewish membership. In the 1960s, the other clubs on the beach had restrictive membership policies. It was the most beautiful beach I'd ever seen—the Sand & Sea was at the site of the Marion Davies estate—Malibu to the north, Palos Verdes to the south, framed by the club's white, wooden buildings with dark green trim. We were blessed to be exposed to wealthy Los Angelinos. Doctors. Lawyers. Hollywood movers and shakers. Dad remembers meeting comedians Don Rickles and Bob Newhart. While my parents were engrossed in beach volleyball or paddle tennis games with the members, or were busy giving them free private lessons, I was able to swim in the Olympic-sized pool and romp in the sand in front of the club. This was my playground, too. If you were to compare incomes, ours probably wasn't much more than those of the people who took care of the grounds, and we always were grateful that we had a place like the Sand & Sea to go to. My parents tried to give back to the club, in whatever ways they could, and they were especially mindful of playing sports with some of the older people whom no one else would play with. We made friends for a lifetime, people who embraced us as family, and have allowed us, through the years, to be included in their children's successes.

Although we always seemed to be strapped for money, my parents did what parents do: If there was something I wanted to participate in, they wouldn't say no. They would find a way to pull it off, even if it meant skimping as a family in another area, or more often than not, their going without. If worst came to worst, they'd say, "Go ask your grandparents." If Mom and Dad were scraping the bottom of the bank account, they'd never tell me. They didn't want that knowledge to affect my decisions. They never wanted me to think, "I shouldn't do this because we can't afford it." When I needed braces on my teeth, for example, Mom made a trade-out deal with the orthodontist. As payment for my braces, she'd give her private tennis lessons.

In a city like Los Angeles, where people are defined by their cars, my parents couldn't have cared less about what they looked like sitting behind the wheel. We always had transportation, but it was never top of the line, and it certainly wasn't anything brand new. Usually, my parents drove their vehicles almost into the ground, like their Honda Prelude, which racked up 270,000 miles before Dad handed it over to my half brother Scott. We also were given several used cars, courtesy of my grandparents.

Tucked in between the spectacular beach houses of Malibu and the sprawling mansions of Beverly Hills, the tiny Santa Monica apartment I grew up in was very nondescript. The I-10 freeway, which goes all the way down to the Pacific Coast Highway, separates Santa Monica. The haves are on one side, the have nots on the other. We lived on the south side of the freeway, where the rents were a lot lower. Our unit had no views; it butted up against apartment buildings.

On the first floor, there was a small kitchen, a living room, and a half bath. Upstairs, there were two bedrooms, one beside the other, and one bathroom, with one of those old heaters, where you flipped a switch and the coils turned red. I'll never forget its louver windows. On nights when the wind was blowing hard, the glass would shake. And because there was a problem with the roof, when it rained, water ran down the walls of my bedroom.

While most kids have posters of athletes or rock stars plastered on their bedroom walls, mine were bare. Even to this day, I have a hard time putting anything on the walls of my house. I had a TV and a little trundle bed. If my friends slept over, we'd make caves and sleep under the bed. Our hair would get all tangled up in the springs.

Mom loved the Salvation Army, and our apartment and our wardrobes reflected her favorite place to shop. We called it Sally Ann's. It was located less than two hundred yards from our apartment. My dream one day is to hire an interior designer to make over my house, because we could never afford a luxury like that. We were always the family who got pieces from here and there, put them together, and didn't care what the finished product looked like. None of our couches were comfortable. Some of them had chewed-up pillows. Dad would just put covers on them and flip them over. We rescued three-legged chairs—and knocked off the three legs. Eclectic? Our style was a cross between gypsy and nomad.

Sally Ann's taught me valuable life lessons. Mom and I loved shopping there together. I'd buy little records and whatnot. But there was one time when I only had a certain amount for one record, and I suddenly remembered a story Mom had told me, when she and my aunt Betty Ann had gone to the store to get Band-Aids for my grandmother. The metal containers of Band-Aids were never full enough, so they removed some of the Band-Aids from another container and stuffed them into the one they were going to purchase. Well, I only had money to buy a *Snow White* record, but I also wanted the *Sleeping Beauty* record. So, when no one was looking, I slipped the *Sleeping Beauty* record into the *Snow White* cover. Later that day, Mom discovered what I'd done, marching me right back to return the record.

Even if my parents had had the money to blow on furniture, clothes, cars, toys, or records, those things wouldn't have been important to them. If we'd been millionaires, if we'd won the lottery or if we'd just had a little extra money to throw around, they would've used it to take care of friends who were down on their luck, or to help feed and care for homeless, sick, or stray animals. Whenever they had leftover food at the pizza stand, they always offered it to homeless people.

My parents taught me a person isn't measured by the money or the material things he or she has accumulated, but rather, by the amount of kindness, love, and intangibles given away to others. As they always told me, "You can't keep it unless you give it away." To this day, I live by the adage: The best things in life are . . . just things.

My dad has a favorite illustration of that important lesson. When he was ten and shining shoes on Waikiki, he met a successful businessman named Harry White. Dad says Harry was an orphan, who'd been something of a juvenile delinquent growing up. Harry was given a choice by the courts—join the armed services in the war effort in Korea or go to jail. When he retired from the Navy, he opened up a sheet metal fabrication company in Los Angeles.

In 1963, Dad saw Harry walking on the sidewalk near Muscle Beach.

"Hey, aren't you Harry White?" my dad asked.

"How'd you know, kid?" Harry replied. Dad explained that he'd shined Harry's shoes on Waikiki. Harry bought him a hot dog and a lemonade.

Fifteen years passed before he saw Harry again. On my first birthday, Harry walked by my parents' pizza stand. "Harry White!" Dad yelled. "It's my daughter's birthday, all pizza's free." Harry wadded up a fifty-dollar bill and threw it into the pizza stand.

On my birthday, for the next eight years, Harry sent me a hundred dollars. Dad and Mom always admired him, not only because he'd turned his life around but because he'd never stopped helping others do the same. He'd helped prostitutes get respectable jobs, drug addicts kick their habits. Then, one July 30, we didn't hear from him. Five months later, at holiday time, Mom said, "We never received a Christmas card from Harry."

Dad investigated and discovered he'd had a stroke. He called Harry and asked, "Is there anything I can do for you?" From then on, Dad made it a point to work out with Harry at the gym a few times each week. One day, Harry said, "Butch, how come you have never asked me for money?" Dad didn't miss a beat, "Because I work."

In the years Harry had left, he sent me five hundred dollars every birthday. The money helped pay my volleyball expenses.

After Harry died, Dad received a summons to show up in court. Harry had left the people closest to him a couple million dollars. He left Dad one hundred thousand dollars, awarded in three installments over fifteen years. But Harry added a stipulation: If someone needed the money more than Dad did, he had to give it to that person.

White's act of generosity had quite an impact on me and my family. Mom and Dad said if we were ever privileged enough to help others financially, we certainly would do that. And if we weren't in a financial position to do so, then we'd lend a hand in other ways. Harry's unexpected gift taught me about the value of being nice to others. It taught me about the importance of giving of yourself. It taught me that simple acts of kindness lead to the biggest blessings in life.

# 5

# GIRL FOR ALL SEASONS

I am a huge proponent of kids playing multiple sports. I don't believe in specialization, which is the way of the world these days. It leads to burnout, tunnel vision, and narrow-mindedness. It overworks muscles. It minimizes friendships. I believe kids should be well-rounded—physically, mentally, emotionally, and spiritually. I am a good example of the theory that participating in lots of activities can produce an outstanding athlete and a whole person.

I always was the girl on the elementary school playground, at recess, playing with the boys. I loved any sport. I ran in little Jesse Owens track meets in my Converse high-top sneakers. I always dressed in shorts or slacks. The only time I ever wore dresses was to my friends' birthday parties. I remember riding a Big Wheel bike at one little boy's party. The fabric from the skirt got caught under the wheels, but I kept riding, burning holes in my new dress by continually rubbing it against the cement driveway.

For me, the rewards of sports were, and still are today, the complete and utter joy I'm feeling, and more important, the intensely personal journey I'm undertaking.

My first foray into organized sports happened when I was five. But it wasn't volleyball—it was soccer. I climbed up through the ranks, and I became so good at it that when it came time to start thinking about colleges, one of the dozens of recruiting letters I received came from the University of North Carolina, gauging my interest in the storied women's program. If I'd wanted to, I could have gone to college on an NCAA Division I soccer scholarship. When I started soccer, I was involved with the American Youth Soccer Organization (AYSO) program in Santa Monica. I played on a coed team, the Arrows, because, at that time, there were no all-girls' teams.

Sometimes, being one of the boys led to funny moments on the field. Take the game in Beverly Hills where I scored a goal right out of the gate against a boys' team. Only a couple of seconds were gone on the clock. I sprinted past Scott Caan, the son of actor James Caan, and I slammed the ball into the goal. SCORE!

"How can you let that boy with the long hair take the ball away from you and score?" James Caan ranted.

"Dad, it's not a boy, it's a girl," Scott shouted back.

My first coach, in any sport, was my father. He coached my AYSO teams from the time I was five until I was about nine. I loved playing, and I was very competitive. After every game, my parents and I had a ritual: We'd stop at the bakery on Main Street in Santa Monica for carrot cake with butter cream frosting. I'd wash it down with a pint-sized carton of milk.

In addition to playing soccer, between the ages of five and nine, I competed in swimming meets at Santa Monica College. My friend Carol Luber and I would walk to the school, pay a quarter, and participate in the free swims. There were two pools—a deep pool and a lap pool. There weren't any lane markers floating on top, so you could swim wherever you wanted. To be allowed off the high dive, in the deep end of the deep pool, you had to demonstrate that you were a good swimmer, swimming two lengths and treading water for the lifeguards.

Truth be told, I really hated the deep end. It was scary, with the black lines running along the bottom of the pool. From the moment I saw the movie *Jaws*, I had a huge fear of sharks. As a kid, I was too afraid to wash up in a bathtub because I was convinced a shark was going to shoot up through the drain and chow down on me. When it came to the deep end of the Santa Monica College pool, I couldn't help but envision a school of sharks lurking down below. Those black lines looked so ominous. So I'd jump off the high dive as fast as I could, then quickly hoist myself right out of the water. On the way home from our swims, Carol and I had our special route. We'd stop at Foster Freeze for vanilla ice cream dipped in chocolate. Delicious. Then, we'd walk past the cemetery, holding our breath from one end of the graveyard to the other, because we were so superstitious.

It's a little known fact that I have Olympic swimming deep in my gene pool. Dad's cousin's aunt, Mariechen Wehselau, was an Olympic gold medalist swimmer in the 1924 Paris Summer Games. She was a member of the world-record 4 x 100-meter freestyle relay, along with the famed Gertrude Ederle. She also won a silver medal in the 100-meter freestyle and held the world record in that event from July 19, 1924, until January 28, 1926. She was born, raised, and died in Hawaii. She was inducted into the International Swimming Hall of Fame in Fort Lauderdale, Florida, in 1989, three years before her death at the age of eighty-six. She got hit by a car outside the Outrigger Canoe Club, Dad says, and she never recovered from the injuries she suffered in the accident.

The younger I was, the more I ate up the different sports. From dawn to dusk, I kept occupied with dance lessons, soccer and volleyball games, swimming and track meets. Still, my grandparents had high hopes for me in tennis, and from the time I was five, did everything in their power to steer me toward a career in it. They not only raised three junior tennis stars of their own, but they played the sport themselves, into their sixties and seventies. They believed I could go further in tennis than Mom or my aunt Betty Ann. To my grandparents, tennis was a much more genteel sport than soccer or volleyball. Tennis, my grandparents reasoned, was a better career choice and a much bigger moneymaker.

When I was in first grade, they started a tradition. Every time I hit the ball against the wall, they paid me a nickel. They kept that up until I was in fifth grade. If I could keep a rally going, say, hit the ball against the wall sixty times, it was three dollars. Easy money for me. At one point, my grandfather made the mistake of saying he'd pay me five dollars for every goal I scored in soccer. One game, I made a ton of goals, and he lowered his payments to two dollars each. A few weeks later, he lowered it again, to one dollar per goal. His soccer incentives lasted only a year or two because I scored too much.

Grandparents are, well, grandparents. I loved them so much. How could I ever get mad at them? They always filled the roles of my fairy godparents. If I wanted something that was too expensive, Dad and Mom would laugh and say, "Go ask your grandparents." Take the tooth fairy, for example. I'd lose a tooth, and I don't know why, but the tooth fairy wouldn't take it at my house. So I'd put it under my pillow at Grandma's. I'd play tricks on my poor grandparents, using the same tooth over and over. When I felt I could get away with it, I'd announce, "I've lost another tooth!" The payout was tremendous: two dollars a tooth.

When I was eight, I officially became a beach volleyball player. I entered my first tournament, playing with Dad in a mixed doubles event at Will Rogers State Beach in Pacific Palisades. I was the youngest player by about ten years. Dad passed the whole court, and I set him. When it was my turn to serve, I stood at the back line, balled up my fist as tightly as I could, and swung hard, praying just to clear the net. We finished fifth. He likes to say that I "copped an attitude" with him that day, that I never paid my half of the entry fee and that I refused to referee later matches. Give me a break. What was I supposed to pay with? Tooth fairy money? And why would adults listen to a little kid referee when they wouldn't even listen to adults?

At ten, I was playing in six-on-six beach volleyball tournaments. In those days, I played in volleyball trunks, not bikinis. I was a real jock. But don't get the wrong idea: I truly love bikinis. I got my first one in 1978, when I was a year old, a green and white floral, and it was a gift from a family friend. (I recently had it framed, along with my bikinis from the 2000, 2004, and 2008 Olympics.)

And speaking of provocative uniforms, I'll never forget the time Dad, Mom, my half brother Brack, and I participated in The Gillis, a multi-tournament in Playa del Rey, California. It's a fun event because people dress up in costumes, but it's tough to win. If you do, you're somebody. Your prize? Bragging rights! We called ourselves "The Dysfunctional Family." Each of us wore a tank top spelling out "dysfunctional" by syllables. Dad wore DYS. Mom wore FUNC. I wore TION. Brack was AL. We played in the six-person, mixed division, and the four of us creamed every team we faced. We had a great time, yelling and screaming at each other—we were very dysfunctional, without even trying. At one point, Dad became, well, Dad. We all wanted to have fun, but he wanted to coach us.

"Why don't you get off the court, Dad, then we'll be FUNCTIONAL?" Brack cracked.

Today, I encourage kids to play with athletes who are older, if they want to greatly improve their skills. That's what I did, right from the start. In the case of beach volleyball, I played with and against adults.

One of Dad's all-time favorite Misty stories occurred when I was twelve. I was playing in the 14-and-under age group in the Los Angeles City Tennis Tournament at Griffith Park. After my match, we ran into old family friends, Wink and Ann Davenport, whose daughter Lindsay also was competing in the 14s. Nobody had any clue at the time that she would one day be ranked number one in the world and win three Grand Slams (1998 U.S. Open, 1999 Wimbledon, 2000 Australian Open). Wink was Dad's teammate on the 1968 U.S. Olympic volleyball team.

Suddenly, Lindsay's older sister Shannon, who was sixteen, said, "Come on, Mom! Let's go! I don't want to be late for volleyball tryouts!"

Naturally, our ears perked up.

"Volleyball tryouts?" I said. "Can I go, too?"

"You're only twelve," Shannon said. "You're not old enough." She was trying out for a 16-and-under team, the youngest age group for this particular volleyball club.

However, we weren't deterred. We followed the Davenports to Santa Fe Springs, California, to watch Shannon try out for the Asics Tigers volleyball club. Mollie Kavanagh, the club's director, and Bob Crowell, the head game coach of the 16s, both said they had no problem with my trying out. My age wasn't really a factor, Bob said, because the team was for 16 and *under*. All of the tryouts concluded with a game called "King of the Hill," where the players broke into groups of three or four and played one point. The winner got to stay on the court and play the next group. I played very well, and I hit out of the middle as well as any of the best players trying out for the 16s team.

Afterward, I turned to my parents and said, "Can I quit tennis and play volleyball?"


When I started my indoor volleyball career, at ten, I always played with kids in one age division up (as many as two, three, or four years older). At thirteen, I joined the Asics Tigers, an elite indoor club team, and I challenged myself by playing with the 16s. Asics was one of the top programs in Southern California, and all of the girls were all-stars. I really bonded with club director Mollie Kavanagh, the coach of the 18s. Even today, I still keep in touch with her. Mollie had coached volleyball since 1964, leading Asics to five national championships, and she was one of my early volleyball mentors. As 16s, we intermixed with the 18s during drills, and I got a lot out of watching the older girls.

Dad designated himself my personal trainer, away from the court and the soccer field. We spent time at local recreation centers, first in Santa Monica and later in Costa Mesa, a suburban city in Orange

County, located thirty-seven miles southeast of Los Angeles. We moved there before my eighth-grade year. Dad put me through all sorts of volleyball drills. I'd jump into pickup games with him at the local recreation centers, and in between games, we'd work on serving to others. We'd also go to local parks, where he'd set up cones and run me through soccer drills. I'd hit soccer balls back and forth to him with my feet.

To build up my endurance, he had me run hills and stadium steps. Even up until a few months before the 2008 Beijing Olympics, Dad always insisted I go over to Long Beach State and push my car through one of the parking lots. He had other nutty ideas, too, including jump squats while holding fifteen-pound dumbbells in each hand and running miles and miles on the beach. I used to roll my eyes and say, "You're crazy."

And then, there was his ultimate harebrained idea.

"I can put the car in neutral; once you push it and the car starts getting up momentum, you'll start jogging, and eventually, sprinting," Dad suggested. "Then, I'll start the engine, pull the car out of the way, and you can race by me."

That's what he'd done while training for the 1968 Olympics. Every time he brought it up, I'd protest or just change the subject altogether. That triggered his inner Vince Lombardi.

"You can't rest when everybody else is resting," Dad always told me. "You have to stay one step ahead of them. You have to do just that much more."

In my second year with Asics, I found another powerful role model, Antoinnette White, an assistant coach for our 16s. A second-team All-American at Long Beach State, she was a member of the school's 1989 NCAA championship team, its first in history in women's volleyball. At that time, I was just barely a teenager. I idolized Antoinnette, who was an outside hitter just like me. I wanted to play like her. I wanted to be like her. I could relate to her size. Like me, she wasn't very big, just five feet eight. She had a quick arm swing, was a great passer, and could set.

"She's not that big, but she makes the game look easy," I'd tell myself. "If she can do it, I can do it." As luck would have it, Antoinnette later became my counselor at Long Beach State's summer girls' volleyball camp.

Playing for the Asics Tigers was very beneficial for me. Being surrounded by the older players made me grow up faster. Being surrounded by better players made me better. I didn't mind being pushed. I didn't think of myself as a little kid—"Oh, I'm just a thirteen-year-old."

My first year with Asics, I was the outside hitter, and we finished second in the 16-and-unders at the Junior Olympics in Tampa, Florida. As we were getting ready to play in the gold medal finals, the chairman of the All-American committee came up to Bob Crowell right before the match and told him if our team won, they were going to name "the eighth grader"—me—the MVP. After we lost, I was named first-team All-American. Later, we flew to San Juan, Puerto Rico, where we toured the island with the Puerto Rican Junior National team, playing in the hometowns of their 18s players. The following year, in Albuquerque, New Mexico, we won the 16s—I was one of the middle blockers—and I was named the tournament MVP.

As my Asics teammates will tell you, I was a fierce competitor. I always wanted to win. Our 16s didn't lose.

"I hate losing," I said one day to my friend and teammate Jen Pavley.

"Misty, do you hate losing, or do you love winning?" Jen asked.

She was right: I loved winning more than I hated losing—because then I didn't have to hear it off the court from Dad.

Analyzing it now, playing high-level soccer for so many years gave me a huge advantage in volleyball. It taught me proper footwork. It helped increase my foot speed. It improved my balance, taught me how to center myself. It allowed me to move easily to my right or my left. It instilled toughness in me. I wasn't afraid to get hit with balls— I took them off my face and my chest. One time, I got a soccer ball in my mouth, and I had to rip my lip off my braces.

Throughout my childhood and into my teenage years, Dad and Mom hauled me to all their volleyball tournaments, both on the beach and indoors. Even when I was just learning the game, my parents always made sure to include me on the court. When they were doing passing drills, I was right there with them. When they were bumping the ball, I was bumping it, too. They practiced serving; I practiced serving. They practiced digging; so would I. They weren't afraid to stick me in one of their games, even when I was eight and just starting out.

I watched, and I listened, for years and years.

Eileen Clancy McClintock, Dad's longtime beach volleyball partner, tells stories about me as a little girl, growing up at Muscle Beach, describing how I'd saunter into huddles during Dad's strategy sessions with her or any of his teammates. I'd lap it all up. Dad and I always went to Mom's indoor tournaments, where he'd point things out to me for hours at a time. "Watch this person," he'd tell me. "Did you see what that person just did?" Sometimes, I'd be the water girl for Mom's team, and I'd squeeze into the huddle during time-outs, soaking up the strategy.

Very early on, Dad and Mom realized how sharp and aware I was. When I was just a kid, Dad says he knew because he had to cheat to beat me at Go Fish. But could he or Mom beat me at Pac-Man? Not in a million years. Not at Pac-Man or any other video game, thanks to my excellent hand-eye coordination. And, of course, my mountainous pile of quarters. Whenever my parents stopped in at the Mucky Duck, a British-style pub in Santa Monica, they were sitting ducks if they took me on at video games. Our Muscle Beach family always gave me their change. Dad would walk by and see ten dollars' worth of quarters on my table. He was notorious for having only three dollars in his pocket.

"Misty, can I have a few quarters?" he'd ask.

"No, Dad, this is for Kong," I'd reply.

# 6

## ALCOHOLISM

A lcohol has always been part of beach volleyball culture. At some amateur tournaments, the winning prizes are free pitchers of beer at a local sponsoring tavern. At others, sponsored by beer companies, competitors are welcome to take leftover beer at the conclusion of the event. Then, it's "Everybody over to my house for a barbecue!" time. I remember my parents bringing home stacks of six-packs of Labatt beer after amateur tournaments. And beer wasn't consumed only after tournaments. I recall being at amateur events where people drank and played simultaneously.

Alcohol also plays an integral role in professional beach volleyball. Through the years, the Association of Volleyball Professionals' sponsors have included tequila, rum, beer, and wine companies. Fans at AVP events come for the party as much as for the competition, to drink in the atmosphere and the alcohol, even if it is legally banned on that particular beach. Spectators still may try to find their way around the law, and typically, there are designated local bars for post-tournament parties.

I understand the relationship between alcohol and beach volleyball all too well. I've lived it, every day of my life, not only on the sand, but inside my family's home.

While I've never talked about it publicly until now, my parents got swept up in the partying aspect of beach volleyball, and later in their lives, their drinking created major problems. It caused me a lot of heartache, embarrassment, shame, and insecurity. Although my father hasn't had a drink in more than twenty years, and my mother was sober almost eleven years when she died in 2002, even today their alcoholism still has a profound impact on me. Trying to cope with their drinking problems shaped my personality, from the time I became aware of their issues, when I was four, until they'd both sobered up, by the time I was fifteen. It's the reason I'm so quiet. It's the reason I don't express my feelings well. It's the reason I can't talk about what's really going on inside me.

Oh, I've tried to party, and I've been successful at it. It's the afterward I've been unsuccessful with. At Long Beach State, when I experimented for the first time with alcohol, I got sick. Early in my pro career, when I drank to be social with my colleagues, I couldn't drive myself home. I even had trouble enjoying a drink at my own wedding, where guests handed me gin and tonics and glasses of champagne. At the end of the evening, I ended up facedown, in my wedding gown, sprawled across a hotel room bed. Today, if I'm at a dinner party or at a social gathering, I'll have a beer or a glass of wine, but that's about it. It doesn't take long before the taste starts bothering me, and it carries me back to my turbulent childhood. I get to thinking, "Don't screw up your life, Misty. You've worked so hard to get to where you are." Plus, I hate waking up the next day with a hangover.

From day one, drinking was part of my parents' lives. After their first date playing volleyball at Muscle Beach, they went to a local bar for some celebratory beers. At that time, Mom was much more into alcohol than Dad. She'd lied to him, claiming to be twenty-one, when she was just nineteen. As time went on, my parents began celebrating everything from birthdays, anniversaries, and holidays to tournament victories with their Muscle Beach cronies. They became more than husband and wife: They became each other's best drinking buddy. I was the odd man out, the little girl playing video games in the back of the bar. Except for those times when they'd offer me sips of their beer; then I'd join in the celebrations. Eventually, it got to the point where my parents didn't need an event to toast in order to drink. They'd celebrate the end of their workdays by having beer (Dad) or brandy and coffee (Mom).

And somehow, it all spun out of control from there.

Neither of them was really quite sure when or why it happened. Dad wonders if it was the Hollywood movie industry culture or the long hours he put in at the MGM film lab that contributed to their drinking problems. Perhaps Dad drank to unwind from work. Perhaps Mom drank because she was lonely. Whatever the case, Dad wasn't afraid to work as many as forty-three hours straight as an assistant to the film colorist. There were two bars near MGM's film lab in Culver City—the Retake Room and the Backstage—and a third bar, Dear John's, a little way down Culver Boulevard. It wasn't unusual for Dad to stop in during his lunch breaks. After a Trader Joe's market was built near MGM, he joked that he "went around the world every day," drinking a six- or eight-pack of beers from Tahiti, New Zealand, and God knows where else during lunch breaks.

Why do I think my parents drank? Because they both suffered from the same disease: alcoholism. It's as simple as that, although everything else about their disease made my life complicated. There was never any rhyme or reason to their getting drunk. I couldn't predict if, or when, it was going to happen. It was never a specific day, or time, like, say, at 5:00 P.M. (cocktail time). Typically, Mom started drinking when she got home from work. Dad, meanwhile, usually had a couple of beers after he got off. Truly, the only thing I could predict, in terms of their drinking, was how angry and upset I was going to get, how small and scared and out of control I was going to feel.

Alcohol affected each of my parents differently. Dad is a laid-back, fly-by-night kind of guy. He was the same when he was drinking. I think Dad could control himself a little better when he was drinking than Mom could. She was a warm, sweet, funny woman—until she got hold of that alcohol. Then, she wasn't sweet, and she wasn't funny. She became mean, violent, and belligerent.

When I was five or six Dad began using me as his beer mule for sporting events at the Los Angeles Coliseum. We'd go to watch motorcycle racing, and I'd carry the beer, half a case of it, as well as bottles of brandy and schnapps, all rolled up in Dad's extra large Goodyear tire jacket. Dad knew the security guys would never question a little girl. They would never check underneath the bulky jacket draped over my shoulders. And they certainly wouldn't pat me down.

As my parents started drinking, they'd begin arguing. As they reached various stages of drunkenness, the arguing escalated. They'd ratchet themselves up, one drink at a time. It got louder and louder, nastier and nastier, more and more cruel. At times, it got physical. Very physical. If Dad came home from work and discovered Mom drunk, which was often the case, he slowed down, or even curtailed, his drinking, figuring he needed to keep it together for my sake, but her drunkenness always ignited a fight. He'd see she'd already consumed a bottle of liquor and was diving into a second, and that would tick him off. And those fights instantly hit outrageous levels. Soon, Mom was transformed into someone I didn't know, and she wreaked havoc on Dad, me, or our apartment. She punched holes in the walls. She smashed windshields. She broke plates, glasses, lamps, and other household items. She threw Dad's volleyball trophies at him.

One time, before I was born, Mom was so out of control that Dad actually called the police. He had no choice. She was crazed, smashing things, and the neighbors had called their apartment, worried that Dad was killing her.

"What do you want to do, sir?" the policeman asked Dad.

"Let Barbara go," he said.

"One of you will have to leave the house for the night," the cop said.

So Dad slept down the street, in his van, well out of eyesight, and the destructive path, of Mom.

I'll never forget the time Mom became so enraged that she broke through the bathroom door. She'd had only a couple of drinks. But I set her off, the alcohol didn't. I was supposed to have cleaned my bedroom and taken a shower, and I dawdled. I was all wrapped up in listening to New Kids on the Block.

"Misty, your room better be clean, and you'd better be taking a shower!" Mom yelled. "I'm coming up the stairs to check on you!"

"Your room better be clean, and you'd better be taking a shower," I repeated, mimicking her.

"Have you cleaned your room and taken a shower?" Mom asked again.

"Have you cleaned your room and taken a shower?" I mimicked her again.

At that point, Mom said, sternly, "You'd better do it, or I'm going to give you the what-for."

"I'm going to give you the what-for, ———," I mimicked, calling her a nasty word.

Mom exploded. I realized that she was only two steps away from the top of the stairs when I'd sassed her, and I immediately sprinted into the bathroom and locked the door to try to protect myself.

"Dad, help me!" I yelled.

"At this point, I can't!" Dad said.

Mom punched a hole right through the bathroom door, reached inside, and unlocked it. She burst into the bathroom and walloped me, which I deserved. She had a hit for every syllable: Don't. You. Ever. Talk. To. Me. Like. That. Ever. Again.

That was the last time I ever talked back to Mom.


For the most part, beginning from when I was a little kid, I took myself out of the firing line as quickly as possible. I'd head upstairs to my bedroom, and I'd lock the door. I'd slip on my Walkman headphones, and I'd turn up my music as loud as I could, but that still didn't completely drown out the screaming or the destruction. Since we lived in a small apartment building, I'm sure all of the neighbors lived through the madness, right along with me. Most of the time, I was too embarrassed about my parents' drinking to invite my friends to our house. And there were plenty of nights I slept at my grandparents' or my friends' houses to remove myself from the volatile environment. Although I never told them about what was really going on behind closed doors at our place.

That is, not until it became so unbearable I finally had to tattle on Dad and Mom. One night, when I was eight, they were both drinking heavily. They were yelling, pitching things left and right, and I was worried for my safety. So I picked up the phone, and I called my grandparents. They had no idea their daughter had a drinking problem, because we'd all managed to keep it a secret from them. However, that night, I had no choice. Their drinking, and their fighting, had gotten so bad that I just wanted out of the house. When my grandfather arrived, he was mortified by Mom's condition and our ransacked apartment. He loved Mom; he thought she hung the moon. Instead of blaming her for the situation, he pointed the finger at Dad.

"Barbie's drinking because of you," my grandfather said, accusingly, to Dad.

Dad was seething. He may have wanted to say, "Have you ever told your daughter that you loved her?" But instead, he said, "I don't think she's drinking because of me. If you want to believe that, I'm okay with it. Ask Misty who she wants to live with."

Then, my grandfather looked at me and said, "Darling, do you want to stay here? Who do you want to live with? Your mother or your father?"

I didn't have to think too long to come up with my answer.

"I want to go with my dad," I blurted out.

Mom started crying. She was so drunk, she could barely talk. However, she managed to get out these words: "Fine, go live with your father!"

I think, deep down, somewhere, she was together just enough to understand why, at that moment, I would rather have lived with Dad.

I loved Mom dearly, but I didn't want to live with her like that. It was painful to watch her destroying herself. Dad, on the other hand, was better able to hold his liquor. Truth be told, a lot of nights after that episode, I slept at my grandparents' house. They insisted on keeping me out of harm's way, and I wanted, and needed, the security and stability they offered. My aunt Betty Ann says, in all seriousness, that I was their favorite grandchild. In fact, she maintains they loved me more than their own three children, because, she says, they felt so sorry for me having to grow up with alcoholic parents.

Wouldn't you have thought my revelation, choosing Dad over Mom, would've been life-changing for her? An aha moment? It wasn't. It took six more years before Mom quit drinking. Fortunately, for me, it took only two more years before Dad stopped.

One night, in 1988, when I was eleven, Dad's drinking came to a screeching halt. Literally. He'd just left a bar in Orange County and had climbed into his truck to drive home to Santa Monica. He and his buddies had been celebrating a victory in a beach volleyball tournament. He was drunk, of course, and he never should have gotten behind the wheel. And never mind the fact he already had one driving under the influence (DUI) blemish on his record. He was acting irresponsibly.

In the blink of an eye, his life changed. And so did our family's.

Suddenly, out of nowhere, while he was crossing an intersection, a motorcyclist, racing one hundred miles an hour, slammed into the front end of Dad's truck. Miraculously, he escaped injury, but the motorcyclist wasn't as lucky. Dad says he'll never forget trying to assist him. The guy's six-foot body was "folded over." His arms, his legs, everything, were wrapped around his torso. He recalls the guy spitting his teeth into Dad's left hand. As Dad was being handcuffed and thrown into the back of a police car, the arresting officer said, "Buddy, you'll never fart again."

Now Dad was facing prison time, twelve years.

I'll never forget Mom receiving the call to go pick him up at the Orange County jail. It wasn't the first time she and I had been through that scenario. But this time was different. This time, for all Dad knew, he'd killed somebody. When he left the accident scene, the motorcyclist was being evacuated by air to a trauma center and was clinging to life. I cried my eyes out that night, after Dad told me he might be headed to prison. Twelve years? I'd have graduated from college by then.

Over the next few days, Dad did his best to pretend things were normal. He went right back to work at MGM. But the accident was eating him up inside. On the sly, he telephoned Ralph and Dixie Johnson, the loggers from Loyalton, California, who'd taken him in when he was a homeless rodeo bull rider. They'd opened their home and their hearts to him. Dad thought of them as his second set of parents, and they'd always been an important part of my extended family as well. With the possibility of prison time hanging over his head, Dad asked Ralph and Dixie if they'd take Mom and me in. If he was locked up, he knew that Mom couldn't support the two of us on her tennis teacher's salary. He also knew that, because of her drinking problem, I wasn't safe. Without skipping a beat, Ralph and Dixie agreed.

Also unbeknownst to Mom and me, Dad had talked to one of his buddies, Jim Oppliger, a former lifeguard and volleyball player at Muscle Beach who was then a deputy district attorney in Fresno. One weekend, soon after the accident, Oppliger was playing in an amateur tournament at State Beach, and Dad was the tournament director. He told Oppliger the details of the accident. He said his blood alcohol level at the scene had been .08, the legal limit, and it had been taken twice more, including at the jail, where it was 1.0. He also told Oppliger he'd recently contacted the best DUI attorney he could afford.

"Before you go spending money, let me find out what your case is all about," Oppliger offered. "Let me also ask around about who's a good lawyer for you. The cost between an attorney for a felony and a misdemeanor DUI is a world of difference."

When Oppliger returned to his office on Monday, he phoned the supervisor of the prosecuting unit in Orange County. Oppliger was told the accident was caused by the victim. He also was told the case had been filed as a felony, but that it clearly was a misdemeanor. The following day, Oppliger phoned Dad and explained that he was guilty of DUI, but not of causing the accident. He said that the best defense attorney couldn't get Dad out of this mess. However, if the district attorney ended up reducing it to a misdemeanor, he told Dad to jump on it.

And then, Oppliger gave Dad the most stunning news: The motorcyclist who hit his truck hadn't died. As it turned out, he was on the run from the Huntington Beach police at the time of the accident. They'd arrested him at the hospital. Oppliger told Dad that he didn't have to worry about a long prison sentence, but he'd have to do some jail time.

"That was my lotto ticket," Dad still says today, even though he has never defended what happened that night. It still doesn't excuse his actions, he says. The motorcyclist was rendered a quadriplegic. Whenever he talks about the accident, Dad always says, "It changed everything about my life." It changed everything about mine, too. If Dad hadn't been forced to change his behavior, if he hadn't stopped drinking, I wouldn't be the person I am today.

Two weeks later, Dad faced the music, without legal counsel. Because he had a clean record—his previous DUI had happened several years before—Dad was sentenced to three days in the Orange County jail. His sentence also included six months of alcohol and drug rehabilitation, and daily attendance at ninety Alcoholics Anonymous (AA) meetings. He was fined forty-two hundred dollars.

Before the accident, Dad had been vaguely familiar with AA and its twelve-step program. His sentence for his previous DUI had included AA meetings, but he'd gone to one, and said, "I can't get anything out of this." Then, instead of getting the secretary for the AA meetings to sign off on his court card, Dad signed them himself. All sixteen of them.

If life is truly better the second time around, then so is AA, at least from Dad's perspective. Right from the start, Dad was told by recovering alcoholics in his AA meetings to "shut up and listen." The most valuable lesson he learned was the Serenity Prayer, which he still relies on daily, as do I:

*God, grant me the serenity*
*To accept the things I cannot change;*
*The courage to change the things I can,*
*And the wisdom to know the difference.*

After six months of AA meetings, Dad recognized he was suffering from a disease, the disease of alcoholism, and most important, he understood he was powerless against it. He realized he had defects of character and had to learn to control his shortcomings. It was the stuff on the inside that had to be changed, Dad says, and in the process of doing that, he'd become comfortable in his own skin.

As an aside, one of Dad's shortcomings is, and always has been, his inability to read the fine print. So when he scanned a listing of AA meetings near our apartment, he never bothered to look at the bottom of the page to see what the asterisk next to particular dates and places denoted. One day, when I was eleven, Dad decided to take me to an AA meeting for the first time. He was three months sober, a completely different person, and I was very happy about this turn of events. We arrived at a Santa Monica restaurant, and we were met by a man at a door to a side room.

"So you're one of us?" the man asked Dad.

"Yup," Dad said.

"How long have you known?" the man wondered.

"Three months," Dad replied.

They introduced themselves to each other and continued to exchange pleasantries.

"So you're one of us?" the man asked again.

"Yup," Dad said.

"How long have you known you were gay?" the man asked.

After that, Dad read the fine print, when it came to AA meetings. He never again made "an asterisk" of himself.

Once he got sober, Dad was able to witness the unhealthy environment in which I lived: Mom continued drinking for another four years. It wasn't pretty, and it wasn't safe.

Dad always told me, "Don't get into the car with Mom if she is drinking." Oftentimes, I didn't realize she was drunk until we were on the road. At that point, it was too late. I'd tell her, "Mom, you're not staying in the proper lane. I'd rather get out than drive with you." Once, I was staying at Carol Luber's house, and I was young, so I had to be picked up. Mom retrieved me, and we almost hit a tree on the way home. Mom put her foot on the brake, slowly. I slammed the transmission into park. I jumped out of the car and ran the mile back to Carol's house.

Why didn't Mom stop drinking after Dad got sober? I'm still dumbfounded by that. Dad says it's because "she didn't find it necessary." Again, I just don't think she could disengage herself from alcohol's stranglehold. It was a strong, strong addiction for her. Dad says you've got to hit rock bottom before you make radical changes in your life. He also says every bottom has a trapdoor. Well, Mom just hadn't bottomed out yet. She kept finding trapdoors. She drank a lot at night, after she came home from teaching tennis. With her being drunk, and Dad putting in so much time at MGM, there were many hours when nobody was looking after me. That ended my childhood long before it should have. I had to become an adult well before I was ready. All those nights, at home, alone with Mom, a beautiful, loving woman, who turned into someone else as the evenings, and the drinking, wore on, hurt me deeply. Often, I had to be the responsible one in the household: "Mom, you can't get into the car and drive." Or, "Mom, you've left dinner in the oven and burned it. Let's order a pizza." Or, "Mom, you're not making sense. It's time for you to go to bed."

One night, Mom called Dad at MGM, drunk and in a panic.

"Somebody stole Misty!" she cried.

Dad explained the situation to his boss, admitted Mom's drinking problem, and was excused from work.

"Whatever it takes, go home and find Misty," his boss told him.

When Dad got home, Mom already had the neighbors out combing the area, searching for me. They were walking the streets, knocking on doors. Before he joined the search party, though, he headed upstairs to my bedroom. He just had a hunch. Sure enough, there I was, asleep in my bed, buried underneath a warm pile of laundry. It turned out Mom had done several loads of wash that night, then folded the clothes and dumped them on top of me. She'd been too drunk and disoriented to notice me sleeping.

Being the only child of alcoholic parents could be extremely lonely, especially when both Dad and Mom were drinking. I was too embarrassed to tell anyone—my friends, my grandparents, my teachers, my guidance counselors, my coaches, my teammates—about what was going on inside my world. At times, I felt as if I were the only kid on earth who had such a topsy-turvy life. So instead of talking about it, I just tried to deal with it on my own. I'd lock myself into my bedroom and do something to try to distract myself. Listen to music. Do homework. Work on jigsaw puzzles. And cry. I'd always cry.

I often worried that their fighting would eventually lead to divorce. Dad says his Muscle Beach friends told him to leave Mom once he was sober. They were concerned about our welfare. But Dad was deeply in love with Mom. He says he never came close to leaving her after he'd sobered up. He had faith in Mom, faith that someday the light would go on and she'd realize she had to get sober. He didn't want to walk away, he says, because then he'd always wonder.

There were times when Mom's drinking got so out of control that Dad and I both had to leave the house. We'd go to movies, hoping that by the time we came home she'd be sobered up. Or passed out.

Even now, I can't recall why she finally stopped drinking in 1992. Perhaps it was because she saw all the progress Dad was making. Perhaps it was because she recognized all the opportunities unfolding in front of me. Or maybe, just maybe, it was because she finally understood it was no fun being miserable all by herself. She was sick and tired of being sick and tired.

For years, Mom used to paw through Dad's dresser drawers, rummage through his stuff in the garage, dig through his truck, looking for booze. She couldn't understand why he came home from AA meetings so upbeat. She couldn't figure out what was making him so happy. He must have been drinking, she thought. Eventually, she figured it out: He was happy because he was sober. Dad likes to call AA "a program of attraction." One day, Mom finally went to Dad and said, "I think I might have a problem."

"Come to a meeting, and we'll find out," Dad suggested.

Mom's first AA meeting didn't go well at all. She listened to others tell their stories, and she absolutely hated it. "That's not me," she told Dad. But he was so faithful about attending AA meetings, and he was so encouraging of Mom's sobriety, that she kept right on going. At most meetings, she'd get into it with the recovering alcoholics, to the point of cursing at them. If she heard an answer she didn't like, she'd take it personally. A few months into the process, Mom announced, "I'm through with AA!" She stopped attending AA meetings, and to her credit, she was able to remain sober. She never fell off the wagon, never even came close. She stayed sober because of her own sheer willpower. She stayed clean because Dad stayed clean. She stopped drinking so she could be present for me. One day, Dad found her in the kitchen, pouring twenty bottles of liquor down the drain.

Even today, I'm grateful, every single minute, that my parents got sober before my volleyball career really took off. While I was living in their tumultuous, alcoholic hell, though, I promised myself I wouldn't let them pull me, and my future, down the drain along with them. I made secret plans to live with my grandparents, or someone else (whom I wasn't sure), in a more stable environment. If I'd had to live apart from one or both of my parents, I would've, in order to save myself.

In the process of becoming sober, Mom became happier, more open, and more centered. She recognized her character defects and learned how to manage her shortcomings. Most important, she learned that quitting booze was only the tip of the iceberg: Just because you stop drinking, it doesn't mean your problems stop, too. Through her own self-analysis, she realized her drinking stemmed from her childhood. One of the things Mom always had longed to hear was her parents saying, "I love you, Barbie." But it was difficult for them to say. Eventually, Mom came to terms with it, and she filled that hole in her life by helping them in their old age.

Now, I'd have to say alcoholism actually brought my parents and me closer as a family. Once Dad and Mom got sober, we did a lot more family things. We talked more. We tried to address our problems, not bury them. Our lives together became much more meaningful. We always started our days grateful, happy, and hopeful. I have vivid recollections of waking up each morning to the blaring sounds of the Three Tenors. At the crack of dawn, my parents would slip in a videotape of their favorite PBS program and crank up Luciano Pavarotti, Placido Domingo, and Jose Carreras. Their songs were so uplifting, such a far cry from the darkness. Mom would be busy cleaning the house, and Dad would be gardening in the backyard, and I'd hear them both singing along with the Three Tenors. Thinking about the scene still brings a smile to my face.

As the years passed, the three of us were able to celebrate our past. Dad is proud of his AA sobriety chips, celebrating various sobriety milestones, five years, ten years, fifteen years, twenty years. He and I always made a big deal of Mom's sobriety milestones, too. We all finally reached the point where we could laugh about our darkest days. If Dad got uptight or edgy, Mom and I would always poke fun at him and say, "You need an AA meeting." Without getting teed off, he'd agree. "Yeah, Serenity Prayer," he'd proclaim, thrusting his fist in the air, and off he'd go to another AA meeting to straighten himself out.

# 7

## High School

My two biggest assets in life are passion and commitment. I'm fully invested in being exceptional, especially in volleyball. You've really got to love what you do for it to be extremely powerful. You've got to feel it, from your head to your toes, down through to your bones, right to the center of your heart. I'm talking goose-bumps-all-over-my-body, the-hair-standing-up-on-the-back-of-my-neck territory. I can't hide my passion. It's extremely evident. I exude it from every pore when I'm on the field of play.

I've made a lot of sacrifices to get to where I am today, although, in the scheme of things, I didn't give up a whole lot. I attended only three high school dances, and now I tell girls, "High school dances are overrated." When you're part of a team, you don't want to miss practice. When you're having fun with your teammates, you don't want to miss a single minute. Give it everything you've got.

I learned some of my most valuable life lessons during my high school years, when I was emerging as the best young volleyball player in the country.

From the moment we moved to Orange County my eighth-grade year, I felt like an outsider. My parents moved into a 1,040-square-foot, three-bedroom house in Costa Mesa. We finally had a house! I could take advantage of the area's superior academics and athletics. It also was closer to my maternal grandparents, who lived in Laguna Hills. I was sad to leave my old friends, but Dad and Mom assured me sports would be my entrée to new ones. However, fitting in was more difficult than they'd planned.

We were leaving our Muscle Beach sanctuary, the acceptance, the familiarity, the comfort, and the security of our extended family. That colorful cast of characters of all colors, ages, shapes, and sizes laid all of their cards right out on the table. They never put up racial, gender, religious, or socioeconomic barriers. Now we were entering affluent, predominantly white Orange County, and more specifically, Newport Beach, one of the wealthiest communities in the nation.

It wasn't my first brush with prejudice. That happened when I was ten and attended the Kamehameha Schools Ho'omaka'ika'I Explorations summer program. It's the admissions policy of the Kamehameha Schools to give preference to applicants of Hawaiian ancestry to the extent permitted by law. The one-week boarding Explorations program centers on foundational themes and activities such as Hawaiian values, mele, hula, Hawaiian crafts, and much more. Because I was whiter than everybody else—I'm three-sixteenths Hawaiian—few people talked to me. By the third day, I couldn't keep down any food and had diarrhea. Dad received a call from someone affiliated with the program, who told him I was sick.

So Dad pulled some strings. He called his close friend Gordon Pi'ianaia. He'd attended and taught at the Kamehameha Schools, and he'd played volleyball at the University of Hawaii. Thanks to Gordon's help, I soon was assigned a mentor from Ni'ihau, the smallest inhabited Hawaiian island. It's the only Hawaiian island where the Hawaiian language is spoken as a primary language. Instantly, I was steeped in Hawaiian culture. It was amazing. I learned Hawaiian values and crafts. I mastered the hula. I won all of the swimming races. And, most important, I finally fit in.

When I got home from Hawaii, Dad took me to see the movie *Mississippi Burning*, which dealt with racial prejudice in the South.

Afterward, we talked about how it felt for me not to be completely accepted in Hawaii as Hawaiian.

"So what do you think about Hawaii now?" Dad asked.

"Hawaii always will hold a special place in my heart," I said.

However, my lack of acceptance in Newport Beach wasn't about racial prejudice. It was about socioeconomic prejudice. When I arrived on the scene as an eighth grader, I was a talented athlete whose reputation preceded her. All of the girls in town had played together for years, in various sports, on public school teams, recreation league teams, and club teams. Instead of being welcomed because, in coming years, I could make the Newport Harbor High girls' teams better, I was looked at with raised eyebrows. More hurtful yet, I was looked down upon because I was a lower-middle-class kid, who lived on the wrong side of the tracks. This was something I'd never encountered before. For example, a lot of the girls in the eighth and ninth grades would have birthday parties, and I wouldn't be invited because I wasn't part of the group.

Fortunately, while I was working hard to make inroads through sports, I met two very nice girls, both of whom came from mixed race families, which also had made it difficult for them to fit in: Tina Bowman, my badminton partner in eighth-grade physical education class, and Cara Heads, the point guard on my eighth-grade basketball team. She later placed seventh at the 2000 Olympics in weightlifting. Tina and Cara could relate to the social challenges I was facing in the predominantly white, affluent community. I respected, embraced, and celebrated their diversity. Through the years, Tina and Cara have remained my close friends.

I learned one of my most valuable life lessons in my freshman year at Newport Harbor High, when I was a member of the varsity volleyball team. Early in fall 1991, we were entered in a tournament in Santa Barbara, which fell on the same weekend as a family reunion. My parents asked head coach Dan Glenn if they could drive me to Santa Barbara, instead of my going on the team bus. Coach Glenn initially told them no, but finally relented, as long as I was in the gym an hour before the first game. Dad and Mom assured him I'd be there in plenty of time. Well, I wasn't. A sailboat came off a trailer, closing the freeway we were on for ninety minutes. As I watched the clock tick down to game time, I got more and more nervous. Sure enough, I didn't arrive until after the team had started warming up.

"I told you if she was late, she wouldn't play," Coach Glenn told Dad.

Dad explained what had happened, but Coach Glenn didn't budge. He didn't even allow me to participate in warm-ups. In fact, Coach Glenn completely ignored me. After the first or second match, Dad said, "We're out of here!" And we drove home.

A few days later, Coach Glenn laid down the law.

"This stuff can't happen, Misty," Coach Glenn said. "You've only known me for a couple of months. You've known your parents all your life. I don't expect you not to listen to your parents. I just need you to be here."

Years later, Coach Glenn admitted he was irritated with me that day because, in his view, I hadn't come sprinting into the gym, apologizing profusely for my tardiness. What really ticked him off, he recalls now, was the "nonchalant manner" with which I walked through the gym door. Realistically, because I was a freshman, Coach Glenn says, he knew I probably wasn't going to play in the tournament. The team had several seniors, including girls who'd played for him for three or four years. But Coach Glenn admits he used that incident to teach me exactly what he expected from his athletes. He wanted me to understand that nobody, not even a rising young star, got special treatment. Coach Glenn had high hopes for me. He already was thinking down the road to my junior and senior years, when he wanted me to be a leader.

Sometimes, the head coach teaches you life lessons verbally. Other times, you learn them the hard way. For a week after the incident, Coach Glenn subjected me to rigorous drills, including "Coach on One" and "Marble Mania." In "Coach on One," a defensive drill, he'd set a time clock at one minute, then he'd toss a ball, anywhere on the court, and

I'd have to get it up. If I didn't touch the ball, ten seconds were tacked on to the minute. In "Marble Mania," he'd roll the balls all over the floor, and I couldn't let them roll out of bounds. If I did, again, he'd add ten seconds to the minute. The drills weren't fun; they were exhausting. But this was my penalty, and I accepted it. The way I handled the adversity, Coach Glenn says, earned me the respect of my teammates.

As my freshman season went on, I ended up starting and doing a phenomenal job. At five feet seven, I was the setter on a team featuring four-year varsity players. I was the only freshman named to the all-tournament team at the Orange County Championships. Coach Glenn says he believed we had the best team in the state that year, and he was devastated (and so were we) when we lost in the CIF quarterfinals in five games. Laguna Beach won the state championship that year, and we'd defeated Laguna pretty handily during the season. So the quarterfinal loss was especially painful. We knew we were better than that. We knew we'd blown a golden opportunity.

In fall 1992, my sophomore year, we had a very young team. Coach Glenn started four sophomores, including me, a junior, and a senior. He moved me to outside hitter, and I excelled at the new position. His reasoning was this: If I were playing at outside hitter, I'd be touching the ball when I passed it, and I'd also get to hit it. So every time the ball crossed the net, I'd have a good chance of touching it twice, as opposed to being the setter, where I'd have only one shot at the ball. He thought I'd be more dynamic at outside hitter, and he admits he used Karch's career as the measuring stick in making the switch. Karch had been a setter at UCLA, but on the U.S. Olympic indoor team he was an outside hitter. Now, Coach Glenn says he wishes he'd kept me at setter.

We were a young, scrappy bunch. We relished our underdog label. We weren't very big, but we were extremely talented. We went on to win the 1992 CIF Division III State Championship behind my thirty-one kills in the title game. A small school, we always played up in Division I. After losing in the semis to Laguna Beach, we weren't eligible for the Division I state playoffs. So Coach Glenn decided we'd step down to Division III. What a smart move. I was named Division III State Player of the Year.

In my first two years at Newport Harbor, I also participated in soccer and track. I was asked to go out for basketball, but I declined because I felt I'd had enough gym time already. Also, I was very passionate about soccer, which was held the same time of the year as basketball. That didn't mean I didn't play basketball for fun, though. One day, while we were practicing approach jumps for volleyball, and we were measuring our vertical leap, Coach Glenn said, "Misty, you're close to touching the basketball rim."

Close? I took that word as a challenge. A week later, as practice was getting started, I said, "Coach, watch this!" I did an approach and touched the rim. Outwardly, Coach Glenn was unfazed. "That's great," he said. "But the true test is if you can touch it three times in a row." Years later, Coach Glenn told me, inside he was saying to himself, "Are you kidding?" Two weeks later, I burst into the gym and said, "Coach, check this out!" I touched the rim three times in a row off an approach. If you challenge me, I'm going to rise to the occasion. I've got a lot of drive, but it's very quiet. I think people always have underestimated my drive because it's so deep under the surface.

Another great example of my drive occurred later my sophomore year, when I was competing in track. I ran the 100, 200, and 4x100- (third runner) and 4x400- (anchor) meter relays and high jumped. As a sophomore, I competed against future Olympian Marion Jones, then a senior at Thousand Oaks High, but I never beat her. In one meet, I came close, though. Well, not really. Because it was a staggered start, I was ahead of her when the gun went off. Marion caught me on the turn, and everybody jumped to their feet as if to say, "You've got to be kidding me." Running side by side with Marion lasted all of a second or two. Suddenly, she flipped an internal switch, shifted into a higher gear, and poof! Dad and Mom always said I had a beautiful stride, that they loved watching me run.

I did manage to outrun a couple of the best sprinters on Newport Harbor's team, but it didn't grab any headlines, although it did ruffle some feathers. According to Dad, the parents threatened to pull their daughters off the team if I were running the sprints. So I ran the 100 only once.

That didn't faze me, though, because I was focused on the high jump. I stunned a lot of people in that event, including myself, and not always for the right reasons. The best high jumper in the school was my friend Tina Bowman, who easily cleared the bar with her Fosbury Flop technique, with its characteristic backward-over-the-bar appearance. When I started high jumping, I was so green, I just grabbed my knees and went over the bar as if I were doing a cannonball into a swimming pool. At one of my track meets, Mom caught my technique out of the corner of her eye.

"Who's that ugly thing who just went over the bar?" she asked.

"Your daughter," Dad replied.

"Oh, my God," Mom gasped. "We've got to get her some lessons."

At that time, my parents didn't follow through with their vow to get me high-jump lessons. Instead, I worked on my technique with my friend Tina, as well as Newport Harbor's track coaches. Eventually, I opened quite a few eyes.

In high school competition in California, you have to clear the high-jump bar at predetermined heights in order to qualify for each of the major meets (league, CIF, Masters, State) at the conclusion of the season. I competed in CIF, but I didn't win. However, my jump did qualify me for the Masters meet. That's where I became locked into a jump-off for a spot in the state meet. It showed everybody what I was made of. I'd never cleared five feet eight, and then, under pressure, I didn't just clear it once, I cleared it three times, qualifying for state. Then, the following week, in the state finals, I cleared five feet ten and finished second. That jump-off taught me about perseverance, how to compete one-on-one. In the heat of battle, it's all about which of you can outlast the other. That jump-off also taught me it's about you and the bar, not the other person.

What helped me in high jump was positive visualization. First, my coach had us watch tapes of Cuba's Javier Sotomayor, the 1992 Olympic gold medalist and world-record holder in the high jump, as well as top European high jumpers. Second, he had us practice jumping six feet, using springboards to get us up in the air. Falling from six feet was scary, so his theory was you had to prepare yourself for those falls. Third, when my opponents jumped, I refused to watch them. I knew their misses could derail me, that I'd be telling myself, "Uh-oh, I hope I make it over." Instead, I'd turn away. Then, when it was my turn to jump, I'd take a deep breath, focus, and say, "Get it!"

I learned a handful of other life lessons in my junior and senior years: I learned, as I got older and better, that I couldn't be the girl for all seasons any longer. It was important to concentrate on one sport. I was spreading myself too thin. I was running from one high school or club practice to another. I also was cherry-picking events, competing in those I deemed important and skipping those I thought weren't as big a deal. That wasn't fair to me, to my coaches, or to my teammates.

Before my junior year, I gave up soccer. Track was the next sport to fall by the wayside. Two incidents prompted that change. Although I had done well as a sophomore in the high jump, I struggled as a junior. That spurred my parents to seek out private coaching to allow me to more fully realize my potential. In those days, it wasn't as common as it is now to pay for private, specialized coaching. When the school got wind of it, the athletic director became angry with my parents. He already had had a problem with us earlier that year, when I quit soccer to join my friends on the basketball team. He'd said I couldn't jump from one team to another, and he didn't allow me to play basketball. In his opinion, the technical coaching I was receiving at Newport Harbor was more than adequate, and he said he didn't appreciate our going outside the school for extra coaching.

And then, there was the straw that broke the camel's back. One weekend, I had a scheduling conflict. My Newport Harbor track team had a meet, and my Ichiban volleyball club team had Junior Olympics qualifying. I weighed my options. The Orange County meet was inconsequential, I thought, while the Junior Olympics was the most prestigious volleyball tournament for a club-level team. Only thirty-two teams were invited. You either had to be number one in your region, or you had to win certain qualifying tournaments.

I explained my dilemma to the athletic director. I told him what I thought were the pros and cons of the situation. Finally, I said, "I think the Junior Olympics qualifying is a much more important event, so I'm going to do that." He was furious. "If you do that, don't come back." With that, I was thrown off the Newport Harbor track team, weeks before the state championship.

Now, with almost two decades of perspective, I realize it must have been extremely difficult for my coaches, at every level, and yes, even still today, to coach a kid whose parents were outstanding athletes and accomplished volleyball players. Not to mention successful volleyball coaches. Sadly, Dad and Mom were automatically considered a coach's worst nightmare.

"But we've never interfered with any of her coaches," Dad once told the *Long Beach Press Telegram*, in reference to their reputation as overly knowledgeable parents throughout my athletic career. "We've just kind of debriefed her."

And I added: "He's tried talking to coaches before, but egos get in the way. So he kind of tells me things I should try to do differently. I listen to him, because he's smart and his coaches were good. The stuff he says makes sense. I've never really shut anyone out. I listen to everybody."

In the end, being told by two coaches to only play volleyball, being forced to put all my time and energy into one sport, turned out to be one of the best things that ever happened to me.

In 1993, my junior year, we won the Sea View League title, twice beating Corona del Mar High. Then we turned around and lost to them at the CIF Finals. We went on the road and beat some really good teams—Bakersfield, Poway (featuring six players who went on to play in NCAA Division I), and St. Mary's (at the University of the Pacific in front of two thousand people)—to get a chance to play Corona del Mar again; we lost to them in the state title match in five games. Another crushing defeat, which I still vividly remember, in part, because I lost my head in the heat of battle.

When things got tight, I suddenly snapped, yelling at my team-mates and shouting at Coach Glenn. Instantly, he subbed me out, and he told me to sit on the end of the bench. After a few points, I went to him and apologized. "Sorry, Coach, I got really frustrated," I said. He reminded me never to lose my cool on the court. "It won't happen again," I said. And then he subbed me back in.

Coach Glenn made the right decision to pull me. If I'd been the coach, and one of my players had snapped like that, I'd have done the same thing. I still don't know what came over me. Maybe I wanted to win too much. Whatever the case, my flare-up had embarrassed me, and I realized I'd have to keep my wits about me, if I ever hoped to be a great player and a world-class person.

I went on to be named the Division I State Player of the Year.

Much to my dismay, my outburst in the state final stayed with me. Not that Coach Glenn or I ever brought it up. Rather, it was others who made it a big deal. I heard all the gossip: "Can Dan Glenn and Misty May get along? Can they win the big game?" Well, talk about making people eat their words.

As a senior, I learned a lot of important life lessons. Not the least of which was that, because I was a superstar, everything I did got examined closely, sometimes too closely, that I could be put up on a pedestal as quickly as I could be knocked off it.

That season, Coach Glenn kept repeating this phrase to me: "You will be judged on how much better you make your teammates."

We lost only one match all season. It happened in the Santa Bar-bara Tournament of Champions, where we were defeated in the quar-terfinals by San Jose's Archbishop Mitty High, led by Kerri Walsh. In my mind, it was an important turning point: We became a much better team, a lot tougher and much hungrier, for having gone through that loss.

In the end, we were finally able to accomplish what had eluded us for four years: We won the 1994 CIF Division I State Championship, beating St. Mary's of Stockton in three games. I was the 1994 Mizuno High School National Player of the Year and at the top of the *Volleyball Monthly* Fab 50 list. I was named Division I State MVP for the second straight year, after recording 302 digs, 92 assists, and a national-record 548 kills, and Newport Harbor finished with a 33–1 record. During my four years, our overall record was 106–12.

And I topped it all off by appearing in *Sports Illustrated*'s Faces in the Crowd.


While my days at Newport Harbor High turned out to be an important time of growth, both on and off the athletic field, what truly helped me grow into the top high school volleyball recruit in the U.S. in 1995 was my participation on the Ichiban volleyball club team in Long Beach. Ichiban is the Japanese word for number one, and it certainly was one of the most prominent, successful volleyball clubs in the nation in the 1990s.

While volleyball is dominated by upper-middle-class kids, Ichiban's players tended to come from blue-collar backgrounds. Ichiban's directors kept the cost low to make it affordable for lower-income families. The geographical area from which Ichiban pulled its players tended to entice more minorities. The directors allowed my family and others who were strapped for money to subsidize club dues through fund-raisers and snack bar duty, and to keep the cost of road trips down by traveling the most economical way. At that time, the cost to join was about eight hundred dollars. Today, the average volleyball club dues are closer to five thousand dollars, an outrageous sum of money. This prevents a lot of great kids from participating in club volleyball, which is a must, if you want to get a college scholarship. If club dues had been that astronomical when I was growing up, it would have been impossible for me to participate.

Tryouts for Ichiban were held at the end of October, when the high school season was drawing to a close. Training began in November. Competition ran from January until almost the Fourth of July, culminating in the Junior Olympics. Ichiban's program had about a hundred girls, playing in four age brackets from 12-and-under to 18-and-under.

In my first year with Ichiban, in 1994, as a junior at Newport Harbor, I played for the club's top 18-and-under team. I joined a team filled with All-Americans who'd grown up in the club. Throughout the season, we were one of the top two teams in the nation. We won most of the major tournaments across the U.S. Unfortunately, we lost in the 18-open gold medal match to Sports Performance Volleyball Club (Warrenville, Illinois) at the Junior Olympics in Austin, Texas.

I was extremely disappointed, but I didn't cry. I'm not a big crier in real life. However, I did have to comfort and console my teammates. Very quickly, however, I made it clear to them that we had to use the loss as a motivating force, that we had to come back, respond, and put ourselves in the same position the following year.

My two seasons at Ichiban taught me how to be an effective leader. I have an innate ability to make those around me better and more productive. I'm the kind of athlete who leads by example, reading others' minds on both sides of the net, anticipating many shots ahead. Assistant coach Lee Maes used to say that I had "a magic" about me, that I had "an uncanny sense" of how to play the game, that I was able to see the whole court, and that I had "a sixth sense" of how to react. I am also the kind of athlete who inspires through my ability to cultivate relationships. It's important to me that people want to play with, and for, me. I want my teammates to follow me on the court, to respond to me when I'm playing with them. I set an example through my work ethic, my attitude and behavior, and my coachability.

True, I'm an only child, which means I can easily, and happily, spend time alone. However, I believe, inherently, I'm a people person. I lead in a subtle, effortless way. I do it with my ability to communicate, by being extremely giving of myself, which makes people feel comfortable and secure. My biggest plus is my sense of humor. I'm a total goofball. I love making people laugh, in a wide variety of ways, through my quick tongue, pranks, imitations, costumes, or skits. Ultimately, in a team sport, it's how cohesive a unit you are that will dictate success.

My second season with Ichiban, 1995, I was one of the few high school seniors on the team. We had a great group of juniors who'd come up through the ranks, but they didn't have as much experience as the previous year's group. We played Sports Performance Volleyball Club again, at the Junior Olympics in Orlando, Florida. This time, though, it was in the semifinal match, and sadly, we lost and went home with the bronze medal. Here's an interesting tidbit: Kerri Walsh and Team Mizuno (San Jose, California) won the gold medal, defeating Sports Performance in the very next match.

# 8

## MOM

My mother is my compass. It has been that way from the moment I took my first breath, and it will be so until I take my last.

I still have her favorite Mother's Day card, which I wrote to her when I was four:

*Why do I love my Mom?*
*Because she lets me steer the car when we're pulling out of the garage.*
*Because she lets me help her push the shopping cart at the grocery store.*
*Because she lets me dress up my cats.*
*And most of all, I love my Mom because she lets me kill cockroaches.*

Dad is the type who lets you burn your hand before telling you the fire is hot. Afterward, he'll thoroughly explain the situation. Mom, meanwhile, made sure you knew all of the ramifications ahead of time, as well as how to avoid every single pitfall.

In stories written about me, Dad always is referred to as "Butch May, the beach volleyball legend," and he gets most of the credit for my career. But Mom deserves a lot of credit, too, much more than she ever has been given. True, Dad was the only parent present when

I won two Olympic gold medals. He has worked with me for count-less hours in training sessions on the beach. He has traveled to tour-naments across the globe. He'd watch me in warm-ups, and if I were having issues, he'd fix them before the matches started. He has given his opinion on coaches, teammates, opponents, trainers, and heal-ers. He has brainstormed with me about ways to improve my game, inspire my partners, and defeat my opponents.

However, there's so much more that has to be taken care of behind the scenes, and that's where Mom came in. She handled the family's important paperwork. She kept detailed calendars of our schedules. She paid the bills on time. She double-checked my homework assign-ments. She made me redo papers that weren't well-written or well-researched. She planned our sports-related trips.

My mother was the sensible, organized parent.

Friday nights, heading into weekend club volleyball tournaments, she'd say as I paddled off to bed, "Your lunch will be packed, along with everything else you'll need, and it'll all be waiting by the front door in the morning. We'll meet up with you later." Saturdays and Sundays, she'd run the snack bar at my club tournaments to defray the cost of dues, registration, and travel. Dad helped her unload the car, then he'd rush off to the beach to play a few games before head-ing back to catch mine. If I had a couple of matches off, I'd pitch in behind the snack bar counter. I couldn't have afforded to play club volleyball any other way.

I loved the snack bar. We had some yummy items. Hot dogs with chili. Nachos with cheese. Mom and I went to Costco to purchase the food. She served fresh doughnuts and cinnamon rolls in the morn-ing. She made turkey croissants for lunch. Mom put in long, long hours. It was a labor of love. One of the things I regret is that I didn't thank her enough. Some of the best times of my life were working the snack bar with Mom.

Even Dad would wholeheartedly agree: Mom was the responsible parent.

After all, she brought him kicking and screaming into the computer age. One day, they pulled up to an ATM. Dad got out of the car and punched in a bunch of numbers. As they were waiting for the money to spit out, Mom yelled, "Well?"

"Nothing is happening," Dad replied.

"Where'd you insert the ATM card?" she asked.

He'd put it in the deposit slot.

Being the child of two outstanding athletes, I am always asked, "What part of you is your father and what part is your mother?" Well, I've got Dad's butt and Mom's hands. I've got both of their gorgeous legs (as well as my maternal grandmother's). I've got Dad's laid-back, Hawaiian approach to life. I've got Mom's intelligence and honesty—she always was in the background, telling it like it is. Mom was very studious. She'd read something once and get it. In college, she helped tutor my teammates and me in various subjects. When I was on road trips, she went to my classes and took notes. She loved school. When it comes to education, I take after my Dad. If he were weighing what to do in his free time, "Beach or books?" he'd always choose beach, and so would I.

My mother was, and always will be, the foundation of our family.

It took a lot of courage for her to marry Dad. Her parents thought he was a beach rat, that he wasn't good enough for her, and they never completely accepted him. There always was an underlying uneasiness in Dad's relationship with my grandparents, and I could sense Mom's disappointment in the situation. When the four of them were together, and her parents set her off, she'd look at Dad and shake her head. He'd bite his tongue, and she'd thank him later for that.

Over the years, my parents compensated for this lack of acceptance by creating their own extended family. Dad adopted people who needed help. He embraced them and took care of them. Mom adopted stray animals. She always had a menagerie at our house. She had numerous dogs (Noodles, Sandy, Claudia, Kolohe, Madison, Holly, Chewy, Katie) and cats (Mr. Peepers, Lola, Spike, Pokey, Red, Speedo), along with a yard filled with birds. Dad and Mom taught me a valuable lesson, in this regard: Families are what you make them.

They come in all sizes, shapes, and forms. And they even come with fur, feathers, four legs, and wings.

Mom never questioned her decision to marry Dad. She never gave it a second thought. I learned some valuable lessons in her bold, controversial move. The importance of having the courage of your convictions, of doing what you think or feel is right even when others disagree. The richness of the rewards that come from following your heart and taking the road less traveled. The strength and wisdom you gain from being true to yourself.

With Dad keeping his distance from my grandparents, and they from him, it changed the dynamics of our family. It made the three of us extremely close. We were the Three Musketeers, one for all and all for one, loyal to each other through thick and thin. No one would, or could, ever come between us. We got the best, and the worst, of each other. We lived in a hermetically sealed world, our own special, little, impenetrable bubble. Mom created it, and as time went on, Dad understood the benefits of it, too. She was of the mind-set, "This is now our family."

Complicating matters, Dad had been married twice before, to the same woman, Linda Stutsman. Although they weren't married very long either time, together they had had two sons, Brack and Scott. Basically, Dad married Linda a few months before each of the boys was born, then they divorced soon after. There was, and still is, a lot of acrimony. Dad recalls Linda instructing the boys to call him "Uncle" after the divorces. It was, and still is, a very painful situation for all of them.

Growing up, I didn't see my half brothers all that much, mostly during the summers. They didn't see Dad a whole lot either because of his crazy work and volleyball schedules. Dad's mother, Mele May, who lived in San Francisco, or Dad's sister Genevieve Vanek, who lived in Fremont, California, would phone Linda and ask to see the boys. Then Dad magically appeared for a visit with them.

In my parents' minds, their special, little, impenetrable bubble was necessary, so I didn't become encumbered by negative emotions.

Dad got a hard time from Linda, and Mom got a hard time from her folks. It hurt them both, very deeply, but they coped with it, figuring there was no reason to subject me to the hard feelings, too.

In their way of thinking, that special, little, impenetrable bubble was necessary, in order for all of their concentration to be on me. That was especially true after they both got sober. That bubble was their excuse not to have to be with everybody else, to shut out all of the bad influences, to focus on something more positive and a whole lot healthier than whatever the dysfunction was. I was the focal point. In addition, Dad promised himself when I was born that he'd be a better father to me than he had been to Brack and Scott. He threw all of his energy behind me, into my well-being and my future. I became his mission.

I also think that special, little, impenetrable bubble was important to Dad and Mom because it shielded them from alcohol. They'd both been great athletes earlier in their lives, but they'd had some sort of deficiency that had kept them from becoming as great as they could have been or had hoped to be. My parents certainly weren't going to let that happen to me. Perhaps it was the drinking. Perhaps it was not having somebody to take them to their athletic competitions. Perhaps it was not having someone to introduce them to the right people. Whatever the reason, Dad and Mom failed to realize their potential in sports, and they were going to make sure I had every opportunity.

What kinds of values did Mom teach me?

*To love yourself.* On the outside, Mom was not a stereotypical Southern California beauty. She was a large, muscular woman. She weighed about two hundred pounds. Strong arms. Powerful legs. Aggressive. Competitive. Tough. Growing up, she and I competed in "nose-offs." We'd stand side by side and stick our noses in the air to see who was taller. When I was a sophomore at Long Beach State, I lost the "nose-off" for good (I stopped growing): Mom was five feet ten, I was five feet eight and a half. Back in Mom's day, when women's sports weren't as accepted by society, there was a term used to describe her and other sports-minded females: tomboys. Nobody ever called me a tomboy, which shows how far women have come.

It didn't bother Mom that she wasn't a supermodel. She wasn't fazed by the wrinkles on her face, from years of playing tennis, paddle tennis, and beach volleyball in the blazing sun. She didn't dress in the latest fashions, and she wasn't a size 0. She wore my old stuff, mostly shorts and T-shirts. I remember her wearing a dress only once.

"You don't want to embarrass Misty," her girlfriends would say, before my banquets and awards ceremonies. "Are you sure you've got something nice to wear?"

Of course, I always held my breath, wondering what getups Mom and Dad would show up in. For instance, Dad didn't have an outfit to wear to the 1999 Honda-Broderick Cup reception in Reno, Nevada, when I was named the nation's outstanding collegiate female athlete. So he went shopping at a local western wear shop. When he sauntered into the ballroom, I gasped. Wrangler jeans. Quilted western shirt. Bolo tie. Leather jacket. Cowboy boots. He looked as if he'd stepped out of the movie *Lonesome Dove*.

Because of Mom's influence, I've never had an eating disorder or a body image problem. I've never been hung up on how I look physically. I'm proud of my body. My ideal playing weight is 150 to 155 pounds. At one time, I weighed almost 170 pounds, but I also was bench pressing about 145 pounds.

Just like Mom, I'm also not interested in clothes. "Life's not a fashion show," my parents always taught me. I've had a difficult time breaking out of that mind-set. Even today, I hate trying things on, I have a horrible eye for clothes and I despise spending money. I like shopping, but I have no fashion sense. If I'm really stuck, a friend, who's a stylist, will dress me. Fashion is just really hard for me. It's tiresome to have to think about it.

*To be compassionate.* Mom and Dad opened their hearts to people and animals. Without thinking twice, they'd give you the shirts off their backs. Mom helped families raise funds to participate in our club volleyball programs. Giving to others was a prominent part of growing up for me. It wasn't unnatural. You give to others without asking for anything in return. You just give, and give, and give . . . and things will come back to you in little ways, in different ways.

*To be charitable.* Mom never turned down any charity that asked for help. Dad had no clue how much money she'd donated until after she died. Then he studied the family checkbook. She always said, "If you don't ask, Butch, you won't be upset." It wasn't in the hundreds of dollars—it was well into the thousands. She felt her $25, $50, or $100 check would make the difference to whatever cause her heart was behind. Mom always had canned food, granola bars, and clothing packed in the car, to give out to the homeless and less fortunate.

*To be generous.* Mom was a great coach, always willing to instill her passion and share her knowledge, especially with teams I wasn't involved in. She coached tennis for the Beverly Hills and Culver City parks and recreation departments. She coached paddle tennis at the Sand & Sea Club. She coached boys' and girls' volleyball teams at Saints Simon and Jude, a parochial school in Orange County. She also coached at Santa Monica College. She always felt if she helped one person, she'd done her job, especially if she'd touched kids who'd never play again, after leaving middle or high school.

*To be inclusive.* At the beach, there'd be people who wouldn't be included in games because they were older, disabled, new to beach volleyball or paddle tennis, or just not part of the "in" crowd. Mom and Dad always were the first to say, "Would you like to play?" They remembered how important it was to them to be included, especially when they were starting out in beach volleyball. They knew how painful it was to be an outsider, and they liked making people feel comfortable.

They had a friend, Gwen Foledar, a member of the Sand & Sea Club, who was physically challenged. She had a genetic condition that caused her to be unusually small. She'd never tried paddle tennis, and

Mom sensed Gwen always was on the outside looking in. One day, Mom asked Gwen, "Would you like to play paddle tennis with me?"

"Oh, no, I can't play," Gwen said.

"How do you know? You haven't tried," Mom said.

Gwen was so grateful to be included, when she took the court, she was shaking. Mom was inspired by Gwen to work on a master's degree in adapted physical education. Gwen encouraged Mom, telling her she'd be great with the disabled. Gwen was with Mom when I was born. In fact, Gwen held me before Dad even saw me.

*To be a positive role model.* Mom taught me that you can learn something from everybody, that nobody is more special or important than anybody else, that you never know who you're going to run into or how you're going to affect someone. For instance, I could take my Olympic gold medals to "Show and Tell" at an elementary school, and the next thing you know, some kid is doing something extraordinary. It was an aha moment: "Oh, my gosh, it wasn't until I saw that Olympic gold medal that I knew I could do this." If you affect one person, and that person affects another, it's a trickle-down effect. I learned a long time ago you only need one grain of sand to make a pro.

*To live passionately.* One of my favorite Mom stories has to do with her Fountain Valley volleyball league crew. There were about thirty-five regulars, or five teams or so. You know how some people say, "We just play for the fun of it"? That wasn't Mom and her girl-friends. In fact, her nickname, on the beach and indoors, was "Killer B." If you were playing the middle, and you made three mistakes, she'd say, "You're outta here." She was determined not to lose. Why? Because the first-place team didn't have to bring lunch the following week. She prided herself on not having to cook.

*To never back down*—especially not from Dad. My family's most infamous volleyball story occurred when Mom and Dad were playing as partners in the 1975 Marine Street Mixed Open. I hadn't come along yet. They were ahead, 12–9, in a fifteen-point game in the finals of the winners bracket. They had to win it to advance to the championship. One thing led to another, and it didn't take long for Dad to start coaching, or rather overcoaching. Soon, they both were hotter than the Southern California sand, and they were letting their opponents Buzz Swartz and Nina Grouwinkle back into the game.

"Hey, B., why didn't you get that one?" Dad asked. "Put it up on one, and I'll put it away."

"Well, if you think you can put it away, how come you didn't put the fourth one away?" she snapped.

"I'm the captain, I'm going to have the last word," he lectured.

"Well, if you're the captain, you'd put more balls down," she argued. "Just deal with it."

"If you want to be the captain, set the ball up higher and closer," he snarled.

"Just deal with it," she said.

Just deal with it? Dad was infuriated. He didn't like being challenged on the volleyball court. And he was such a talented player that he could hit any spot he wanted to. That's a dangerous combination. As he went back to serve, he said, "Move up. Watch the first pass coming over."

She groaned.

"Just deal with it," she said, loudly.

Just deal with it? Mom pushed Dad's buttons again. Finally, he muttered under his breath, "The hell with it!" He used a top-spin serve, threw up the ball as hard as he could, then he bopped Mom on the back of her head.

Their friend Sandy Malpee, officiating the match, came to Mom's rescue.

"Barb, he did it on purpose!" Sandy said.

With that, Mom and Dad stormed off the court, quitting the tournament and forfeiting their chance for a second-place finish. They loaded their stuff into their van, and roared away. It was a seventeen-minute drive to their apartment in Santa Monica, without traffic. That day, though, it felt like seventeen hours. They hit every red light. When they reached Ocean and Lincoln, just two blocks from Muscle

Beach, Dad said, "Hey, B., want to go down to the beach and finish that tournament?"

"With you?" Mom asked, disgustedly.

"Yeah," Dad said.

"Oh, all right," she moaned.

And off they went to pretend to finish the Marine Street Mixed Open.

The next day, Dad's temper tantrum made the sports pages of the *South Bay Daily Breeze*, under the headline, "Butch May Goes Berserk."

# 9

# Long Beach State

As the top high school recruit in the country, I had my pick of colleges. I received more than three hundred recruiting letters, and my final list was a Who's Who of the nation's best programs: Stanford, Hawaii, Arizona, University of the Pacific, and Long Beach State.

Having the freedom to go anywhere should have made my choice a no-brainer. I couldn't have made the wrong choice if I picked the school by throwing at a dart board, right? Wrong. College helps you discover who you are, who you can become, and what life is all about. It was important for me not to make a decision just to make a decision, but rather to put a lot of thought into what I wanted to get out of volleyball and what I wanted to do after I was done playing. I had to be mature, intelligent, and strategic.

I know this now, in part because, early in the process, without doing my research, I'd made an emotional decision, verbally committing to the University of the Pacific. One day, I got completely carried away, thanks to Elsa Stegemann, a friend I'd played against in club volleyball. Out of the blue, we suddenly promised we'd play together in college. Elsa wanted to attend UOP; I wasn't clear about my choice. But since we were a package deal, I verbally committed to UOP, too, as a sophomore at Newport Harbor. However, until you sign an NCAA letter of intent, you aren't legally bound to a program. Soon after committing, I started re-examining my decision.

If you'd asked me, when I was a freshman in high school, what I wanted to be when I grew up, I would've said a professional soccer player. By my junior year, though, I began seeing myself playing professional indoor volleyball, in an international league. I also thought I had a shot at the U.S. Olympic indoor team.

Although I was a highly touted outside hitter, I believed my pro and Olympic career hinged on becoming a setter. While I'm considered tall in the real world, I'm shorter than the prototypical world-class indoor volleyball player. Actually, I'm a midget. These days, the best college and pro outside hitters are about six foot three. I'm only five foot eight and a half. Being a setter, I figured, would give me more cachet. When I was growing up, Dad insisted I learn every position because you never know when a teammate will suffer an injury and you'll have to fill in for her. That was one of the most important volleyball lessons Dad ever taught me. Knowing how to play every position has made me the player I am. Sadly, these days, kids specialize in one position.

While researching college programs, I'd ask, "Who's the best setting coach?" Time and again, the same name came up: Debbie Green, Long Beach State assistant coach. Experts called her "the best female U.S. setter ever." A two-time All-American at USC, she led the Trojans to two national championships. She also was a member of the 1980 Olympic team (the U.S. boycotted the 1980 Moscow Olympics, so she didn't go) and then led the U.S. to a silver medal at the 1984 Los Angeles Olympics.

And so, in August, before my junior year at Newport Harbor, I phoned Brian Gimmillaro, Long Beach State's head women's volleyball coach, and verbally committed to being a part of his program. Under Brian, the 49ers had won two NCAA championships (1989, 1993). You would've thought the first words out of his mouth would be: "Yippee! I've just landed the number one recruit in the country!" Instead, he said, "Who's playing a prank on me?" (That was Debbie's reaction, too, when Brian told her about my call.) They were stunned by my decision, since I hadn't yet made an "official" visit to campus.

Truthfully, I didn't need to go through that exercise. I'd attended Long Beach State's girls' volleyball camps every summer from the time I was in sixth grade. I liked the coaching staff, the players, the program, and the school. There were other pluses, too. It was twenty minutes from Costa Mesa. My parents could see me play. I could go home for laundry, meals, and money. In addition, Long Beach State had a good kinesiology program, which is what I planned to major in. Originally, I'd wanted to become a veterinarian, but Long Beach State didn't have a veterinary program. Also, that major would've required a lot of schooling, which wasn't realistic, given my dreams of a pro volleyball career. I'd also thought about marine biology, but with field trips, I couldn't focus on the requirements of that major and play volleyball at the same time.

After giving Brian the good news, the next call I made was to UOP's head coach, John Dunning, explaining I'd decided to go to Long Beach State. It was bad form to renege on a commitment, and I felt horrible about having to make that call. I'd genuinely wanted to play with Elsa, but I never should have made the decision without doing my home-work. I'll chalk the embarrassing episode up to immaturity.

From the get-go, Brian and Debbie understood that I wanted to learn to set, and their plan was to gradually teach me the position. Then, perhaps, by my junior or senior year, I'd become the full-time setter. In the meantime, I'd play outside hitter. However, Lori Price, the team's starting setter, came into camp out of shape. (She later transferred to William and Mary.) So three days into my freshman season, I was the 49ers' starting setter, and my foray into the new position was baptism by fire.

Early in the season, during the team's two-a-day practices, it was just Debbie and me. The first session, I worked out, without a ball and away from the team, for three hours. The second session, I worked with the team. Debbie taught me the basics, including footwork and hand position. I nicknamed her "my shadow," because she was always right next to me, catching my sets. During the season, I also worked with Debbie after practice. Freshman outside hitter Jessica Alvarado served as the "ball baby." (Perhaps most important, Jessica was the one who ran ahead after practice to make sure we got to the cafeteria before they stopped serving dinner.)

I threw myself into setting. I worked and worked at it. It was the most difficult aspect of volleyball I've ever had to learn, and sometimes I looked ridiculous transitioning to my new position. In those days, because of NCAA rules, in spring training we could practice only two hours a week, for eight weeks, and believe it or not, we couldn't touch the ball. So Debbie and I concentrated on footwork. Standing in front of a mirror, I pretended to set an invisible ball.

As a setter, you run the offense, much like the quarterback on a football team or a point guard on a basketball team. You make the plays happen. If the first contact isn't good, you position the ball better so your team can get a point. You keep the team together, mentally, after they've made mistakes. There's a lot of leadership involved in the position. Most important, as the setter, you're the only player on the team who always has one of three contacts every time the ball is on your side of the net.

I'm glad I was a hitter before I was a setter, because I was better able to adjust the set to a hitter, depending on the situation. I also anticipated hitters' mistakes and knew how best to motivate them. As a hitter, I knew where the sets should be. I knew their timing. And beyond all of that, once a hitter, always a hitter: I was a huge threat from the setter position. My teammates could set me, forcing opponents to defend three hitters.

In the spring of my freshman year, because I seemed to have some free time, I joined the Long Beach State women's track team. But that adventure didn't last long. Running from spring volleyball practice to track practice, and trying to keep my grades up, soon became stressful. So stressful, in fact, my body fat dropped to 9 percent, and I stopped menstruating. I went to the school's student health center and learned I was suffering from athletic amenorrhoea. It is suspected that low body fat levels and exercise-related chemicals (beta endorphins and cat-echolamines) disrupt the interplay of the sex hormones estrogen and progesterone. Long-term complications of untreated athletic amenor-rhoea include susceptibility to broken bones and premature aging.

The ideal body fat for average females is 22 to 25 percent; for aver-age males, it's 15 to 18 percent. The ideal body fat for female athletes is less than 17 percent; for male athletes, it's less than 10 percent. The doctors told me to eat enough food to take in enough calories for my workouts and to make sure I had enough calcium in my diet. They put me on progesterone and birth control pills. (I was thankful for the birth control pills because my menstrual periods were, and still are, extremely painful and debilitating, often including migraines. I need Advil, Motrin, ice packs, and bed rest.)

In addition to the physical toll of playing two sports, it didn't help matters that the first time I performed a high jump in track practice, per a coach's orders, I was so close to the bar, I ended up hitting a stan-dard with my head. I needed two stitches to close the cut in my scalp.

That was my short-lived college track career.

From then on, it was all volleyball.

I picked up the mental aspect of setting the fastest, getting used to the quick decision-making the position demanded right away. During our sessions my freshman year, Debbie talked to me about leadership and communication as a setter. I kept reminding her I was playing with upperclassmen. I told her I did not want to appear bossy. I admitted I was hesitant to proclaim myself a team leader.

"But I'm only a freshman," I kept telling Debbie.

"It doesn't matter, Misty," she'd reply. "You're the setter. That's the role you have to play."


A little-known fact: I couldn't set in warm-ups as a freshman and sophomore. I had a complete mental block, until the game started. It's like a quarterback not being able to complete passes in warm-ups, then connecting in the heat of battle.

As a result, I got picked on in practice every day.

"Come on, you can figure it out," Brian would always say.

But I just couldn't get it.

One day, after warm-ups, I ran off the court, crying. I just couldn't take the criticism anymore.

"I can't do this," I sobbed to Debbie.

She took me into the laundry room, handed me a piece of paper, and told me to sign my name.

"Now, I want you to look at it and sign it exactly how you did it before," she said.

When I tried to do it so exactly, I couldn't do it. Then Debbie asked me to close my eyes, and when I opened them, I was looking at a blank piece of paper. Again, she had me sign my name, and lo and behold, it looked exactly like the original signature. Her exercise taught me if you try to be too perfect, if you overthink, you'll mess up. Just go with the flow. That was one of the most important lessons I've ever learned.

Debbie was right; eventually, I got it. However, even when my setting was clicking, I never took it for granted. How did I break out of my mental block? By telling myself, "Clear your mind." Once the whistle blew, the game unfolded so quickly, and I was focused on so many elements, I didn't have time to overthink. Then, I was fine. But there were moments, here and there, when I was standing back at the service line, thinking, "I hope I get this ball in." And I'd always serve it out because I was focused on not being able to do it.

By my junior year, Brian says I was "the best setter ever to have played in college," and by my senior year, he says, I had a profound impact on how the sport was played.

"Misty May did for volleyball what Wayne Gretzky did for hockey, and Magic Johnson did for basketball," Brian always says. "They all changed the way the game was played."

I am deeply touched by Brian's words, because he's one of the best volleyball minds in the country.

"It's very hard in a sport to control and tackle the rhythm of a game, especially if you can't stop the ball," Brian has said. "Misty could control the rhythm of the match, just by setting the match, which I haven't seen done before, and that is remarkable when you think that it's done without stopping the ball.

"She could take the height of the ball, the speed of it, the release of it, and make it easier for defenders to take the ball, or for people to pass it. Or she could take the height, speed, and location of a pass and change that rhythm to suit the needs of the hitters. And she could confuse the opposition by changing the way she released the ball, changing her body position, changing the speed and height of the ball.

"That's harder than people think because it involves changing the center of gravity, changing the time the ball is in your hands, changing your hand position on the ball, changing your body position. She is the best I have ever seen do it, and do it on purpose, and she can even do that in a time between plays, when she is served, or when her teammates served; she was able to control and tackle the rhythm of the match."

Here's an example of where I think I took the position: During my senior year, I learned to jump set. When I was in the front row, I'd jump up and set with my feet off the ground. As a setter, you're supposed to be a threat, because when you're in the front row, you have two hitters on your side of the net, but your opponent has three blockers on her side. So you want to be a threat by attacking on the second ball. Instead of setting, you hit it or dump it. I became so good at jump setting, so acrobatic in the air, blockers would jump up with me, and my hitters would not have to deal with blocks. I became so deceptive, my own teammates didn't know which way I was setting.

There were lighthearted moments, too. I was known for my ability to have fun.

Take my pigtails, for example.

Inexplicably, to me, when I was at Long Beach State, my pigtails became all the rage in volleyball. They never were part of a grandiose plan to generate publicity or to set me apart from the other women. It was very simple. One day, I got my hair cut, and it became too short to pull back into a ponytail. I had to keep my hair out of my face, so I just pulled it back into pigtails. Who would've imagined pigtails could set off such a firestorm? Little girls in pigtails began showing up for our games at Long Beach State's Pyramid. A local sportswriter referred to me as "Pigtails" instead of Misty May. And, at a match at UOP, an adult male fan wore a pigtailed wig atop his head. After the match, I gave him some advice: "Sir, please straighten your pigtails. They're crooked."

I enjoyed making my Long Beach State coaches and teammates laugh. I still love cracking people up. I take after Dad in this area.

My voracious appetite always is great for laughs. I'll eat anything put in front of me, if it's remotely edible. I attribute my love of food to being raised in a family of Hawaiians. Whenever I've been in Hawaii, it's always been a nonstop eating marathon.

My fear of the boogeyman has made me the brunt of many jokes. Teammate Brandy Barratt, also a roommate, can't get over what a wimp I can be. As a kid, I was afraid to be home alone. When Dad and Mom weren't around at night, I'd make sure to turn on all of the lights in our apartment. When the wind rattled through our louver windows, I was sure the night stalker was lurking outside. In college, I got hooked on the TV show *America's Most Wanted,* although it convinced me that criminals could burst through our front door. I'd run through the house, flipping on lights, every time the show was on. One night, as a junior, I was at home with Kristin Harris, one of my two roommates. We were watching TV in her room, and we heard a strange noise. We got so scared that we barricaded ourselves in her bathroom. Two and a half hours later, Brandy walked in the front door.

"Hello! Anybody home?" she yelled.

"Brandy, knock three times on the bathroom door, if it's you," I said.

As it turned out, the strange noise was nothing more than a tree branch that had rubbed against a window.

At the team's annual volleyball banquet at the end of each season, I was always at my comic best. My sophomore year, Brandy and I dressed up in seventies disco outfits, complete with psychedelic bell-bottoms, platform shoes, Afro wigs, and sunglasses. We danced to "Saturday Night" by the Bay City Rollers. We threw everybody into an uproar—and started a tradition.

My parents were never far from the fun, either. Dad and Mom knew better than to sit with the other players' parents. They'd hide out in the back of the stands because they knew nobody wanted to listen to what Dad had to say.

"Take her out!" he'd scream, if I made a bad play.

"Lucky!" he'd holler, if I made a good play.

My comic relief contributed to our accomplishments at Long Beach State. It made our hard work seem easier. It lightened disappointments. It brought us together, as teammates, classmates, and women. Brian referred to us as "the sisterhood." Most important, the humor greased the skids for the serious moments.


Before I go any further, I want to come clean about two serious moments, two mistakes that I made at Long Beach State that I'm not proud of. As a freshman, I learned there were certain ways I had to act because I was the star of the team. The first serious moment: I was late to practice because I'd gone to get a hot dog at Wienerschnitzel, my favorite fast food joint. I got caught in a slow drive-through line, and when I realized what was happening, it was too late to back up. I walked into practice after everybody else, and Brian was so mad that he kicked me out. The incident taught me I had to do a better job of planning my schedule and that nothing could ever interfere with practice.

The second serious moment: I'd gone out partying on a Sunday night, and I was still so sick and hungover on Monday afternoon that I couldn't make practice. Or, maybe I should say, I couldn't bring myself to go to practice. I knew I'd done something wrong. As I was throwing up into the toilet, I told myself, "I want to quit volleyball," which was a cop-out. I should've faced the fact that I'd made a mistake, that I'd screwed up and hurt my teammates, and dealt with it. I didn't have my parents there to tell me to be in at a certain time, not to do this or that. I got mixed up with the wrong group of kids.

Later, Debbie talked to me about the incident.

"You really didn't want to quit," she said.

"No," I admitted.

After that, drinking was a big no-no. College helped me realize that people had their eyes on me, no matter what I was doing. I had to be conscious of that. I was a role model. Little kids were starting to look up to me. I had to set the best example. And that's exactly what I did, once I set myself straight.

In 1995, I became the first freshman to start at setter for Long Beach State since Sheri Sanders in 1986, although I also played six matches at outside hitter in an attempt to shore up the team's passing and defense. It's not like I became a superstar setter when the whistle blew. I'd do okay, but I had to learn. I'd describe it as a roller-coaster season. I had good games and bad games. The coaches called plays for me because I didn't understand. We had a fairly young team. We finished with a 22–10 record, losing at San Diego State in the second round of the NCAAs.

In 1996, when I was a sophomore, we put together a fine regular season, especially given changing lineups and game plans, travel snafus, and a rash of injuries. We went undefeated longer than any team in the nation, rising to number three despite the obstacles. We finished 32–2, drawing a first-round bye in the NCAA tournament. We were the number two seed in the Central Regional and the number seven seed in the entire NCAA bracket. Unfortunately, Michigan State upset us in the regional semifinal.

Early that season, against Cal Poly San Luis Obispo on November

1, I dove for a ball and all my weight landed on my bent left knee. I heard it make a noise, but since I'd never injured it before, I figured I'd nailed my funny bone. On the next play, I did the same thing. The result? I partially tore the posterior cruciate ligament (PCL) in my left knee. I spent five matches on the sidelines, rehabbing my knee, strengthening the ligaments around the tear. But I was never the same physically after that. I returned for the Big West Conference tournament at University of California–Santa Barbara, where we were the number one seed for the Western Division. It inspired the team. We mowed down North Texas in the first round, 15–10, 15–9, and 15–4. That victory set up a semifinal match with UCSB, our third meeting of the season. We played one of our finest matches ever in the Thunderdome, with an incredible 18–16 win in the second game, which propelled us to a three-game sweep. Then, in the finals, we lost in five games to UOP. I was named the 1996 Big West Player of the Year, and I led the way for the 49ers to top the conference in team hitting percentage. I was ranked among the top ten in the Big West in hitting percentage (fifth), assists per game (fifth), and digs per game (ninth).

In August 1997, I was faced with a personal crisis: I was sexually assaulted. It was a very painful time in my life. Until now, I've never spoken about it publicly. To this day, few people know it occurred. It wasn't something I talked about, not even to my coaches, my teammates, or my closest friends. It was mortifying. It was humiliating. And although I later had to testify at a trial, the word never got out about the incident because, back then, I wasn't a volleyball icon, I wasn't in the media spotlight, and quite frankly, the media was a lot less aggressive and Internet driven. It happened at the rental house I was living in off-campus. My roommates and I had been to a party, and I'd gone to bed about 1:30 A.M. Normally, I locked my bedroom door at night, but for some unknown reason, this time I didn't.

I was startled from a deep sleep. I sensed a shadow over me. I called out my boyfriend's name, but there was no answer. Once I became more awake, I realized a man was on top of me, groping my private parts. Mom always had taught me if I was in a situation like that to kick the guy in the groin, which is exactly what I did. He ran out of my bedroom. I thought I'd recognized him—he looked like the family friend of one of my roommates, who'd been visiting earlier that evening. I woke up my buddy Zach Caiger-Greaves, who'd been sleeping on the sofa in the living room, and I told him what had happened. I woke up my roommates, too. We all decided I had to notify the police.

Then I phoned my parents. Mom answered, and I explained the situation. I told her I was all right, but I was very upset, and I wanted her and Dad to meet me at the hospital for moral support while I went through interviews and a physical examination. I figured she'd be hesitant about waking Dad because she knew how furious he'd be with the guy, and that if he ever saw him face to face, he'd probably pummel him.

The authorities came to my house, collected my clothes and my bedding, and put me through a preliminary interview. For evidentiary reasons, I was told not to shower or bathe, brush or comb my hair, use the restroom, brush my teeth or gargle, eat or drink anything, or put on makeup. Then I went to the hospital.

When Mom and Dad arrived, I was being set up for the examination room. By this time, the suspect had been apprehended at the John Wayne Airport in Santa Ana—indeed, he was the family friend of a roommate—and he was in another examination room. I was a jumble of emotions. I was angry. I was embarrassed. I was confused. Why hadn't I locked my door? Was I to blame for this? I was in a pool of tears. Mom held me, and Dad kept saying, "I'm going to kill that son of a bitch." Sure enough, the cops had to restrain Dad to make sure he didn't get a chance to act on his threat.

First, I underwent a sexual assault forensic examination, which is also known as a "rape kit." I was physically examined by a highly trained rape trauma team, which collected any evidence necessary to establish that a crime had occurred, and if possible, to establish who'd committed the crime. I was swabbed to determine whether there'd been physical or penile penetration. My hair and pubic hair were plucked, as well as combed through to collect any foreign matter. A series of photographs also were taken. Next, I underwent an extensive interview with a rape counselor and a representative from the district attorney's office. I relived the incident and explained in great detail what had happened. After that, notes from my interview and examination were compared to determine whether I was telling the truth.

And then, I was asked one final question: Do you want to press charges? I said yes. I never wavered. I never wavered on anything I said, or did, that night. At about 5:30 A.M., Dad recalls the district attorney telling him and Mom that a lewd and lascivious act had occurred, that I'd been touched and fondled inappropriately, and that I'd never wavered in the interview or the examination. Dad recalls the district attorney saying that the evidence against the suspect was overwhelming.

Choosing to follow through by pressing charges gave me a feeling of accomplishment and empowerment. I knew I was protecting myself and others from being victimized. It still makes me feel good to know that I fought back. I'm proud of the fact that when faced with a situation like that I wasn't afraid. I wasn't afraid to phone the police, to show up at the hospital, to go through the physical examination, to press charges, or to testify at the trial, which led to a conviction. I did the right thing.

To this day, I've never undergone any form of counseling for the sexual assault. I was strong enough to work through it, thanks to a lot of emotional support from my parents, who always were there to listen whenever I needed to talk. I was able to keep it from affecting me in school and on the volleyball court, and I went on to thrive in healthy relationships with men.

In 1997, my junior season, we stayed at the number one spot in the nation for seven weeks in a row in the USA Today/American Volleyball Coaches Association (AVCA) Top 25 Poll. We took over the top spot November 2 and remained there until the conclusion of the season. The last time the 49ers had been ranked number one in the nation during the regular season in the AVCA poll was September 28, 1993. From top to bottom, we believed we were destined to win the NCAA Championship. The expectations the coaches had for us were sky high, but we actually wanted more from ourselves than they could've ever imagined. We worked our butts off. We stayed extremely focused. We were determined to be the best team in the nation, when all was said and done.

The turning point of the 1997 season came in our two-game series against number two Florida, in Gainesville. We beat the Gators the first night, 15–8, 15–6, 15–12, then lost to them the second, 15–12, 10–15, 12–15, 15–11, 15–11. It was our first defeat of the season. Afterward we set our team goals in stone. We had a two-hour team meeting in the locker room, longer than any I can remember.

"How good do you want to be?" Brian asked us.

We told him we wanted to be NCAA champions, and when we came back to practice Monday, it was game on! Practices, which hadn't been easy to begin with, became dreadfully hard, thanks, in large part, to Brian's telling us we needed to step it up, if we wanted to reach our goals. I don't know who pushed harder, Brian or us. We were so hungry to win the NCAA Championship we ran through walls for him.

Then the team was dealt two devastating blows.

First, in practice November 13, Jessica broke the third metacarpal on her left hand. Then, two weeks before the fifty-six-team NCAA tournament, we were passed over for the number one seed. That went to Penn State. We were seeded second, Stanford was third, and Florida fourth. Being seeded second meant we'd have to face the defending national champions, Stanford, in one of the semifinals at the Final Four in Spokane, Washington. When the seedings were announced, we were all very upset. We should have been playing the fourth seed, and Stanford and Penn State should have been playing each other. Brian was so outraged that he made his feelings known in the media.

His worst fears were quickly realized: It was one and done in Spokane. We beat Stanford the first set, then we just fell apart. They were such a strong team. They had quite a few seniors. At one point in the match, I was on such a mission to win the NCAA Championship that I looked like a Cirque du Soleil performer. Falling to the court, I took a bad pass a few feet above the floor and shot it within inches of a far corner for a side out. Still, it wasn't enough. Brian pulled out all the stops, inserting Jessica into Game 4, when we were down, 12–3. She was an immediate spark. We went on a 7–0 run and eventually went ahead, 15–14. But Stanford never let up. The Cardinal beat us, 9–15, 15–10, 15–4, 17–15, in front of 10,284 at the Spokane Arena.

We had a tough time that day trying to thwart Stanford's Kerri Walsh (twenty-two kills) and Kristin Folkl and Paula McNamee (thirteen). As a team, we were number one in the nation in hitting percentage, yet we'd struggled all match behind a poor .155 attack. However, we were able to limit the Cardinal to a .209 hitting percentage, as if that was any consolation. It wasn't. My being named AVCA Division I Player of the Year, a first-team All-American, and *Volleyball* magazine's Player of the Year didn't lessen the sting either.

After Stanford beat us, we congregated in the locker room.

"What do you want?" Brian asked us.

"We want to be the best team in the country," I said.

Then Jessica, a junior and one of our most vocal leaders, took it one step further.

"I don't want to lose a match all season," she said.

I think it's important to set a far-fetched goal. We all wanted to win, but nobody wanted to step up, except for Jessica, and say, "I want to go undefeated." It was in the back of everyone's mind, but Jessica wasn't afraid to say it. Her attitude and her fearlessness rubbed off on everybody else. We rallied behind her proclamation.

I've always said the best team we competed against in the 1998 season was our B side in practice. Why? Because they said, "We're going to compete with the starters in practice and make them the best team in the country. We're vital members of this team." I give Brian a lot of credit for our all-for-one, one-for-all attitude. During my first three years at Long Beach State, he'd molded us into one powerful unit. I remember wondering, for example, why he made us wear the same color hair ties, why he wouldn't let us wear bows in our hair. Everything was so regimented, I thought, "This is a little over the top." But then, I read a book by John Wooden, the legendary UCLA basketball coach, and it dawned on me, "Now I know why Brian does what he does." Bill Walton's hair was too long, and Wooden told him he'd have to cut it. He wanted everybody on the same level on the court. Everybody's got to be in uniform.

That's what was so great about our 1998 Long Beach State team: When we had that meeting after losing to Stanford in the 1997 NCAA semifinals, we knew we were all in it together.

Case in point: Brian had asked everybody to play beach volleyball that summer. I'd given him the idea, and he understood playing on the beach would help my teammates identify strengths and weaknesses in their games. Since there are only two people covering the court, using beach volleyball as cross training for indoor volleyball, you learn to pick up different shots. Then, when you go back indoors, with six people per side, it makes the game much easier. Playing on the beach taught me every skill. Outdoors, the timing is different because of the sand. When you jump, you're not jumping as high. The wind also plays a role in your performance. Indoors, you have a little less freedom as a player because you're each responsible for certain zones. Because I was training with the U.S. National A1 team that summer, I didn't put in time at the beach. However, all of my Long Beach State teammates did. I definitely noticed a difference in our team's overall performance. Everybody's skills picked up. Everybody loved it because, like I said, we knew what we wanted, and then we had to ask ourselves, How were we going to get there?

So what happened? We were undefeated in the regular season. We were a powerful machine, mowing down opponents left and right.

We blanked California, San Diego State, Cal State Fullerton, Idaho, New Mexico State, and UC–Irvine in 15–0 games. If we did that at home games, every fan in attendance got a free bagel at a local bagel shop the next day. And if we won in less than sixty minutes, everybody got free In-N-Out burgers. That became such a popular promotion, Long Beach State fans booed opponents who took time-outs late in games, threatening to ace them out of free burgers.

Brian, the 1998 AVCA National Coach of the Year, pushed all the right buttons. Physically, we were in the best shape of our lives, thanks to his relentless practices. Mentally, no team in the nation was tougher.

The season was monumental for me, and my family, for another reason: At our Thanksgiving Tournament at the Pyramid, Long Beach State's arena, the school retired my number five jersey. As Mom, Dad, and I stood together on the court, the lights were turned down, and a single spotlight shone on my number five jersey, which was hanging from the rafters. I became the fourth 49ers women's volleyball player—and only the seventh athlete in school history—to have her jersey number retired.

Naturally, I turned it into a light moment.

"Does this mean I get another jersey?" I kidded after receiving the honor.

The next evening, the team gathered at Cirivello's on Viking Way in Long Beach to watch the announcement of the national pairings: We were the number one seed in the nation.

"It's our year," I told the Long Beach Press Telegram. "This is the first team since I've been here that, when we play a team that's really not at our level, we still play with the same intensity. Past teams I've been on will maybe have a 15–11 game with one of those teams. But this team has all been on the same page, just going for one thing. I feel like the time is right."

We blew through the first round, obliterating Southern University, 15–0, 15–0, 15–0, in forty-nine minutes. We tied the NCAA playoff record for least points allowed in a match. We set a school record with a .615 hitting percentage and tied the 49ers' second-best effort for service aces with fifteen. Southern, Southwestern Athletic Conference champions, playing in their first NCAA tournament and seeded last in the sixty-four-team tournament, almost scored a point in the third game, which would have made the score 9–1, but they had the wrong player serving.

We knocked off nineteenth-ranked Arizona, 15–11, 15–4, 15–11. I was awarded a yellow card (penalty) for celebrating too much after spiking the ball in the Wildcats' court for a side out.

Next up, Illinois. A funny thing happened on the way to that NCAA regional semifinal. Brandy and I had just walked up to the door of the Pyramid, where fans were standing in a long line at the ticket window. I was dressed in my practice sweats, Brandy had on her 49ers' jacket. A little girl, wearing a Long Beach State volleyball T-shirt, approached us. We figured she wanted an autograph. Instead, she pulled out an extra ticket and said, "Would you guys like to buy this?" Brandy and I rolled our eyes and said, "Is she joking?" But no. She hadn't recognized us. We busted up laughing. I gently broke it to our young fan that we didn't need a ticket for admission because we were playing in the match. Then we went inside and bumped off Illinois, 16–14, 15–4, 15–11.

And finally, we defeated Texas, 15–9, 15–9, 15–2, to advance to the Final Four in Madison, Wisconsin. The celebrating seemed to last forever. We ran through the Pyramid, high-fiving everybody in the gym. Before we left the Pyramid for the last time in our college careers, Jessica, Benishe Dillard, and I kissed the floor.

After only one major upset in the first four rounds, the NCAA tournament held to form, with the top four seeds advancing to the Final Four. We were matched up against number four Florida in the semifinals, while number two Penn State would play number three Nebraska. It would be the first time we'd played Florida since splitting two regular-season matches in Gainesville the year before.

The 49ers' associate athletic director, Cindy Masner, went to great lengths to turn it into a home game for us: She hired the Wisconsin band to perform. All decked out in 49ers' attire, the UW band opened up with "On Wisconsin," then played the 49ers' fight song. We did our part, too, with a .500 attack, committing only two errors on twenty-two attempts.

We won our thirty-fifth consecutive match, eliminating the Gators, 15–2, 15–8, 15–10, to win our sixty-seventh consecutive game and record our thirty-first sweep in front of 12,327 at the Kohl Center. At that time, it was the largest crowd ever to watch a women's volleyball match. I recorded my sixth triple-double (thirty-two assists, fifteen digs, and eleven kills), and I had a couple of service aces to set an NCAA tournament record.

Ironically, several of my teammates and I were fighting colds, and we wore down as the match went on. It hadn't begun until 10:15 P.M. Central Standard Time and didn't end until 11:45 P.M. We'd waited two hours and twenty-seven minutes for the first semifinal to be played. Penn State defeated Nebraska, 3–1. And then, after meeting with the media after the game, I was selected by the NCAA for random drug testing. That made my night, and Brian's, even longer. I was suffering from bronchitis, and I was dehydrated. I didn't get back to the hotel until after 1:00 A.M., and I didn't fall asleep until almost 3:00 A.M.

Our semifinal victory set up the title match everybody had been dreaming of since the summer, when we'd both laid claim to the number one ranking: Long Beach State versus Penn State. We both were undefeated with 35–0 records. It was believed to be the first time in NCAA tournament history that teams with perfect records would meet in the NCAA title match.

"This is what we've been waiting for," I told the Long Beach Press Telegram.

We had a day off before the final, and Brian limited practice to one hour, figuring it would be best for us to get some rest.

The championship match was an epic battle, and our most harrowing, thanks to a hostile crowd and a Penn State team that just wouldn't quit. But we all knew it would be. In addition, the Nittany Lions just rubbed us the wrong way. In a November article in USA Today, their players were quoted as saying to forget about the rankings, which had

Long Beach State number one. *They* were number one in the nation, in their minds. Jessica was so perturbed by Penn State's arrogance that she carried that article in her duffel bag from that point on.

When we fell behind in the final game, Brian called time-out and made the most important speech of his career.

"We can't lose! We've come too far, and we've worked too hard to lose!" he said. "Forget all the noise. Just concentrate on what we do best."

We fell further and further behind. 7–2. 8–4. And then, suddenly, we took command. In my mind, I was just waiting for the last ball to drop, so we could all start jumping around. Finally, it did.

We defeated Penn State, 15–3, 15–10, 13–15, 14–16, 15–12, in front of an NCAA-record crowd of 13,194. The two-day total of 25,521 broke by more than 4,000 the record set the year before in Spokane, Washington. We'd won one for the underdogs—Long Beach State's annual athletic budget was $5 million, compared to Penn State's $40-plus million. We'd saved the best for last: We'd hit a magnificent .556 in Game 5, committing only one hitting error on eighteen attempts.

We threw ourselves on top of one another on the court.

I was named co-MVP of the 1998 Final Four, with nine kills, seventy assists, and four blocked shots in the title game. I set an NCAA tournament record with twenty service aces in six matches, shattering the previous mark of thirteen set by UCLA's Natalie Williams in 1991. I also was named the AVCA Division I NCAA Player of the Year for the second consecutive season, the first back-to-back winner since the 49ers' Tara Cross won in 1989 and 1990. We'd posted a perfect 36–0 mark, the first time in NCAA history a women's volleyball team had gone through the season undefeated. Arguably, we were the greatest women's volleyball team in college history. It was the perfect ending to my Long Beach State career.

In early February 1999, we came together again for a magnificent evening, this time at our NCAA Championship banquet at the Ramada Renaissance hotel. The year before, after we'd lost to Stanford in the semis, our annual banquet had been held at the Pyramid, with only a few hundred family, friends, and boosters attending. This time, though, seven hundred people filled the second-floor Renaissance ballroom. So much excitement still swirled around our volleyball program that there was a buzz in the room. It was a three-hour lovefest, filled with laughter and tears.

Always the class clown, when I was introduced, I got behind the podium and asked the audience to please remain standing.

"I'd like to sing the national anthem," I joked, referring to a threat I'd made a few years before.

For me, it was all about leaving 'em laughing.

The evening closed with highlight clips of our perfect season, set to Andrea Bocelli and Sarah Brightman singing, "Time to Say Goodbye."

All that was left was a visit to the White House, which has become routine for outstanding athletes and championship teams. But instead of going to Washington, D.C., to meet President Bill Clinton, he came to us. In May, we met him on the tarmac, next to *Air Force One,* at the Los Angeles airport. He was on a four-day, five-stop tour through California, Washington, and Nevada. President Clinton praised us for our accomplishment, and he told us how much he appreciated our sport. I believe it was the first time a women's college volleyball team had met the president of the United States.

My years at Long Beach State were life-changing. I couldn't have asked for better teammates. At the time, I thought, "This is a very special group of people." But now, so many years later, I realize just how special they were, and still are. It was such a great team to be part of. No other team ever would, or could, mean as much to me.

In fact, in October 2008, I suggested we get back together for our ten-year reunion. We hadn't all seen each other since we'd won the 1998 NCAA Championship. It was a simply amazing weekend; it felt like we'd never left campus. Because I'd had surgery for a ruptured Achilles tendon, I was getting around on a motorized scooter. Interestingly, some of my teammates had no idea I was recovering from an injury I'd sustained on ABC's *Dancing with the Stars.* Not everybody watches TV, I guess. In fact, they just figured I was using the scooter to make them laugh, that I was just being Misty May.

# 10

# U.S. NATIONAL TEAM

On a whim, a few months after my team had won the 1998 NCAA Championship, I decided to dip my toes in the sand.

Valinda Hilleary Roche, who worked in my physical therapist's office, asked me to play with her in a pro beach volleyball tournament. I thought, "Why not?" However, it was a little more complicated than throwing on a bikini and hitting the beach. First, we played in an AVP qualifier in Santa Monica. Then I scraped together the cash to get me to my first official pro tournament, an AVP Pro Beach Tour event, May 1 and 2 in Clearwater, Florida.

Jim Steele, our dear family friend, suggested I approach the Long Beach Century Club for help. Founded in 1957 by a group of prominent sports enthusiasts, the nonprofit corporation is dedicated to the promotion of amateur athletics in the city. It has supported thousands of Long Beach athletes and teams. The club gave me vouchers for Southwest Airlines and money to cover my other expenses. At that time, all I had was a Discover credit card with a five-hundred-dollar limit. To save a few bucks, I stayed with my high school friend and former track teammate Tina Bowman.

Valinda and I finished ninth in Clearwater. I remember it well because I felt so lost all weekend, traveling on my own to a volleyball tournament for the first time in my life. And I'll never forget our generic uniforms—black bikini bottoms and black cotton sports bras from Mervyns. We won two thousand dollars, but I didn't take any money because I wanted to maintain my amateur status. In our second tournament, a USA Volleyball event in Huntington Beach, we finished thirteenth and won three thousand dollars. Again, I didn't take the money. However, when I made my first big pro paycheck, I paid back the Century Club, and I've been a big supporter of the organization ever since. It wouldn't have been possible for me to get my start if they hadn't helped me.

A month or so after that tournament, I received a surprise phone call from Holly McPeak, the best female beach volleyball player in the world and a three-time MVP on the domestic beach circuit. She and her partner Nancy Reno had just split up, after defeating the world's number one team, Brazil's Adriana Behar and Shelda Bede, in an event sanctioned by the FIVB (Fédération Internationale de Volleyball) in Toronto, Canada.

"Can we have dinner?" Holly asked.

At that time, Holly was thirty, and the sport's It Girl. She'd been playing beach volleyball part-time since 1987 and full-time since 1992. She'd won every major professional beach volleyball title, except for the Olympic gold medal, which had eluded her. She and Nancy had dominated the sport, domestically and internationally, leading up to the 1996 Atlanta Games. Then they'd beaten themselves, twice breaking up their partnership for personal reasons. They'd never regained their form, and in Atlanta, finished fifth.

When the doorbell rang, my housemates and I pulled back the drapes and peeked out the kitchen window to scope out Holly and her black Mercedes. You would've thought Madonna was standing on my front porch. I had to pinch myself in Holly's car, on the way to dinner, I was so in awe. We went to Claim Jumper, and today we both laugh at our one-sided conversation. I mostly listened, as she told me how much fun it would be to play together, how she'd teach me the ins and outs of the beach game, how she'd show me what it takes to be a professional athlete. She also filled me in about beach volleyball's financial rewards. Finally, she threw out the kicker: If I joined her on the beach, we could try to qualify for the 2000 Sydney Olympics.

By the end of dinner, my head was spinning. Playing in the Olympics was a dream of mine. Playing with the number one woman in the world was the opportunity of a lifetime. Playing on the beach was something I was very familiar with. It all sounded so exciting, and it all felt so right. I asked Holly if I could take some time to think about her offer. Over the next several days, I wrestled with my decision. I pride myself on being a woman of my word, and I'd already made a commitment to the U.S. national team to play indoor volleyball. Finally, I phoned Holly and declined. I had to honor my promise.

From my early days at Newport Harbor, I'd been fast-tracking through the USA Volleyball system. In summer 1993, before my junior year, I became a member of the USA Volleyball youth girls national team. The next summer, I was the only high school player to take part in the 1994 U.S. Olympic Festival in St. Louis, Missouri. At first, I wasn't even going to be allowed to try out because I was too young. And the following summer, I was one of only four incoming college freshmen to play in the 1995 U.S. Olympic Festival in Boulder, Colorado.

As a freshman and sophomore at Long Beach State, I played on the U.S. national A2 team, and then, the summer after my junior year, I was promoted to the ultimate spot: the U.S. national A1 team, which was composed of the best women players in the country. I was one of the youngest members of the team, and I was fearless.

"You have to make a name for yourself, especially when you're the youngest," I told the *Los Angeles Times*. "You know people are talking about you, with opinions on whether you're good enough. But it was just a different level of competition, and I figured out right away that I could play for them."

Finally, in June 1999, the summer after my senior year, I became a full-time member of the U.S. national A1 team, living and training at the U.S. Olympic Training Center in Colorado Springs, Colorado.

Head coach Mick Haley had pushed me to join the team six months earlier, weeks after we'd won the 1998 NCAA Championship. I'd declined because I'd wanted to finish my spring semester.

When you're in residence at the U.S. Olympic Training Center, you feel like a character in the movie *Groundhog Day*. You have twice-daily practices, and in between, you sandwich meals, naps, weight training, and aerobic conditioning. You go to sleep at night, you wake up the next morning, and you do it all over again. Because the U.S. women's indoor team hadn't yet qualified for Sydney, there was a lot of anxiety surrounding it. So it was just me and my U.S. teammates, and volleyball, volleyball, volleyball, for days on end.

Doing nothing but training is a luxury, and I was grateful to be a member of the U.S. national team, except for the fact that I wasn't being given much of an opportunity to play. From the outset, Haley told my parents and me that I most likely wouldn't be the starting setter for at least a year and a half. At the time, I thought it was a curious statement. I'd just completed one of the most successful collegiate careers ever, establishing myself as one of the most dominating players and one of the best setters in college and U.S. history. Now, with some perspective, I think the reasoning behind Haley's decision to sit me for a year and a half had to do with three things: I was one of the younger players, I had to learn a new system (which was very different from Brian's fast-moving, quick-hitting philosophy), and I lacked foreign playing experience.

In addition, it probably didn't help matters that, at five foot eight and a half, I was one of the shortest players on the U.S. national team. And it probably worked against me that I'd chosen to stick around Long Beach State until June, rather than move to Colorado Springs six months earlier as Haley would've preferred.

Of course, Dad has a very different view. To this day, he's convinced Haley's decision to sit me for a year and a half was political. Dad believes the issues he had at the 1968 Olympics with Jim Coleman, his U.S. team's head coach, influenced how I was treated by Haley thirty years later. At that point in time, Coleman was the general manager of national teams for USA Volleyball, which meant he oversaw my women's team. While Haley may have had a solid reason to treat me the way he did, it wasn't evident to me or my family. Even today, Dad continues to apologize to me about what he wholeheartedly believes was his negative impact on my shot as the starting setter for the U.S. national team.

"I've been around volleyball long enough to know that it's very political, that you make enemies for life because the people that are in this thing never forget," Dad always says. He'll apologize to me, then he'll say, "We'll never know how good you could've been indoors, pal."

One thing Haley said still sticks out in my mind. He told me that, as a setter, I was "too deceptive." I thought, "But isn't that what you want from your setter?" At Long Beach State, Debbie had taught me deception is a huge plus. Dad had drummed that into me, too. "Keep 'em guessing," he'd tell me. Maybe Haley thought I was too deceptive for my own teammates.

Regardless, it was clear from the get-go that Haley and I had a major difference of opinion over the philosophy of setting. He tried to change my setting style. He wanted me to set every ball at the same height. I wanted to hit each ball at the height I thought was best for each individual. Being a setter on a volleyball team, to my mind, is like being an NFL quarterback. In football, not every receiver wants the ball thrown to him exactly the same way. Some guys like it higher, some guys like absolute rockets.

After I got to the U.S. national team, we participated in a handful of tournaments and exhibitions. One was in New Orleans, where I didn't get off the bench; another was in Japan, where I played sporadically. (Ironically, a lot of the girls who came to watch me in New Orleans were wearing pigtails, mimicking my signature hairstyle.) I was disappointed by my lack of playing time, but it wasn't until I got to the Pan American Games, July 23 to August 8, in Winnipeg, Canada, that I started to ask questions. There, I ran into Jen Pavley, a volleyball player from Agoura Hills, California. She'd been a club teammate of mine. She was competing in beach volleyball. (She and partner Marsha Miller ended up winning the Pan Am Games silver medal.) She told me that she was on her way to see a movie. A movie? What a concept—doing something to take your mind off volleyball!

When you're part of a team, there's a pack mentality. If one person goes to the bathroom, everybody goes. If you go to dinner or to the movies, everybody else goes, too. There's no deviating from the group. I was getting tired of that mind-set.

"How are you dealing with all of this team stuff?" I asked Jen.

"I'm playing beach volleyball. We each have our own schedule," Jen said. "That's why I can go to the movies if I want to."

"Wow, that must be nice," I replied.

The wheels in my brain started turning. I wanted the challenges, connections, excitement, and growth I'd experienced at Long Beach State. I wanted the laughter, lunacy, relationships, and fun I'd experienced with my parents and their friends at Muscle Beach. Most of all, I wanted the freedom of self-expression I'd always felt when I played volleyball. How was I going to get that?

Toward the end of the summer, I was moved back to the A2 team to get some more playing time. My parents were working at a volleyball clinic in Colorado, so I asked them to drive over and watch practice. We were playing mini-tournaments against each other, and I wanted them to take a look at my game, as well as catch the vibe of the team and its coaching staff. Plus, I was homesick and unhappy, and I wanted to see familiar faces.

After the clinic, they drove eight hours, fighting traffic and road construction, to see me. When Dad took one look at the practice, he flipped out. He recalls Haley reading the newspaper and talking on his cell phone throughout the two hours we were on the floor. He remembers me setting balls, and my teammates shooting them every which way, with no correction by the coaching staff. Dad was fuming.

"Butch, keep your mouth shut," Mom instructed.

At the end, Haley asked Dad what he thought of practice.

"When does practice start?" Dad sarcastically replied.

One thing led to another, and then Haley said, "I told Misty she'd have to sit for a year and a half."

In hindsight, not being given much of an opportunity to play for the U.S. national A1 team is one of the best things that ever happened to me. It was the impetus I needed to think about what I wanted out of my volleyball career. It was the impetus I needed to ask myself, "What makes me happy?"

Truth be told, I was getting more and more depressed. I'd started losing the fire. Worst of all, I was losing my love of volleyball. And that really worried me. I wanted to quit, and I wasn't raised to be a quitter. My emotional state was the big reason why I'd phoned my parents and asked them to visit. I'd wanted their opinion of practice, but most of all, I'd wanted them to know how I was feeling about volleyball.

After practice, my parents and I went out to dinner, and I said, "Well, what do you think?" As always, Dad was brutally honest. He made it very clear that he wasn't at all happy about my situation.

"What do you want to do, Misty?" he asked.

"I don't want to be here anymore," I said. "Are you going to be mad at me if I quit?"

"Absolutely not," Dad said.

As it became clear throughout the summer I wasn't going to play a major role with the U.S. national A1 team, at least not at this point, I began soul searching. Over and over, I asked myself, "What can I do to make a change before I end up completely hating volleyball?" I'd seen friends come to despise the sport because they were driven so hard as kids. I didn't want that to happen to me, because volleyball was such a meaningful part of life for me and my parents. I've always valued my parents' opinions, and I knew they'd shoot straight with me. Of course, Dad's view would be absolutely black and white, while Mom's would have shades of gray.

"Maybe it's time for a change," Mom said.

She'd always wanted me to play beach volleyball. She felt that's where my heart was, and she believed that my body would last a lot longer playing on the beach.

A few minutes later, I decided I was officially finished with the U.S. national team.

"I'm going to try this beach thing," I announced to my parents.

Brian and Debbie tried to talk me into sticking it out indoors. However, while they were a little skeptical about how well I'd do on the beach, they also knew my heart wasn't with the U.S. national team. It might have been different, if Brian had taken the U.S. national team's head coaching job when it was offered to him a few years earlier.

"We wanted to see Misty represent the country as the Olympic team setter because that's the goal of anyone who has played indoors," Brian told the *Long Beach Press Telegram* in 1999. "But Misty has a quality I've rarely seen in athletes. I believe she can be a success at whatever she chooses. I think she'll be one of the best beach volley-ball players in a few years; it just may not be until 2004 before she can get to the Olympics because she started late."

# First Olympics

A fter quitting the U.S. national team in August 1999, the first person I called was Holly McPeak. Since we'd last talked, she'd struggled throughout the summer, playing in FIVB, AVP, and USA Volleyball events with Gabrielle Reece and Karolyn Kirby, and she'd had mediocre results with both partners. The word had gotten out that I was pursuing a professional beach volleyball career, but I wanted Holly to hear it directly from me. I needed her to know that if she was still willing to take me on as her partner, I was ready to go.

"Are you truly serious about this, Misty?" Holly asked, sternly.

She proceeded to impress upon me that qualifying for the 2000 Olympics wasn't going to be easy. There were spots for four U.S. teams in Sydney, two men's and two women's, but because I'd dilly-dallied with the U.S. national team all summer, we now were ten months and six tournaments behind the other U.S. contenders in the Olympic qualifying process.

In the two years leading up to an Olympics, beach volleyball teams try to qualify for the Games by playing in worldwide events sanctioned by the FIVB, the governing body for the sport. Points are awarded at each tour stop, depending on where each team finishes. Some events award double points. At the conclusion of the qualifying period, each team's best eight finishes are added together, and the two teams with the highest point totals represent the United States.

Holly explained that we were behind the eight ball: We had only ten FIVB events in which to get eight world-best finishes. Just one tour stop was in the United States, and it also was the only tournament with double qualifying points. The two leading U.S. women's teams—Annett Davis and Jenny Johnson Jordan, and Liz Masakayan and Elaine Youngs—had big points leads, and they also had the advantage of having had good finishes in the 1999 World Championships in Marseille, France, a double-points qualifier. (A silly FIVB qualifying procedure placed too much emphasis on old points.)

I quickly glanced at their cumulative points totals. In my mind, I calculated that to qualify for Sydney, we'd have to finish in the top four in every event, and we'd always have to finish higher than those two teams. I thought it was doable. At the time, though, I was so young and so naïve, I didn't truly grasp what a monumental task it was going to be, how many thousands of miles we would have to travel, and what a physical and emotional toll it would take on us both. I also had no clue about Holly's drive, or her workouts, which were a regular topic of conversation in beach volleyball, described as falling between army bootcamp and hell. What's that saying? Ignorance is bliss?

And then I asked Holly, "Why do you want to play with me?"

Her response cemented it for me: "Because I know you want to win."

After speaking to Holly, I called Dad and Mom.

"Guess who I just talked to?" I said.

"Who?" Dad replied.

"Holly McPeak," I said. "She and I are going to make a run at the 2000 Olympics!"

"What are your odds of qualifying?" Dad asked.

"A million to one," I said, laughing.

"That sounds pretty good," Dad said. "Great, we're going to Sydney!"

What had Dad wanted to say? "Are you freakin' crazy?!" What he hadn't told me was that Holly had called him a few days earlier to feel him out about partnering with me and that he'd given her his and Mom's blessing. What Dad also hadn't told me was that when it had become clear I was going to pursue a career on the beach, he'd phoned Karch.

"I want Misty to be the next Karch Kiraly," Dad told him.

"No, Butch, she's going to be the first and only Misty May," Karch replied.

In September 1999, Holly and I began seriously training. Little did I know the depth of her commitment to the sport or her intense will to win. We'd meet in Manhattan Beach, at the courts near the big, peach, three-story house Holly shared with her longtime boy-friend Leonard Armato, a sports agent who represented Los Angeles Lakers center Shaquille O'Neal, and a cofounder of the AVP, who later became its chairman, commissioner, and CEO. We started from square one, with Holly teaching me basic skills. Although I'd played beach volleyball, and had a good feel for the game, Holly kept reminding me that I didn't know its nuances. She was all about fierce defense and her trademark was perfect passing.

"Don't worry, in a month, you'll get it, and say, 'Wow!'" Holly kept telling me. Time and again, as I added skill after skill to my beach repertoire, she proved to be right.

Soon after we began training, Holly suggested we travel to Brazil. Because we were a "small team"—Holly at five foot seven and me at five foot eight and a half—she said we needed to excel in a lot of areas to defeat the taller teams. The Brazilians focused on excellent ball control, a style she envisioned us playing. There were some great female players in Brazil, as well as some great coaches. We'd received a wild card entry into the final event on the 1999 FIVB tour, in Salvador de Bahia, Brazil. So off we went.

I was up for the challenge, although still very much a kid. I hadn't done much growing up on my own. Throughout my life, my parents had always taken care of things for me, and when I was at Long Beach

State, my coaches had handled the details and provided the structure. In fact, I was so accustomed to everybody else taking charge, I showed up at the Los Angeles airport without my passport. Mom had to race home to retrieve it.

Holly and I spent a couple of weeks in Brazil, and the best part of the trip was being in Rio de Janeiro with Shelda Bede and Adriana Behar, the rock stars of women's beach volleyball. We stayed at Shelda's house, thanks to Holly's friendship with her. On that trip, I eyeballed the best Brazilian players, male and female, and I spent hours studying their games. That's what my parents had taught me to do, ever since I was a little girl. "Pick out the best, see what they're doing," they'd instruct. Then I tried to find a way to incorporate their strengths into my game. The first two I picked out? Shelda and Adriana. They were a "small team" with awesome skills, and they'd been on top forever.

Holly and I finished tied for ninth in Salvador. We each won $2,250 and received sixty-eight points. It wasn't good enough to count toward Olympic qualifying, but it was respectable for a team getting its feet wet. Regardless, we knew we had a lot going for us in our Olympic quest. We both were hard workers, extremely self-motivated. We both had been setters in college, highly skilled in every aspect of indoor volleyball. Holly played three years at the University of California–Berkeley before completing her collegiate career at UCLA in 1990 with an NCAA Championship.

After we got back from Brazil, Holly and I did nothing but practice, practice, practice. Her training regimen was harder than anything I'd ever experienced. Her father, Chuck, was a former marine lieutenant, and it was clear the apple didn't fall far from the tree. Again and again, she repeated her mantras: "This is our goal." "We can't take our eye off the prize." "It's not going to be a cakewalk." Trainingwise, I didn't know anything besides what I'd done in college, so I often overtrained. If Holly was doing a particular workout, I did it, too. I tried a lot of different things, per her orders, like bikram yoga, and this and that, and very quickly, I became a rat on a wheel, racing from workout to workout, spending hours and hours in my car. I often felt nervous, anxious, and stressed out. I knew if we wanted to qualify for Sydney, I had to give it my all—and then some—and that I couldn't make any mistakes.

Holly became the driving force behind our Olympic quest. She kept us moving, full steam ahead. She hired Gene Selznick, who was in his seventies, to be our coach. Gene was one of the most dominant indoor players in the history of the game and a celebrated member of the 1960 and 1966 U.S. Volleyball World Championship teams. An early proponent of Southern California beach volleyball, dating back to 1949, Gene was nicknamed "the First King of Beach Volleyball." Even with a coach, nobody pushed me harder, on or off the court, than Holly. She steered me to talented healers who could help me recover quickly from nagging injuries. She taught me how to be a responsible adult. And she called me out when I made rookie decisions.

One time we planned to practice at Manhattan Beach at 9:00 A.M. When I hadn't shown up by 9:15 A.M., she ran up to her house and phoned me. I had a severe migraine, and had decided to stay home.

"Well, you need to call me and tell me," Holly scolded. "We're a team, a partnership. We're trying to do something, together, that's really big. This isn't just a day at the beach, Misty. This isn't just a casual thing. This is the Olympics."

Holly can best be described in one word: INTENSE. She brings out the best in everybody she plays with. She is a hard worker and a very dedicated player. However, it was tough for me, at twenty-two, to get into her demanding regimen. Throughout our growing pains as teammates, and my growing pains as a young woman, Holly continually reminded me, "This is what we're trying to do. This is where we're trying to go. We can't mess around."

My parents stepped aside and let Holly take the reins. They completely entrusted me to her. She had to be thinking, "Here are two parents who know a lot about beach volleyball. They could be at every practice. They could be pretty controlling, if they wanted to be." But my parents never interfered. Mom, battling back pain since my last year or two at Long Beach State, watched practice, but not often. Meanwhile, Dad ran me through "extra credit" workout sessions. After Holly and I'd finished practicing, he'd drill me at Huntington Beach. Beyond that, though, they just played supportive roles.

Thanks to Holly, I worked harder than ever. I grew into a professional athlete. She was my mentor, I was her protégée. I always deferred to her. She'd ask which bikini I wanted to wear. We had ten from which to choose. "You pick, I don't care," I'd tell her. She'd ask where I wanted to eat on road trips. "You pick, it doesn't matter to me," I'd reply. She'd ask if I wanted to wake up at 6:30 A.M. or 7:00 A.M. "Whatever you think," I'd say. Thanks to her impetus, I signed sponsorship deals, launched a website, bought a home in Long Beach, and started an investment portfolio. In the process, Holly and I had a great time together. Today, she'll admit there were plenty of times she thought she was traveling with her thirteen-year-old sister rather than a young woman who'd just finished four years of college. Now, I can understand Holly's perspective: I always say that I gave her a lot of gray hair.

Holly was my mother away from home, and more often than not, she was my big sister. She endured my ever-changing hair color. Jet black. Brunette with sun streaks. Honey blonde. She played a role in my endless pranks, like trying to pass off friends as family members to the media. She rolled her eyes at the crazy situations I got myself into, like staying up until 1:30 A.M. downing one-dollar tacos. (I tied my personal record of ten.) She laughed at the goofy stuff that came out of my mouth, like when a reporter from the *San Diego Union-Tribune* asked about my website, www.mistymay.com, and I replied, straight-faced, "I know it isn't creative, but I didn't want somebody stealing my name. You know how they get a name and turn it into a porn site." She taught me a lot about life and introduced me to elements of it as only a big sister could.

Like getting my first bikini wax.

Holly took me to Pink Cheeks in Los Angeles. Afterward, I found out it was the place for Hollywood celebrities, but I had no clue at the time. I was more concerned that the esthetician took a lot off. Actually, she took everything off. I was in complete shock. Holly hadn't prepared me to be scalped. It was painful. Going to the gynecologist was bad enough, but now this? And just when I thought the esthetician was finished doing her job, she suddenly barked out an order: "All fours, please!" Yikes. But I quickly told myself, "If it's good enough for Holly, it's good enough for me." When I got up from the table, my butt cheeks stuck together when I walked. After the ordeal was over, Holly informed me bikini waxes were just part of being a pro.

In our first four months together, things went quite well. We believed the 2000 Olympics were within our reach, even if few others did. Then, in January 2000, I got a phone call I wasn't prepared for.

"I have cancer," Mom said.

My first thought was, "My mom's going to die." I burst into tears. The only people I'd ever known who'd had cancer were my grandparents, Mom's parents, and they'd both died from the disease. My mind began racing. I thought about my grandfather, who'd had prostate cancer. I thought about my grandmother, who'd had uterine cancer. I thought about all of the great things I wanted to accomplish, in volleyball and in life. And I thought about how my mother, who'd played such a prominent role in my success, might not be around to see my plans come to fruition, to share all of my victories with me and Dad. Would she live to see me get to the Olympics? Win gold medals? Get married? Have children?

In my head, I kept hearing myself say, "This is the end of the world." Suddenly, I blurted out through my tears, "I want to live at home." Her cancer diagnosis had turned me back into Mama's Little Girl.

My mother was stoic, calm. She did her best to hold it together. "Everything will be fine," she assured me. She'd never wanted anybody to worry about her. But I knew she'd been crying. I could hear a faint nasal sound in her voice.

For two years, Mom had complained about back pain. As a life-long athlete, she'd figured she just had an arthritic problem in her spine. Or perhaps she'd tweaked her back by swinging too hard at a ball while playing with her girlfriends. She'd had massages and chiropractic adjustments, but they'd only provided temporary relief. The pain quickly returned, cropping up in different areas of her back. X-rays were inconclusive. One day, Dad went to see Dr. William Stetson for his arthritic knees. Stetson got to chatting with Dad about the family, and Dad told him about Mom's persistent, moving back pain.

"That doesn't sound right," Stetson said. "Have her come in to have an MRI."

Then, boom. A day or so after the MRI, Stetson phoned Dad and said, "We'll keep Barbara's appointment for tomorrow, but I want you to come in with her."

"What's up?" Dad said.

"She has cancer," Stetson said.

Stetson explained to Mom that the MRI showed spots in her upper back, just below her shoulders. The cancer already had metastasized, so she underwent numerous tests to determine its origin. She never had a biopsy or surgery, and the doctors never figured out what kind of cancer it was. It moved from her lungs to her spine to her hip to the base of her skull. It was all very confusing to Dad and to me—it still is—because it was discovered so late.

Mom subjected herself to extensive radiation and chemotherapy treatments. She wasn't going down without a fight. An athletic, strong-willed woman, she tolerated a large combination and high dosage of chemotherapy drugs. However, the potent poison made her extremely ill. It yanked at her emotions, upset her stomach, zapped her energy, and left a tinny taste in her mouth. Sometimes, she slept with a bag of potpourri next to her nose to overpower the taste. The doctors kept cheering her on, telling her the chemotherapy was working, insisting she was getting better. They used cyclist Lance Armstrong as a beacon of hope: Diagnosed in October 1996, at twenty-five, with stage-three testicular cancer which had spread to his lungs, abdomen, and brain, he'd undergone surgery and chemotherapy to save his life. His doctor admitted he had less than a 40 percent chance to survive. He'd proven the medical experts wrong, conquering cancer, then winning the Tour de France seven times (three times during Mom's battle).

Dad and I, and all of Mom's girlfriends, were enthused by the doctors' words, but Mom wasn't buying any of it. She felt like crap. She was ornery. Everything bothered her, just one thing after another. She kept talking about how much she missed having her mother rub her forehead and promise her everything would be okay. Now that was somebody whose words she could trust. To make herself feel better, Mom cuddled with an old red and white cotton jacket that had belonged to my grandmother.

"My major fear is not dying, it's my crappy thinking," Mom said. "Feeling sorry for yourself leads to 'Why should I live?' If you're not happy on the inside, how can you be happy on the outside?"

To pull herself out of her doldrums, Mom consulted a healer, Petra, who focused on improving the spirit. She taught Mom visualization techniques to renew her body, mind, and soul. She had Mom keep a grateful journal. She put Mom on a macrobiotic diet. For some semblance of normalcy, during her weeks off from chemotherapy, Mom took to the volleyball court with her girlfriends. Even if she couldn't jump, swing at the ball, or hit very hard, she still had the desire to get out there. She was a competitor, through and through, and she loved competing with her girlfriends. The chemotherapy couldn't kill her passion for volleyball, and it certainly couldn't diminish her sense of humor. She actually got to the point where she'd laugh at the bandanna covering her bald head. "I look like one of the Seven Dwarfs," she joked. She threatened to paste a fake beard on her face. "I'll tell people my hair grew back, but in the wrong place," she kidded.

Eileen Clancy McClintock, Dad's longtime beach volleyball partner, remembers playing with Mom and some of Mom's girlfriends at Sorrento Beach during, or soon after, one of her rounds of chemotherapy treatments. Every time Eileen lovingly got on her, Mom would shoot back, with a smile, "You can't yell at me. I'm a cancer patient!" Eileen still laughs about the scene afterward, when Mom went into the restroom and announced, "Stand back! I'm radioactive!" A few minutes later, a toxic chemical stench wafted from Mom's toilet stall. Everybody pinched their noses and held their breath, except for Mom, who roared loudly.

From day one, my parents sheltered me from Mom's cancer. I went to only one doctor's appointment, and I never accompanied her to treatments. It isn't easy for me to come up with the details of her disease, and her valiant battle, because I don't have much firsthand knowledge. My parents did that on purpose. I was gone a lot, chasing my Olympic quest around the world. I called home every day. Some days, she felt good, others she felt lousy. But my parents never gave me the straight scoop. For the longest time, I felt very guilty about not having been there for Mom, but eventually I made peace with myself. Now, it makes a lot more sense to me why my parents didn't want me to become involved in Mom's cancer. Come hell or high water, Mom and Dad weren't going to let anything interfere with my future. And this battle was hell for us. They insisted I carry on with life, that I do everything in my power to get to the 2000 Olympics. Always being the dutiful child, that's exactly what I did.

The 2000 FIVB world tour, and the first of nine Olympic qualifiers, kicked off in Vitoria, Brazil, the first week in February. Holly and I finished fifth. While disappointed, we saw some bright spots: We had upset Brazil's Shelda and Adriana, the number one team in the world, and we had led Liz and E.Y. before dropping a tight match that we could've won.

With only one FIVB event under my belt before the 2000 season, Holly and I were at a severe disadvantage at each tour stop, forced to play in the qualifying round in order to get into the main draw. This made our Olympic quest even tougher: We'd have to play twice as many games as everybody else. That meant more stress, more pressure, and more days on the road. Holly would call Dad to lament our predicament, and he'd tell her it was a blessing in disguise.

"That's great, you get to practice," he'd say, trying to pump her up. "Use those as practice matches."

The next tournament, in mid-April, was a USA Volleyball event in Deerfield Beach, Florida. Although it wasn't an Olympic qualifier, it did wonders for us. It was our first victory, and we split twenty thousand dollars. We dominated the competition. I had 19 kills in only my second final. I became the youngest woman to win a U.S. pro beach title.

"I don't know what makes us so successful, we're a brand-new team," Holly told reporters after the match. "The chemistry is definitely there. I knew we had chemistry from the beginning. We both grew up on the beach playing, so we have the background. We are a long shot to make the Olympic team, but we believe in our chances. If we play the way we did this weekend, we can get there."

Meanwhile, I was stunned and a bit starry-eyed.

"Everything is a learning experience for me," I told the media. "I'm still new at this."

In May, we played in two Beach Volleyball America (BVA) events— Oceanside (second to Lisa Arce and Barbra Fontana after blowing a 5–0 lead) and Santa Monica (third). Again, the tournaments had no impact on Olympic qualifying, but they represented an important milestone for women's beach volleyball, and that was very meaningful to us. After the 1997 season, the Women's Professional Volleyball Association went belly up, about $1.2 million in debt. Now, thanks to software multimillionaire Charlie Jackson, the BVA's owner and operator, the women pros were back in business. Each of the seven BVA tournaments would have a seventy-five-thousand-dollar purse, the winning teams splitting fifteen thousand dollars.

After finishing second in Virginia Beach, Virginia, a USA Volleyball event in late May, we headed into a hellacious, two-and-a-half-month, eight-FIVB-tournament stretch that would hopscotch the globe.

We kicked it all off in Rosarito, Mexico. We played well through-out the event, the only glitch occurring the morning of the final. I was late meeting Holly for warm-ups because I'd gone to have corn-rows put in my hair. The braiding took forever, and by the time I came dashing onto the court, Holly was livid.

"Where have you been?" she snapped.

"Having my hair braided," I replied.

Holly rolled her eyes in disgust. We ended up losing to Shelda and Adriana, and I wound up paying for it in another way: severely sun-burned scalp. Because I was rushing to our warm-ups, I hadn't had time to put sunscreen on the exposed skin, which was now all over my head, thanks to the cornrows.

A few days later, we left for Europe and Asia on our six-week Olympic qualifying odyssey. I arrived at the Los Angeles airport for my first-ever extended international tour with an enormous suitcase. I packed about twenty-one days' worth of outfits—one for morning, one for noon, and one for night—because I couldn't fathom how I was going to do laundry in the beach volleyball outposts we'd be playing in. Holly took one look at my suitcase, shook her head, and said, "Where are you going?"

"To Europe with you," I replied.

"It's a business trip, not a summer vacation," Holly said.

All Holly had was one small suitcase and a carry-on bag. She nick-named my bag "Big Bertha." Holly always told me exactly the way it was. She was, and still is, no-nonsense. She's the only person I know who emails, then follows up with an email saying, "Did you get my email?" As Dad says, "If a tournament application has to be turned in in five days, Holly gets it in with five days to spare." She was, and still is, all business. It worked for her, and it worked for me.

"Some days, some people don't want to be there," Holly told the Los Angeles Times. "Misty's fired up and ready to learn every day. Her youth and excitement for the game, the energy she gives off, definitely help. Last year, I played with partners I felt sucked my energy."

Our first stop was Cagliari, Italy, the capital of the island of Sardinia. It has one of the longest and most beautiful beaches throughout the Mediterranean. The Poetto Beach stretches for eleven kilometers and is famous for its fine-grained, white sand. We finished fifth. We didn't panic, though, and we didn't lose faith in our Olympic quest. We just kept moving forward. After the match, Holly sat me down, and we analyzed our performance for a couple of hours. From there on out, self-analysis and team critiques became vital parts of our post-tournament routine.

We flew to Toronto, Canada, for the following week's FIVB event, the Canadian Open. The qualifier turned out to be no fun. It was pouring rain—the court resembled a lake—and Holly and I wore garbage bags over our bikinis. The ball was so wet and so heavy, we had to underhand it. However, we persevered. We lost in the final, again, to Shelda and Adriana, finishing second.

We crossed the Atlantic Ocean again, this time flying to the next week's FIVB event in Gstaad, Switzerland, one of the world's most exclusive ski resorts. Beach volleyball? It was a brand-new FIVB event, and at that time, it was women only. The stadium was located in the heart of Gstaad, or the "holiday village," as the Swiss like to refer to it. Although it was mid-June, it was so cold that we wore booties on our feet during matches. We lost in the final, again, to Shelda and Adriana, finishing second. The best part was our trophies: We were awarded big, beautiful Swiss cowbells. I still cherish mine.

The following week, the FIVB stop was in Chicago, Illinois, a double-points qualifying event. We won three qualification matches to earn a berth in the thirty-two-team main draw. One of my most vivid recollections is playing against a German team on an outside court. It was a hot, humid day, and I was wearing a pair of Oakley sunglasses, which fit too closely to my face. They fogged up. Holly served, and it was short. Germany dove and passed it over the net. "Hit the ball!" Holly yelled. However, I couldn't see the ball, and it ended up hitting me right in the face. We beat Shelda and Adriana in the final, 15–12, on the Fourth of July. We earned thirty-two thousand dollars and 600 qualifying points. We had 2,062 points total and were closing in fast on Liz and E.Y. (2,284 points) for one of the two U.S. spots.

"Every team that entered this event knew how important it was," Holly told the *Chicago Sun Times*. "To come out with all that pressure on us and play against the best team in the world, it just all came together, and it was a huge win for us."

After Chicago, it was back to Europe for an FIVB event in Berlin, Germany. That's when disaster struck. Holly and I were playing an Italian team on an outside court. I dove for a ball, tearing my abdominal muscle. I continued playing, but every time I swung, I felt a stabbing in my stomach. It never occurred to me to pull out of the tournament, because we needed the qualifying points for Sydney.

"If you're badly hurt, you don't have to keep playing," Holly kept telling me.

No way was I going to give up our Olympic quest. "Just let me play one more match," I said. And then, we kept winning. It was crazy. After every match, Holly phoned Dad, gave him a play-by-play and said, "Butch, every time she serves, she cries." Dad kept telling her, "Holly, don't bother an injured animal." Well, the next thing you know, we beat Australians Tania Gooley and Pauline Manser to win our second straight tournament. It moved us into second place among U.S. women's teams vying for an Olympic berth. It was a huge win for us, and especially rewarding for me, teaching me I could perform at a high level even with excruciating pain.

Several hours later, I flew home from Europe to receive medical attention. Over the next two weeks, I underwent various forms of treatment, but there's not a lot you can do for a torn abdominal muscle, other than rest, and there wasn't time for that. Then, we flew to Osaka, Japan, our second-to-last qualifier. I struggled, serving underhand and unable to hit. Sitting? Painful. Coughing and sneezing? Killers. Why, even getting out of bed hurt. I had intensive physical therapy and acupuncture, practically around the clock. At one point, I saw doubt in Holly's eyes.

"Trust me, Misty, we don't have to do this," Holly said. "Your health is more important."

"I can do this!" I said.

Holly meant well, but she underestimated me. In a gut-wrenching situation, I'm very much Butch May's daughter. Dad had a will unlike any other. He rode bulls for many years, suffering nasty injuries, and he instilled his warrior's attitude in me. I'm relentless. I never give up.

Sure enough, Holly and I finished fourth, pretty spectacular given my condition. But that lower-place finish meant we didn't earn enough points to qualify for Sydney. So we'd have to travel to Dalian, China, for the final FIVB qualifier for one last-ditch effort. Had we finished second or third in Japan, we would've qualified, and I could've flown straight home to nurse my abdominal tear.

Instead, we jetted to China. To clinch the Olympic berth, we had to finish no lower than second. I lay around the hotel and iced my abdominals. I tried to get medical attention, but there wasn't anybody who could help me. We were out in the middle of nowhere. It was awful. I don't know how we got through the tournament. I really don't. We made the Olympic team, after a come-from-behind semifinals victory over Zi Xiong and Rong Chi of China, 17–16. We trailed 14–8 before stunning the home team. It was a miracle. I just toughed it out in all that pain. By the skin of our teeth we qualified for Sydney, edging out Liz and E.Y. for the second spot by a mere 50 points.

On our flight back to Los Angeles, Holly mapped out our schedule for the next five weeks. She was sympathetic about my injury, but stern.

"Misty, you really need to deal with it," Holly said. "You've got to see the best specialist possible."

The next thing I knew, Holly was attacking the challenge of healing my abdominal tear with the same intensity she applied to beach volleyball. She identified Alex McKechnie, a physiotherapist in Vancouver, British Columbia, Canada, as a leading authority on core training and movement integration. He'd come to the Lakers in 1997–98 to work on Shaq's ab muscle tear. She took it from there, setting up an appointment with McKechnie, volunteering to fly to Vancouver so I'd have a second pair of ears, then making our airline and hotel reservations. She told me to meet her at the Los Angeles airport at 9:00 A.M. the following day for a 10:00 A.M. flight. When I hadn't arrived by 9:30 A.M., Holly called me. She became concerned when she couldn't reach me. As the gate agent was closing the door to our flight, I phoned to say I was stuck in traffic.

"I'm giving up my weekend to go to Vancouver with you, and you can't even make it to the airport on time?" Holly barked. "Come on, you've got to be responsible. We're going to try and fix your stomach."

The plane left without her. We sat in the Los Angeles airport for three hours, waiting for the next Vancouver flight. Holly didn't say boo from the time I got to the airport until we touched down in Vancouver. That's how angry she was. Talk about an uncomfortable silence.

We spent two days with McKechnie, and I think it cost me five hundred dollars a day. He introduced me to a series of core exercises. The goal was to get me through Sydney. McKechnie taught me how to segment my abdominals, to recruit muscles around the tear, so that I could relieve some of the pain. Holly trained with me, so she could help me in the future. This episode really illuminated the different weaknesses in my body. I'd never focused on training my core, which is the fundamental muscle source for balance, posture, and overall body strength. Oh, I'd done sit-ups and push-ups to strengthen my midsection, but that's about it.

In the five weeks before the Olympics, I completely laid off volleyball and concentrated solely on strengthening my core. I returned from Vancouver and showed my program to the athletic trainers at Long Beach State, who did whatever they could to jump-start the healing process. It was a frantic time, trying to fool Mother Nature and speed up my body's healing clock. I had a lot of acupuncture. I spent hours in physical therapy, hooked up to electric stimulation units. Electrodes were placed at strategic points on my stomach, sending currents surging through my abdominals to pump out the inflammation.

The frantic feeling followed me off the court, too. Holly recalls my parents being freaked out she was going to dump me and pick up a new partner for the Olympics, which was allowed under the rules.

"You guys, I wouldn't do that," Holly kept trying to reassure my parents. "Misty earned this spot. That girl is amazing, and I'd never bail on her."

I think the real reason my parents were so worried about my Olympic spot had a lot to do with Mom's battle with cancer. While Holly and I were traveling the globe, Mom was moving mountains of her own to get well enough to travel to Australia, should we qualify. All along, Dad and Mom believed we'd get there, and their positive attitude is what helped them believe she could get to Sydney, too. The Olympics gave all of us something to look forward to. That's why I pushed myself so hard. After all, we were the Three Musketeers, one for all and all for one.

Except when it came to shaving my head.

A few weeks before the Olympics, Dad shaved his head in support of Mom, who'd lost all her hair from the chemotherapy treatments. Our family friend Jim Steele did, too. Mom understood it wouldn't be prudent for me to be playing beach volleyball, in the hot, Australian sun, with a bald noggin, so she insisted I not do it. As for Dad, she asked him to grow back his hair because she thought she looked a lot better bald than he did. When it started to come in, I tried to color it.

"You should do like rocker Billy Idol and dye it platinum blond," I suggested.

"It's burning!" Dad screamed, as I applied the dye to his nubby scalp.

"No, it's just stimulating the roots of your hair." I replied.

But I was wrong. It really did burn his scalp, and eventually, we peeled the skin right off Dad's head.

Meanwhile, my parents' friends showed their support for Mom in very generous ways. They threw a big party, hosted by Larry and Chris Rundle, at the Westlake Village Tennis and Swim Club. Larry had played on the 1968 U.S. Olympic team with Dad. Everybody who came donated to my parents' Sydney trip, raising $16,500.

Mom was extremely humble. She didn't want all of the attention. She didn't want people coming over to the house and fussing over her. However, she did appreciate the fact that her cancer allowed her to see how important she was to people, that she had a lot of dear friends. Her close friend Toni Bowermaster told me that before Mom got sick, she hadn't realized how much people loved her. "I think it was a surprise to Barb," Toni now says about the outpouring of emotion toward her.

It was a triumph for Holly and me to qualify for the Olympics, and it was a triumph for Mom to travel to Sydney. For most of the season, she spent a handful of days each week in chemotherapy. She was tired, but she felt good. She still had her sense of humor. When she boarded the plane to Australia, with very little hair on her head, the steward asked, "May I help you, sir?" Mom laughed. "Well, you can help me, but I'm not a sir, I'm a cancer patient," she replied. Needless to say, the steward couldn't have been more accommodating the rest of the trip. Any time Mom asked for something, he got it for her.

Holly was an Olympic veteran, having finished fifth at the 1996 Atlanta Games. She gave me a lot of advice on how to handle the demands of family and friends at an Olympics. She told me that I needed to manage my time, that I couldn't let myself get swept up in the hoopla.

"We're going to Sydney to win the Olympic gold medal," Holly said. "We're not going to sightsee."

But when she suggested we skip Opening Ceremony because we'd be spending a lot of time on our feet, Dad blew a gasket.

"Not march in Opening Ceremony?" he snapped. "That's one of the best experiences you'll ever have. March and put six of those disposable cameras around your neck, so that the memories that aren't in your head will always be in pictures."

I'm glad I listened to Dad, because the Opening Ceremony was the event of a lifetime. It's the only way to understand the meaning of the Olympics, the only way to truly get the goose bumps.

My parents rented a house about three blocks from Bondi Beach, the venue for beach volleyball. Dad and Mom stayed there, along with several members of Misty's Misfits, the motley crew that has supported me at volleyball events throughout the years. My half brothers Brack and Scott, as well as Brack's significant other Krista, stayed in the house, as did dear family friends Loren Woll, Patricia Nohavec, and Ernie Suwara. Two other close family friends, Eileen Clancy McClintock and Jean Brunicardi, who had Parkinson's disease, stayed in a hotel room across from Bondi Beach. Since the rental house had people sleeping everywhere—in beds, on sofas, on air mattresses on the floor—a hotel was easier for Jean to navigate.

When Mom was diagnosed with cancer, she decided to resolve all of the family issues of the past. She believed it was time for us to be a real family. She made an effort to establish strong relationships with Brack and Scott, and she used my volleyball career to correct mistakes and mend hard feelings. Growing up, I hadn't seen them very often, perhaps in the summer or at Thanksgiving at my aunt Gen's house in Northern California. I became the catalyst for bringing all of us Mays back together, and the Sydney Olympics represented a turning point for my family. Mom insisted that Brack and Scott come to Australia, because she knew she was really sick, and she wanted all of us there, to experience it together.

Holly and I stayed in an apartment a few blocks from the beach. My family and friends cooked at the rental house, and I ate meals with them. Every morning, Brack, an incredible chef, bought fresh bakery items. Most evenings, he cooked wonderful dinners with fresh fish and vegetables. The rental house felt like one big Misty's Misfits slumber party, with people jumping all over each other, getting up at the crack of dawn, staying out until the wee hours of the morning.

In addition to playing tour director, Holly added another role in Sydney: physical therapist. McKechnie had prescribed specific exercises for me to do daily, as well as warming up before matches. Every day, except days of matches, she ran me through them, just to make sure I was staying on top of my injury and doing everything possible to make it through the Olympics. I'd grab a big purple exercise ball and she'd grab the smaller blue one and we'd head to the hills for two hours of intense ab and body work.

The toughest thing about beach volleyball training at an Olympics? Being allotted only thirty minutes on the court. Because I'd taken five weeks off, Holly and I were just starting to practice together in Sydney. We went to Australia a week early, to try to get back in the groove with each other, but we were practicing with limited time and opportunities. Worse yet, it had been forever since we'd played a game.

Now, Holly says, "We were out of rhythm, and we just weren't the same team we were before that."

My legs were weak, my stamina lacking.

We went in as the fourth-seeded team, favored by some to win the gold medal, by others to reach the medals podium. Three opponents later, our Olympics were over. Just like that. Poof. We lost to Brazil's Sandra Pires and Adriana Samuel, 16–14, in forty-nine minutes. They'd both won medals at the 1996 Atlanta Olympics, but with different partners. Four times, we evened the score, only to watch the Brazilians fight back and regain a one-point lead, thanks to stellar net play by Pires. Finally, after three match points, Pires smashed in a winner, bursting the magnificent bubble Holly and I had created over the past nine months, sending us to our knees in disbelief. Our Olympic quest was over, two points shy of making the medal round.

Afterward, Dad, Mom, Holly, and I all said we were convinced we could've won a medal, perhaps even gold. If only I'd been healthy. If only we'd been in sync. If only we'd stuck to the game plan Dad and Gene had given us. Later, Holly told reporters, "I felt I should have been more aggressive, and I can't really explain why I wasn't."

We came into the Olympics as one of the best teams in the world, enjoying a meteoric rise to the top, thanks to our globe-trotting Olympic quest, as well as our relentless drive and determination. Unfortunately, my injury put us in a bind. In beach volleyball, rhythm is everything. We'd been playing well as a team, then we'd put on the brakes. We'd completely stopped for almost six weeks. I rested, trying to heal my abdominals. Holly trained, trying to hold "the team" together. Meanwhile, everybody else in the world was fine-tuning their bodies, their partnerships, and their games for the Olympics.

Throughout the Olympics, I thought I'd held it together pretty well. In fact, I don't think I was that bad off, physically or emotionally. And then, in the quarterfinals, against Brazil, something snapped. We didn't do as we'd been told. At times, we tried to do too much. At times, we did too little. Because coaches aren't allowed to instruct during matches or to be near the players, and because there aren't any time-outs to stop the action and regroup, I'll never forget hearing Dad and Gene scrambling to get us back on track. From up in the stands, Dad yelled, "Don't!" followed by Gene screaming, "Block!"

At the conclusion of our Olympics, I was disappointed, but not devastated. Yes, I was quoted in *Volleyball* magazine saying, "I won't lie: It really sucked to lose." And, yes, I cried after our final match. Dad, Mom, Brack, and Scott kept assuring me there'd be a next time. But having witnessed Mom's cancer battle, I knew there were worse things in life than losing a volleyball match, even in the Olympics.

Truthfully, what we'd accomplished to get there, all three of us, Holly and I and Mom, made the fifth place finish sweet. Learning beach volleyball from the ground up was a victory. Qualifying for the Olympics was a victory. Growing as a person, on and off the court, was a victory. Coping with excruciating pain and pushing myself to achieve great things was a victory. And having Mom there to see me play was the biggest victory of all. It's still the highlight of my career.

What my Olympic experience taught me, firsthand, was that time waits for no one. You must identify your passion and follow your heart. You must never back down from challenges. You must never, ever give up. You must do everything possible to seek out, embrace, and savor the special moments in life. You must cherish family and friends. You must always go for the gold. Because you never know what tomorrow may bring.

I'll always remember looking up into the stands in Sydney, after Holly and I had lost, and thinking how lucky I was to be Barbara May's daughter.

# 12

# KERRI WALSH

I'd just finished the final match in Sydney, and I hadn't even mentally or emotionally processed my Olympic quest, when talk of the 2004 Olympics began.

Leonard Armato, Holly's significant other, a sports agent, and a cofounder of the AVP, told Dad they'd like me to sign a five-year contract to play with Holly through the Athens Games. Dad said he couldn't promise that I'd continue as Holly's partner, but he also wouldn't speak for me. Mom, meanwhile, was much more blunt.

"No way!" she barked, still smarting from the loss and our inability to follow Dad and Gene's game plan.

Fortunately, I was out of earshot.

After all those weeks on the Olympic quest merry-go-round, I was completely worn out. I had to slow the breakneck speed with which I'd approached my rookie season on the beach. I had to dial back the intensity of my training. I had to stop the constant analysis of my game. I had to end the relentless drive for perfection. I wanted to enjoy the journey, as much as, if not more than, the destination. For me, beach volleyball is all about the journey. So is life. They always have been, and they always will be.

I had to stop feeling as if somebody were holding my head under-water and not letting me come up for air.

I wanted to breathe.

After Holly and I finished fifth, my parents were so disappointed we hadn't advanced to the medal round that they immediately began talking about finding a new partner for me. As luck would have it, the very next evening, Dad and Mom stumbled upon the perfect candidate: Kerri Walsh. We were eating dinner at the AT&T hospitality center for U.S. Olympians and their family and friends. We had Misty's Misfits in tow, and more, about seventeen people in all, including my parents and me. Dad noticed Tim and Marge Walsh, Kerri's parents, across the room.

"What are you looking at?" Mom asked Dad.

"Kerri Walsh's parents," he replied.

Then, he turned to me and said, "Misty, what about playing with Kerri Walsh?"

"She doesn't play beach," I replied.

"You can ask her to try," Dad said.

For several minutes, Dad and Mom discussed the upside of my playing with Kerri. Finally, Dad walked over to Tim and extended his hand.

"I'd like to introduce myself," Dad said. "I'm Butch May, Misty's father."

"Sure, Butch, we know who you are," Tim said. "How are you?"

"Well, I was just wondering, would Kerri like to play beach?" Dad asked.

"Why?" Tim replied.

"Because my wife, Barbara, and I think she'd be a great beach player," Dad said. "We'd like Kerri to come down to Southern California to see Misty for a couple of days, get the two of them out on the sand and give it a try."

"Are you serious about this?" Tim asked.

"Absolutely," Dad said.

It wasn't that I didn't want to play with Holly any longer. She was a great partner and a great person. Even today, when Dad sees Holly, he thanks her for pushing me through the threshold. It was an honor for me to have played with her. She was a great teacher and an excellent player-coach on the court. She was successful for so many years because of her intensity. She was relentless in trying to get better every day, and while being exposed to her attitude was incredibly instructive, keeping the flame burning so brightly 24/7 was also tremendously draining for me.

I wanted to enjoy the process, and Holly's crash course in beach volleyball hadn't allowed me to do that. The more my parents talked about the possibilities playing with Kerri offered, the more I realized it was the right time to move on to a new partner, the perfect moment to start over again from the beginning with a younger, taller player. Deep down, I wanted, and needed, to learn the game slowly and to grow with a partner over time.

Picking Kerri as a partner for me was a stroke of genius on my parents' part. At that time, Kerri was twenty-two, almost ten years younger than Holly, and considered the nation's best young female indoor player. A year younger than I, Kerri was six foot three, and from the moment she stepped onto the sand, she'd become one of the tallest, if not the tallest, women in beach volleyball. Instantly, my role would change. With Holly, I was "the big player"; with Kerri, I'd become "the little player." That would play to my strength as a defensive player.

Kerri grew up in Northern California, born in Santa Clara and raised in Saratoga. The nearest beach was in Santa Cruz, about thirty minutes south, where she'd participated in Junior Lifeguards and spent her free time, swimming in the ocean and hanging out on the sand. She'd made a conscious effort not to play beach volleyball because she thought she'd be too terrible at it, or in her own words, she was worried she'd "look like an idiot."

Kerri was a smart woman with impeccable volleyball credentials. She'd led Stanford to two NCAA Championships (1996 and 1997); was a four-year, first-team All-American, Final Four MVP (1996), and co–National Player of the Year (1999). Just like me, she had strong, athletic genes: Her father, Tim, who was six foot eight, had pitched in the Oakland A's organization and made it to the Triple-A level. He'd also played semipro basketball. Her mother, Marge, was a two-time volleyball MVP at Santa Clara University.

Kerri and I already knew a lot about each other. Volleyball is a tight-knit community, and you always hear about the standouts. At that point in time, she might be best described as the Northern California version of me. We'd played against each other twice during our high school years—I was at Newport Harbor, and she was at Archbishop Mitty in San Jose—and once in college. Stanford had defeated Long Beach State in the semifinals of the 1997 Final Four. Kerri later told a story about how, as a high school player, she'd been so nervous about playing against me in the Tournament of Champions in Santa Barbara she couldn't breathe. She remembers tearing up after her team won because it made her a little sad for me. Another time, also in high school, she'd asked for my autograph at a tournament in Stockton. She was in tears because she was so anxious about approaching me. Her parents told her to just walk up and ask me, and she finally approached me, handing me her lucky number nine towel and a pen to sign it.

"I won't bite you," I told her. At the time, I couldn't understand why Kerri was acting so goofy. I thought, "I'm just a person like everybody else." I guess she just looked up to me that much.

What I didn't know then was that, as a kid, Kerri was extremely insecure. The first five years of her life, she barely spoke. Her brother Marte, who's eleven months older, did most of the talking for her. Throughout high school, Kerri was very shy, even in small groups. She always leaned on Marte, her support system and her pillar of strength. She'd led her teams to championships in a variety of sports, but she wasn't a vocal leader.

As I later learned, Kerri's Sydney Olympic experience had been bittersweet. Thirty minutes before her first game with the U.S. Olympic indoor team, she was told she couldn't play because a drug test had indicated a suspicious testosterone to epitestosterone ratio. After she was retested, it turned out to be wrong, and Kerri was back on the court a few games later. She and her U.S. Olympic indoor teammates finished a disappointing fourth. Kerri was feeling burned out on volleyball. She didn't want to play professionally overseas because she didn't want to be far away from her family. She also needed a change of pace, so she was considering playing in Puerto Rico, which had a shorter indoor season.

When we both got home from the Olympics, Kerri and I began trading emails. Should I come down? Yeah, come down! It was really casual. Kerri later told me in her head, and in her heart, she was so nervous about what she thought was "an audition" that she tried to prepare for our meeting by getting together a group of players in Northern California to play with her at the beach. From the time she was fourteen, Kerri now admits, she'd always wanted to play volleyball with me.

In early February 2001, five months before Kerri graduated from Stanford with a bachelor's degree in American studies, my parents' matchmaking finally came to fruition. Kerri traveled to Southern California to spend several days with me on the beach. She recalls driving to see me at Huntington Beach, "practically hyperventilating on the freeway."

Instantly, we clicked. Mom was there, trying to get a feel for how we'd mesh as partners. Mom asked Casey Jennings, a pro player, and Steve Curtis, a family friend, both of whom happened to be training at the beach, if they'd play some games against us. She wanted to see Kerri run, jump, and move in the sand. Ironically, Kerri paid zero attention to Casey that day because she was so nervous about "auditioning" for me and my parents. Nobody would've ever guessed they'd later fall in love and get married.

At that point in time, Kerri says, her volleyball skills were "at a level 20 million times below" mine. As always, she's being ridiculously hard on herself. I thought she had all of the skills and fundamentals. It was clear that she, like me, had come from very good junior and collegiate programs. We both were well-rounded players. She was a phenomenal athlete, which was especially impressive given her height. She was quick and explosive. She had good balance and body control. She could move equally well to her left and to her right. She had soft hands. She had the ability to be a force blocking and hitting. She could play defense. A lot of times, taller girls just park themselves at the net. You won't find them running around the court, playing defense.

And while I'm at it, let me clear up something else. Kerri always says my parents and I were "auditioning" her, putting her through "a tryout," that day. That's an overstatement. In my mind, it was as much about seeing if Kerri liked playing on the beach as it was about us seeing if we meshed well as partners. It was just a casual, windy, late afternoon at Huntington Beach. It was "Either you like playing beach, or you don't, Kerri."

Throughout the weekend, Kerri and I continued to play together. Both Dad and Mom were on hand, and they grew more excited by the minute by Kerri's performance. They loved her height. They were impressed by her athletic talent. They were elated she enjoyed playing on the beach. They believed our partnership had a lot of promise. As Dad now says, "Kerri looked like a daddy longlegs spider out on the sand. She had all the makings of a beach volleyball superstar."

Breaking the news to Holly that I'd be moving on to a new partner wasn't easy. She never takes no for an answer. She doesn't go away easily or quietly. In beach volleyball, there's a term for switching partners: "getting dumped." It sounds cruel, but you can't believe how routine dumping partners becomes for some players. A poor showing in a weekend tournament, and the first thing Monday morning, phones are ringing all over the beach volleyball world, as players get jettisoned, while their former partners continue the seemingly endless search for the winning combination.

In April 2001, Holly and I played in our final event together, an FIVB tournament in Macau, where we finished third. We'd signed up for the tournament well ahead of time, so we had no choice but to follow through with our plans. When I explained to Holly I was planning to partner with Kerri, she wasn't at all happy with my decision.

"Why don't you get Kerri a coach for this year and play with her next year?" Holly argued.

I'm sure 2001 would've been a lucrative season for Holly and me because, after killing ourselves to qualify for the Olympics, and becoming a force to be reckoned with worldwide, we probably would've won a lot of tournaments. But, my reasoning was, if I waited until 2002 to solidify a partnership with Kerri, then I'd be right back to where I was with Holly, cramming to teach her the sport while trying to qualify for the 2004 Olympics under an extreme deadline.

At first, the volleyball world thought Dad and Mom and I were crazy to jettison Holly and partner with Kerri. Back then, a lot of people were scratching their heads and saying, "How can Misty May dump one of the all-time winningest players for someone who's a total beginner?" But if you're going to develop a new partnership, especially with someone as green as Kerri, the best time to do it is the year after an Olympics. The timing to move on from Holly was especially important for me, too, given the new, smaller court size that was coming into play in the game, which Dad and Mom, as well as other beach volleyball experts, believed eventually would cater to the taller, more powerful players. The bigger, better athletes would be coming out to the beach, my parents predicted. So it was the right time for me to get a jump on the trend. And beyond all of that, I really wanted to play with someone my own age. It was going to be fun to learn, and grow, together.

Back then, the more appropriate question about my decision to partner with Kerri would have been: "Can Kerri Walsh become a great beach player as quickly as Misty did?" After having lived through our grueling Olympic quest, I would've answered, "Absolutely not!" And that's not a knock on Kerri. Nobody could have survived the crash course I'd endured to get to Sydney. I'm not sure I could do it again if I tried. While nobody will ever forget Kerri's diving digs in the United States' upset victory over Korea at the 2000 Olympics, the rule of thumb in volleyball is that it takes three years to transition from the indoor to the beach game. Not only hadn't Kerri played beach volleyball growing up, but she wouldn't have the benefit of the now-defunct Fours tour, a four-person circuit, which had sped up the transition of former indoor players such as Jenny Johnson Jordan, Annett Davis, and Elaine Youngs. Most important, Kerri wouldn't have the benefit, as I did, of starting her beach career with an experienced veteran like Holly.

Anna Collier was our first coach. My parents picked her, thinking she'd be the perfect teacher for us when it came to beach volleyball skills. We met with Anna two or three times a week, at least two hours at a time. She was very tough, strictly no-nonsense. We were there to work, and she ran us into the ground. Just as I'd hoped for on my second go-round, Anna started from square one. She taught us basic passing and footwork, how to keep everything in perspective, how to move together as a team. She also taught us to never give up, how best to motivate the other person if she got down. She put us through a drill where we each served a ball, then ran in and played defense. If our serve was a lollipop, she wouldn't accept it. We had to go after it as if we were playing a match, as opposed to just putting the ball in play, then casually getting ready for defense. With Anna, it was attack, attack, attack. She worked us so hard in training that when we got into a game situation it was easy. I've always said, "If you aren't in shape after training with Anna Collier, there's no hope for you."

In our first season together, Kerri and I defined our relationship with Anna strictly as being a teacher-and-trainer-on-the-sand, but not in real competition. We didn't bring Anna to tournaments. She never wrote up scouting reports on our opponents, never videotaped our games, never analyzed our performances after matches. Truthfully, we didn't know what we wanted or needed out of a coach. Plus, that first season together was, in our minds, all about learning every aspect of the game. Rather than having somebody tell us what to do, we wanted to learn everything for ourselves. And learn the hard way, if need be. It wasn't until later that we changed our tune, after seeing top Brazilian teams put together an entire army, including technical coaches, scouting coaches, and training coaches, as well as massage therapists and physiotherapists. Once we started analyzing how the best teams were run, we wanted to bring a coach to tournaments, especially internationally.

A lot of people have the misconception that, in the beginning of our partnership, I was the natural and Kerri was the one who had to make the major transition. That's not true. Everybody, including me, has to make the transition from indoor to beach. Deep down, volleyball is volleyball, the same sport and the same skills, indoor or on the beach. The beach game is more freewheeling, and therefore requires a lot more versatility, strength, and stamina. From the outside, it looks very hang-loose, very day-at-the-beach, so to speak. But it takes a lot of mental toughness. Unlike indoor, where you may not touch the ball during a rally, in beach, you're involved in every ball movement, so you have to be able to cover the entire court and make every shot imaginable. True, Kerri and I both made the transition to beach when we were twenty-two. While I might have been a little more seasoned when I stepped onto the sand, having been exposed to the game as a kid, I still was young and immature. Kerri was, too. In one sense, we were girls. We had to grow, not only with each other but as young women, and experience-wise, as far as being on our own.

In indoor volleyball, everything's taken care of. You show up, and, whether you're at the top club level, in college, or on the U.S. national team, your uniforms have been picked out. You're given shoes and knee pads, and you don't have to wash, replace, or repair your equipment. You're told, "We're leaving on this date for this tournament in such and such." Airline tickets, hotel rooms, and meals are handled for you. All you need to do is pack your suitcase and get yourself to the airport, unless there's a team bus. Your biggest responsibility? A current passport. And then there's beach volleyball, where it's, "Okay, we're leaving . . ." And everything is up to you. But I didn't play the role of Mother Hen to Kerri, as Holly had played to me. No, we worked on everything together. Airline, hotel, and train reservations. Packing for extended international trips. Scoping out restaurants. Cutting corners and saving money.

Success didn't happen overnight for Kerri and me. While we immediately meshed in our practice sessions, we didn't instantly click in the heat of competition. It's unrealistic to think success will come instantly for a partnership. It takes time to develop trust and confidence in each other, get the handle on teamwork and the knack for court sense. It takes time to know what your partner is thinking and how she will respond in various situations. It takes time to learn how to communicate, verbally and nonverbally.

As a warm-up to a rigorous FIVB tour, we played two BVA events, one in late April in Clearwater, Florida, the other in late May, in Oceanside, California. Then, in mid-June, we embarked on a nine-tournament jaunt across Europe and Asia. Our decision to play exclusively overseas caused quite a stir. Initially, the AVP wasn't going to allow us to play in FIVB events. In order to secure enough points to stay in the main draw overseas, and ultimately qualify for the 2004 Olympics, we had to sacrifice playing at home. Also, we needed to compete against the best women's teams in the world, which meant playing the FIVB tour, not the AVP.

In our first tournament, in Cagliari, Italy, we finished a disappointing ninth. We were knocked out by Holly and her new partner, Lisa Arce. After that, it was a long and winding road for Kerri and me. We placed third in Gstaad, Switzerland; ninth in Gran Canaria, Spain; and seventh in Marseille, France. We didn't win a tournament until our fifth FIVB event, which was in Espinho, Portugal. Our winner's check was twenty-seven thousand dollars. Then it was back to the roller coaster. We finished ninth in Klagenfurt, Austria; second in Osaka, Japan; and second in Hong Kong.

Still, I could sense that Kerri and I had something very special. Almost immediately, our partnership felt different from Holly's and mine. It was truly magical. At every practice, and in every tournament, we were getting better and better, individually and as a team. In fact, I was so enthused I told myself, "We can be Olympic champions."

But I won't kid you, it was a real grind. People think your life as a professional athlete is so wonderful; they say, "Look at all the places you get to go and see." But it's not a vacation, it's a business trip. If you lose, yes, you might spend some extra time sightseeing, but if you're winning, you're not walking around checking out the town. In fact, you're not doing much of anything, other than eating, sleeping, and playing volleyball.

We did, however, manage to get the flavor of the country by the style of beach volleyball their athletes played and by the site of the tournament. Brazil, in parts, is more like a third world country. They have a lot of poverty there, but both the rich and the poor show up at the beach. They're all there. The beaches are great, they go on for miles, and it's a very active society. It doesn't matter what size they are, everybody's in a bathing suit. The Brazilians love life, no matter how much money or how many material possessions they have.

In Switzerland, we played right next to the Alps, and I always felt compelled to roll down the mountains in my bikini, singing the soundtrack from *The Sound of Music.* Kerri and I fell in love with a salami sandwich at a local hotel. We became so superstitious about it that we always ate it, along with a salad, before tournaments, sometimes as many as three times in one trip. In Austria, we played next to a lake, beside beautiful green foothills. All the food was so fresh. In Marseille, France, we played at a topless beach (but not for us!). While we were playing, we could see people sunbathing with their tops off.

Throughout our first season, Kerri was extremely hard on herself.

I can't believe I was ever such a peanut!

I'm hanging out in front of our family's pizza joint at Muscle Beach. Where are Dad and Mom? Playing beach volleyball, of course.

Mom was a nationally ranked tennis player. Everybody always says we looked a lot alike.

Taking my first steps from Mom to Dad's outstretched hands.

My grandmother and grandfather Betty and Kenneth Grubb.

My sixth birthday. Making a wish, blowing out the candles, and dreaming in gold!

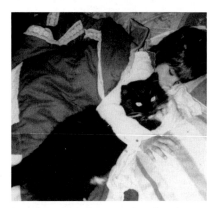

The Tour de Misty. Honk, honk! Beep, beep!

Snoozing with Pokey, one of my favorite cats.

"Yes, Santa, I was a very good girl this year."
(Years later, I learned Dad was behind the beard.)

Eileen Clancy McClintock and I having a blast at a Smurfs concert.

My friend Jessica Jennings and me, two budding ballerinas.

My dance troupe and me (back row, far right). Now you can see why I was destined to be on *Dancing with the Stars*.

My cousin Taylor Dent and me, aka the Future Tennis Pro and Super Girl.

The Arrows, my first soccer team. I'm in the first row, far left, and Dad, my coach, is in the second row, far right.

Ichiban, one of the club volleyball teams I played on as a teenager, helped me grow into the number one high school recruit in the nation. I'm in the second row, second from the left.

I miss playing indoors. I loved it so!

It was an honor to receive the 1999 Honda-Broderick Cup as the nation's most outstanding female collegiate athlete.

Instead of going to the White House, our 1998 NCAA Championship team met President Clinton on the tarmac at the Los Angeles airport during one of his West Coast trips. I'm in the back row, fourth from the left.

I am forever indebted to Debbie Green, a 1984 Olympic silver medalist who is considered the best setter in U.S. history. As the assistant at Long Beach State, Debbie taught me how to set as well as how to be a leader and a world-class athlete.

Dad, Mom, and me at the 2000 Sydney Olympics Bon Voyage Party. Dozens of our family friends gathered to cheer me on, donating $16,500 so my parents could afford to travel to Australia to see me compete with Holly McPeak. What a send-off!

Me and Kerri Walsh, the first beach volleyball team in history, male or female, to win back-to-back Olympic gold medals.

After losing ground internationally, we had to re-create ourselves in 2007. With a new coach and a new attitude, we won our seventh of eight FIVB events, in Phuket, Thailand, to close out the season with a bang.

Opening Ceremony at the 2004 Athens Olympics with President George H. W. Bush and some of the U.S. beach volleyball contingent. From left to right, Nicole Branagh, Sean Rosenthal, Kerri Walsh, President Bush, me, and Jake Gibb.

Our first Christmas card as husband and wife! Our "babies," Gruden (left) and Boogie (right), patiently posing in our backyard in Long Beach.

With Matt on our wedding day, November 13, 2004. (Photo by Sandra Beckman)

I finished fifth in the Pro/Celebrity Race portion of the Toyota Grand Prix of Long Beach in April 2005.

Me and "mini me" on the Great Wall.

Dad and me on the Great Wall of China on a sightseeing trip during the 2008 Beijing Olympics.

Me and Maks Chmerkovskiy, my partner on *Dancing with the Stars,* before taking the floor to perform the mambo.

One of the perks that came with winning the 2004 Olympic gold medal was the invitation to throw out the first pitch before a Chicago Cubs game at Wrigley Field.

At home in Coral Springs, Florida, I cook in catcher's gear. It's safer for everybody!

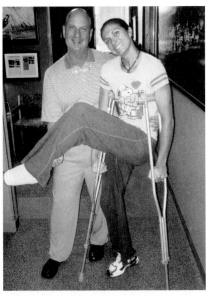

Dr. Bill Schobert and me in his doctor's office the day after he performed surgery on my ruptured left Achilles tendon.

A special moment with the Rydzynski family at Huntington Beach in 2006. Their son Nicholas, one of my Gold Medal Gifts, is wearing my 2004 Olympic gold medal. From left to right, Kirk; Paul, two; Christy; Nicholas, four; and me.

Born to be wild! That's Dad and me! We're fooling around on a souped-up cycle at an AVP event in Dallas.

I cherish the closeness I've developed with my half brothers Brack (left) and Scott (right). We're playing tourists on a family cruise in the British Virgin Islands.

Me and Brazil's Shelda Bede, my all-time favorite beach volleyball player.

In spring 2009, I put together a team in Mom's honor, Barbara's B's, for the Long Beach Relay for Life. For twenty-four consecutive hours, we took turns walking around a track, raising more than three thousand dollars for cancer research, education, and programs.

Matt and me hitching a ride in Thailand.

"I suck," she kept saying to me.

"No, you don't," I kept reassuring her.

From the beginning of 2001, it was evident that Kerri and I were wired differently. We're both competitive. We're both hard workers. We're never satisfied. We're always trying to find ways to get better. We'll both push ourselves to our limits. However, we deal with winning and losing, success and failure, in very different ways. I can shake off a loss in three seconds, hug the opposing team, and run off—my life is more than just volleyball. Kerri lets a loss drag her down for a lot longer, but that spurs her on to be the great player she is. I've found my own way to be the best. For me, that involves not letting things weigh on me, not letting myself be defined by volleyball. Kerri wants everything now, but I'm the type who'll say, "We'll be good, just give it time." In order to be a successful athlete, I think, ultimately, you've got to be able to say to yourself, "Not every day is going to be my day."

That first season was an important bonding time for Kerri and me. The closeness we developed as teammates, business partners, and friends was invaluable. We were away from home for almost nine weeks, and we were together every day, all day. It was such an adventure. We traveled well together, which is the real key in a long-term, pro beach volleyball partnership. Although we had different personalities, on and off the court—my dream job is being a *Saturday Night Live* cast member; hers is, most likely, being a Hollywood stylist or a personal shopper—we got along the whole time.

As Kerri says, "Beach volleyball can be like a soap opera. Ideally you want to find a partner that you can be in sync with physically and mentally." If we hadn't gotten there by the middle of our first season, we certainly were well on our way. I remember coming home at the end of August, after our long overseas tour, unpacking my suitcases, and Kerri calling me and saying, "I miss you, Misty." It had been only six hours since we'd said good-bye to each other at the Los Angeles airport, but she told me she didn't know what to do with herself because I wasn't there.

The 2001 season taught me even more about playing with injuries. My left knee had started to act up again. I'd torn my posterior cruciate ligament (PCL) in 1996, as a sophomore at Long Beach State, but rather than have surgery, I chose to rehabilitate it through weight training and physical therapy. I was cleared to get back onto the court, and played in the playoffs, but I probably shouldn't have. I wore a brace, and because I was so hampered, my Long Beach State team was forced to run a completely different offense to keep me behind the block. After we lost in the playoffs, I saw a new physical therapist, who questioned why I'd played. He told me I needed to be in rehab for at least six weeks. After following his orders, I was able to get back out on the court without a brace, and I had better stability. I played the rest of my college career without any problems.

Then, in 2001, my PCL injury reappeared. Kerri and I were practicing at Huntington Beach. We were doing a dropping drill. We'd take a couple of steps back from the net, Anna would hit the ball to us, and we'd dig it. I stepped in a hole, hyperextended my left knee, and completed the PCL tear. Now, my left PCL was completely gone. Even at that point, doctors still maintain you can play without a PCL, as long as you're diligent about physical therapy. But even though I was religious about my rehab, strengthening the muscles around my left knee, and I still was able to squat and jump, I repeatedly hyperextended it. I tried playing in a brace, but it was too restrictive. After the season, I decided to investigate whether surgery could fix it. I didn't want to live the rest of my life worrying about stepping off a curb, or perhaps just standing, and hyperextending the knee. I went to one of the best surgeons in Los Angeles, and he said he wouldn't do the surgery because it wouldn't be successful. He said that, in all likelihood, if he operated on my knee, I'd never be able to play world-class volleyball again. I was ready to quit, but Dad wouldn't let me.

"Your mother has struggled to stay here on earth, and now you're ready to give in?" he asked. "You never want to leave before the miracle. Be persistent."

I was referred to Dr. Bill Schobert, in Mission Viejo, California, by a number of volleyball players and coaches, including Karch. Among athletes, Dr. Schobert was known as the orthopedist you went to if you needed to have another surgeon's work revised. Dad calls him "Dr. Do-Over." Unbeknownst to me, Dr. Schobert had been working on a technique for PCL reconstruction for quite a while. In the early 1990s, he'd had a young female patient who needed PCL surgery, so he'd decided to apply the principles of anterior cruciate ligament (ACL) surgery in reverse. First, he'd practiced on a cadaver. Then, he'd performed the PCL reconstruction on her knee.

While the standard PCL reconstruction is done with arthroscopic surgery, Dr. Schobert says, even today, it's still an operation that is performed "fairly blindly." It's tricky because the surgeon drills from the front of the knee into the back, through the tibia, directly at the artery and the nerve. If the drill goes through either, Dr. Schobert says, the patient's foot won't work, or he or she could lose his or her leg.

Even today, isolated PCL reconstructions, meaning that no other ligament is injured, are not performed very often, Dr. Schobert says. You'll hear about people having ACL-PCL or MCL-PCL (medial collateral ligament) reconstructions. But you'll seldom hear about somebody having just a PCL reconstruction. Most orthopedic surgeons don't like to perform PCLs at all, Dr. Schobert says. Instead, they'll suggest strengthening the quadriceps muscle on the front of the thigh to help make up for some of the strength and stability lost by having a torn PCL.

After Mom and I visited Dr. Schobert, we reported back to Dad, and the three of us decided, as a family, to put our faith in him. I knew I couldn't keep playing with a torn PCL, and I believed I'd be a better player with a more stable knee. I trusted Dr. Schobert, and I was willing to take the risk. Even though at that point in time, he'd done only fifteen to twenty PCL reconstructions, I really liked his style. He was brutally honest and down to earth like Dad. He was also compassionate, warm, and engaging like Mom.

Ironically, Dr. Schobert now says my 2001 PCL reconstruction was "an exciting little surgery, because partway through it, one of the guides moved, and I initially drilled in an area you don't want to drill in." It was in a spot in the tibia, he says, and he didn't like it. So he had to shift the drill hole, and then get the rest of the procedure done. He repaired my knee with a cadaver's Achilles tendon because it's so big and strong. The two-hour surgery went very, very well.

These days, I never give my PCL reconstruction a second thought. Except when somebody calls me by my nickname. While I was working to regain my strength on the court, I wasn't quick to the ball. My left leg didn't have complete range of motion. I couldn't flex or extend it. So Kerri's boyfriend, Casey, nicknamed me Turtle, and the nickname has stuck with me ever since. (What are Kerri's nicknames? Well, she has several, including "Queen Bee," which is how her family referred to her growing up. And then there are Dad's nicknames for her: "Spiderwoman," "K.W.," and "Long-Legged Galoot.")

Today, Kerri and Casey will admit that calling me Turtle is a lot more sarcastic than true because I'm actually very quick in the sand. What you don't know, though, is that I have an amazing hidden talent: If I tilt my head at an extreme angle and rotate my eyeballs, I look just like a turtle. If ever there was a perfect candidate for David Letterman's "Stupid Human Tricks," it's me.

# 13

# Toughest Year

My mother taught me a lot about girl power.

Throughout early 2001, it was becoming very clear that Mom's cancer treatments weren't accomplishing what the doctors had hoped. She still met her volleyball cronies at the beach, whenever she felt well enough to get there. She talked a bit about her treatments while passing the ball back and forth, but she really just went to the beach to forget about life for a while. She wanted to get lost in the sport that she loved so much. She wanted to feel the sand between her toes, hear the waves tumble onto the beach, and sense the warm sun on her body. She wanted to go back in time, to the days when she was young, vibrant, and healthy. She wanted to be surrounded by her special group of female friends, whose warmth, love, strength, and athletic spirit fortified and empowered her.

Late in summer 2001, Mom placed an emotional call to Sandra Golden, one of her "old" volleyball friends, and asked Sandra if she'd play with her in the Huntsman World Senior Games, in St. George, Utah, that October. Sandra remembers being surprised that Mom wanted to participate in a tournament against some of the world's best senior athletes, since she'd been too weak to play volleyball much of the summer. Without hesitating, Sandra said, "Yes," because she was so honored Mom had asked her.

Indeed, it was a bold move on Mom's part, but then again, she never was one to let the parade pass her by. For fifteen years, she'd played with Alice Sanchez's Mavericks team at the U.S. Senior Nationals. She'd always left everything on the court, and yet she'd always been overlooked for national awards. Alice believes Mom's being passed over had a lot to do with politics. "They just pick people that look flashy and maybe put a ball straight down, where Barbara was just a steady-Eddie player," Alice says. "She was tough, tough, tough. Very, very aggressive, just a very tough personality."

To illustrate Mom's passion, Alice recounts a conversation she had with Mom when she turned sixty-five. Mom, who was forty-eight at the time, proclaimed, "Alice, when I get to be your age, I hope I'm still playing volleyball." Today, Alice is seventy-five-plus—and still playing.

I'll let Sandra tell the rest of the 2001 Huntsman World Senior Games story, as she recently shared in a beautifully written tribute letter for this book. She titled it, "A Barbara May Story," and I cried when I read it. I know I never could have come up with words as meaningful as hers:

> After I hung up, I realized Barbara's call was not about quitting on life or giving up volleyball, something she loved. Not yet! Barb was very emotional about playing competitively again and had decided to play in one more major tournament, the Huntsman World Games, in St. George, Utah. It would be our first appearance at the Games, but it would be the fifteenth anniversary of the Games. Teams from around the world would be present, representing all major sports. Barb had turned fifty in January, which qualified her as a Senior. I was fifty-one at the time, so I was more qualified. We would play on Alice Sanchez's team, the Mavericks, an appropriately named team. . . .
>
> As the tournament approached, Barbara's spirit seemed to lift; I think it gave her something to look forward to. On the other hand, she shared

*with me that she had some concerns because she had not played for a while, and she wanted to play her best. She was also struggling to lose weight due to her cancer treatments; this was a serious goal for her. She wanted to feel her hip bones again. As the tournament drew close, she was at the beach, trying to get in a little bit of play. I heard that her doctors weren't too pleased with her decision to play because the cancer treatments may have weakened her body in more ways than most of us knew. Any hard fall or hit or something unusual could be tragic; chemotherapy evidently weakens the density of the bones. None of this mattered to Barbara, though; she had to play in what she knew would most likely be her last tournament.*

*On Wednesday, October 17, I picked her up at her home in Costa Mesa, to drive to the tournament in St. George, Utah, about a six-hour drive. All the way there we talked about everything that was important to her and little about her health. We hadn't been together for a while because I had been in Europe traveling for four months during the summer. Throughout my trip, I emailed her almost every day so she could share my experiences without being there. We spent much of this trip centered on where I had been and my experiences in previous months. She had seen my pictures and spoke about seeing Europe with Misty someday, realizing that she might not have the chance. She had lots of dreams that we discussed, and we were about to realize one.*

*That evening we attended the Opening Ceremonies at the Tuacahn Amphitheatre, in a natural red rock mountain setting. It was an amazing event, similar to Olympic events, with an Olympic torch, dancers with flags of the world, powerful music, fireworks, and former professional and Olympic athletes making presentations. They had lived through experiences we desired to experience in a smaller way; we were champions for still trying. . . . The event theme was "Reach Higher"; Barbara was about to accomplish this over the next few days.*

*On Thursday, October 18, the tournament would begin, but that Wednesday night, after Opening Ceremonies, would be just as memorable for me. Although Barb and I went to bed early, we didn't get much sleep; she struggled all night with medication, pains, worry, and so much more that I'll never understand. At 4:00 A.M., she was up, and wanted to go out to the pool and sit in the spa so she could warm her body; she wasn't feeling well, and I was beginning to panic. The pool and spa were closed, but I was able to get management to allow us to be there if we were quiet. For about an hour, she sat there thinking about everything, then she became too hot and wanted to go in the pool. My life experiences hadn't prepared me for this situation. I could tell she was suffering with her illness, but I was afraid to say or recommend anything to her because I had no idea if this was normal, based on her condition. Over the next few nights, I realized it was normal for her to be uncomfortable most of the time. Sleep was hard, but so was just living. After a spa and a swim at 4:00 A.M., who can think about playing a volleyball match in four hours? I was exhausted, and I was the healthy one. . . .*

*Over the next two days, our Mavericks team played well enough to continue winning; eventually, we ended up among the final teams and would get a chance to play for the gold medal. Barbara was tired, but so were the rest of us; exhaustion was normal, but we all worried about how this was affecting her. Nobody would say anything to her because we truly didn't know what she was feeling, and we didn't want her to think we expected more of her, because we didn't expect this much. Her play was better than that of most of her peers.*

*Finally, we were going for the gold in the final match. Barb was out there playing hard like she always did. The rest of us were out there pushing ourselves not to lose. We all knew that this would probably be her last tournament and her last match. Everybody wanted to win it with her.*

*After winning the first set, we only had to win one more to win the match. Time between sets centers on coaching strategy, resting, getting water in our empty bottles, and using restrooms. People often disappeared for a few minutes. When the set was about to start, Barbara was nowhere near the court; after a quick search of the building, we still couldn't find her. Just as the referees called us to the court to start, a team member located Barb outside the gym crying. The magnitude of the tournament and this being the last match she might ever play had pushed her to her limits. She apologized to her teammates about not playing hard enough to contribute as she expected. She cried, wanting to play more and not to have the experience end. Her whole life was coming to an end, piece by piece, she later told me in our hotel room. She knew it was her last match, and she didn't want it to start or end.*

*After tremendous patience shown by the referees and the other team, she once again entered the gym and walked onto the court to a tremendous ovation from everyone in the arena who knew her situation. We went on to win the match, and Barbara won our hearts. All of us who played that day will remember her tears, her spirit, and her drive to keep pushing on, in spite of her situation. She became everyone's hero that week and epitomized the motto of the Games to "Reach Higher."*

*The drive home was not as emotional as the drive to the tournament. I think Barb came to realize that she had accomplished what she came to do; winning this event closed another chapter in her life. We didn't talk volleyball on the way home; we talked about her love for her family and her dogs. The more she spoke about them, the greater her enthusiasm rose; it was a beautiful trip.*

After she won her gold medal, Mom's health gradually deteriorated. On January 31, 2002, her friends had a birthday party for her, and she was doing fairly well. Toni Bowermaster remembers Mom and her girlfriends watching the sunset together that evening. However, February wasn't so great. Mom wasn't responding well to her cancer treatment, and now the doctors were worried about a brain tumor, the newest progression of the disease. At the end of February or the beginning of March, she stopped playing volleyball altogether because she started having trouble with her legs. They just gave out on her.

Mom insisted Dad and I maintain a sense of normalcy. So Dad kept working at MGM, and I kept training for the 2002 season. As we'd done the season before, Kerri and I decided to forgo the AVP tour. Our first scheduled FIVB event wasn't until June, in Madrid,

Spain, which allowed me to spend time with Mom. In addition to getting ready for our FIVB season, I was the assistant women's volleyball coach at Irvine (California) Valley College.

Truthfully, I didn't want to play volleyball. I just didn't have it in my heart. After seeing Mom struggling to sleep, tossing and turning in pain, her face burned from radiation treatments, I felt I couldn't leave her alone. She was getting worn out and delirious from the treatments. She'd forget to turn off the burners on the stove, and she'd leave the heater on in the bathroom. I wanted to do everything possible to make her comfortable. I also wanted to support Dad, who was working plus trying to take care of her. I couldn't let him worry so much.

Knowing how important it was to Mom that it be "business as usual" around our house, three of her best girlfriends—Toni, Mary Zant, and Sandy Weaver—and a few of my parents' longtime friends volunteered to help out, so that Dad and I could maintain our daily lives and not be overcome by her cancer. That gave Mom a great sense of relief. Although I protested, saying I'd prefer taking off time from volleyball to pitch in, Dad and Mom both said, no, "Life goes on."

A family friend, Ed (E.T.) Thompson, also lent a hand, planting gardens for Mom, as well as sprucing up the yard. That meant a lot to all of us, because Mom had always loved being surrounded by nature. My parents had met E.T. decades earlier at Muscle Beach, when he'd borrowed a volleyball from Dad, then sold it for a quart of beer. In the mid-1990s, while house-sitting for my parents when they were playing in the U.S. Senior Nationals, E.T. sold Dad's truck for crack cocaine. My parents returned from the tournament, realized the truck was gone, threw E.T. out of the house, and called the police.

Finally, in 1999 or 2000, E.T. sobered up. When Mom was diagnosed with cancer, she decided to reconcile with him. In fact, Mom compiled a list of people who'd affected her negatively or had done her and Dad wrong over the years.

"We've got to forgive them," she told Dad.

So almost a decade after banishing E.T. from our house, Dad and Mom welcomed him back, with open arms.

Despite all of this loving support, it still was an extremely tumultuous time for us. In early February, Dad was hospitalized for a week with an infection. He'd been badly bitten, trying to break up a fight between a couple of their dogs. Before he checked into the hospital, though, he made 1:00 A.M. calls to Mom's girlfriends, scheduling round-the-clock shifts of caretakers to look after her. I don't know how Dad did it. His days seemed a lot longer than twenty-four hours. He loved Mom very much, and he didn't want to see her suffer.

When Dad was discharged, he took over the reins again. He drove Mom to the hospital for more chemotherapy treatments. One day, he says, she walked into the lobby, stopped, turned to him, and said, "No more." Dad obliged, taking her home and trying to make her as comfortable as possible.

But less than a week later, Mom felt so crummy she had to be admitted to the hospital. One evening, she called Dad and said, "I'm still on the toilet. They forgot about me." She'd gone into her bathroom, sat down on the toilet, and was too weak to get up. She'd also summoned the nurses to bring her more pain medicine. Dad assured her the nurses would be in soon to help her. Forty-five minutes later, though, she called Dad again. "I'm still on the toilet," she said. Dad was irate. He phoned and raised a stink with the nursing staff. He says he was told they were overworked and understaffed. He shared the incident with a friend, a nurse at the same hospital, and she asked what floor Mom was on. When Dad told her, she said, "Butch, they've put Barbara on the floor where people go to die." Dad's response? "Those SOBs!"

The next day, Dad retrieved Mom from the hospital and brought her home for good. He and I were very grateful for the peaceful sanctuary her friends had created in her bedroom. The walls were painted a soft coral. Her bed was positioned in a corner, where she could look out a window and see the entire backyard. E.T.'s garden always seemed to be buzzing with activity, thanks to flowers that attracted butterflies and feeders that lured birds. Along the same wall as her window, Mom had placed a beautiful piece of driftwood that had washed up on Muscle Beach. Her girlfriends put little icons and other doodads Mom found inspiring on it, including prayer beads, seashells, and dream catchers.

I learned an extremely important life lesson from Mom: Even with death staring her right in the face, she lived in the moment, and she stayed in the moment, believing that she was going to get better. She kept doing her exercises, even when she couldn't walk, thinking that any day she would beat the disease.

Sometimes, she'd look her best friend Toni in the eye and ask, "Am I going to die?"

"You know what, Barb, not today," Toni would tell her. "You're alive, and you're here, and not today."

Every once in a while, she'd go to the dark side. But not very often. She had her menagerie of rescued dogs and cats around her, and she did a lot of busy work to keep them healthy and fed, cooking for them a couple of times each day. Toni recalls that Mom spent a lot of time when she was at her sickest talking about how "very, very, very, very, very sad" she was for all the years she'd been drinking. Toni says Mom had a lot of regret about her "embarrassing behavior" in my younger years. She was mortified about all of those times I saw her drunk, remarking, "Gosh, I wish I wouldn't have done that." Toni describes their intimate discussions of Mom's alcoholism as being "truly bittersweet." On one hand, Mom was happy she'd gotten sober; on the other hand, she felt guilty about having lost quality time with me.

Mom never discussed any of her regret or guilt with me. If she had, I would've told her she was the most wonderful mother in the world to me. I remember the good times; I don't dwell on the bad. Growing up had its ups and downs. Though some times were worse than others, especially when my parents were drinking, I learned to look past their alcoholism, because both Mom and Dad were loving, giving people. If I could change anything about my life, it would be that Mom never would've gotten sick and died, and that I would've shown her more appreciation.

Today, the Mom I remember is the woman who was my compass,

the woman who taught me all those valuable life lessons. Off the court . . . Be true to yourself. Don't listen to what other people are saying because you're the one who has to live with yourself. You have to do what's right for you. On the court . . . Give your all. Give your best, so you don't have any regrets. Leave it all on the court. Today, I live my life as Mom taught me. I set my goals and stay focused on them.

I bet it was difficult for Mom to be part of the Three Musketeers, sandwiched between Dad and me. Now, I realize she often was pushed to the outside of our spotlights. Eileen Clancy McClintock, Dad's longtime mixed doubles partner, says that, for years and years, Mom had labeled herself in one of two ways—"Butch's wife" or "Misty's mom." When Mom was diagnosed with cancer, and she was showered with an enormous outpouring of love and friendship, it moved her so much that she admitted to Eileen, "Now I realize that people like me for being Barbara, not because I'm 'Butch's wife' or 'Misty's mom.'" The cancer forced Mom to look at herself differently. If there was anything good that came out of her having that horrible disease, it was the knowledge that she was well loved, and especially that she was well loved for being herself.

Sadly, by late April, Mom had reached a point of no return. Everybody told me she was getting close to seeing her final resting place. I kept wishing they were wrong. I hadn't cried in front of her—I'd always kept a stiff upper lip—but one night, I just couldn't control myself. She broke down when I was helping her go to the bathroom. Mom cried so hard she started hyperventilating. Nothing they teach you in college can prepare you for something like that. I didn't want to let Mom go, but I also didn't want to see her suffer. The look in her eyes at that moment absolutely broke my heart. She was scared, she wanted help, but I was powerless.

And still, she soldiered on.

My mother taught me so much about never giving up, about never wanting to lose.

In Mom's final weeks, many people came to see her, to pay their respects. It was a major outpouring of love, which is exactly what

Mom had attracted throughout her lifetime. Love. To help ease the pain, stop the nausea, and lessen the anxiety, Mom smoked marijuana. Smoking marijuana would calm her down, because at the end, she was extremely nervous, jittery, and agitated. E.T., who had the toughest job of all, night duty, says she was afraid to go to sleep at night because she was petrified she might not wake up. She wasn't ready to let go yet. Then, when the sun came up, she'd give herself permission to go to sleep. I tried very hard to comfort her. I'd crawl into bed and hold her. When she was on the morphine drip, if I heard her moan, I'd press the button to shoot the morphine into her system.

However, I never could make her feel completely comfortable. I'd add a pillow here or there. I'd sit her up or lay her down, then I'd help her up and situate her in a chair in the bedroom. Still, she'd be in excruciating pain. She'd say, "Turn me this way, Misty." Then, a few minutes later, she'd say, "No, Misty, turn me that way." It was up, down, up, down. It was especially difficult to satisfy Mom in the days before her death. It was frustrating to me because, deep down, I knew there really was no solution.

At one point, near the end, I lost all my patience.

"Mom, you've got to make up your mind," I snapped.

I wasn't mad at her; I was pissed off at the disease. I wanted to take away the sickness and the pain. It didn't occur to me then that the pain was making her irrational. Mom burst into tears. I turned to Dad and E.T., and I said, "I can't take it! I don't know what to do! I'm leaving!" With that, I stormed out my parents' front door and drove off to a volleyball camp in San Luis Obispo. As a world-class athlete, I'd been taught not to have emotional meltdowns in the heat of battle, but this situation had become much too trying for me. I'd let my feelings of helplessness get the best of me. More than that, I'd realized this was not how I wanted to see, or remember, my mother.

Late Friday evening, after I'd reached San Luis Obispo, Dad and I spoke on the phone. I still was upset about Mom and my behavior toward her. He had to work extra hard on the phone that night to get me calmed down. Then Dad broke the news that Mom was turning, that the hospice nurse had taken her off all drugs except morphine, and that she'd soon die.

Now, I felt even more helpless. Soon, Mom likely would be in a comatose state. How was I ever going to apologize for my outburst and tell her how much she meant to me? I've never been the best communicator, so Dad suggested I write my feelings in a letter. He understood that, at that point, I was incapable of telling Mom how I felt without breaking down. The letter, he said, would allow me to get everything out.

Fortunately, when I got home from San Luis Obispo, I was able to read it to her. I got into bed with Mom, and I wrapped my arms around her. Although she was in and out of a coma, I'm sure she heard my words, and I'd like to believe that she felt me lying beside her. I've been told that people can hear what you're saying, all the way until they take their last breath.

On the day Mom died, Thursday, May 9, 2002, I'd been scheduled to play in a fun little indoor tournament, a Long Beach State fund-raiser. I'd told Dad, "I want to go see Mom." But he'd said, "No, Mom and I want you to play." After the event, I'd just walked in the front door of my Long Beach house when Dad called and said, "You'd better come. Mom's not going to last very long."

I jumped into my car, still wearing my knee pads, and I sped off. I got pulled over by a cop, just down the street from my house. I was crying, pleading, "Please, my mom is dying, please let me go, I need to get to her." The cop didn't believe me; I guess he'd heard that excuse before. I kept saying, "No, really, my mom's dying." I tried calling several people to corroborate my story, but none of them answered their cell phones. I called our family friend Jim Steele, then I handed the phone to the cop, and Jim explained the situation. Finally, the cop let me go, saying, "Be careful."

Because of that traffic stop, I missed Mom's dying by five minutes.

I blamed myself for that.

I blamed myself for a lot of things.

Dad tried comforting me by saying Mom had died peacefully, surrounded by him, E.T., and her girlfriends, Toni, Mary, and Sandy. He told me Mom's journey was complete, that in the end, she'd finally resolved in her head that I was going to be okay, so she felt she could let go. When she passed away, he said, she looked pretty, all dressed in pink and wearing little earrings. Dad and Mom's girlfriends had stood in a circle beside her bed, holding hands and saying prayers as she was transcending.

"We all touched her and assured her she would be okay," Dad said. "We told her it was okay to let go."

Mom's dog Chewy had sensed she'd passed away and jumped up on the bed and lay across her stomach. At one time, Mom had eight mutts and five cats, all of them rescued. She felt love from the animals. But Chewy was Mom's least favorite because he always was trying to attack her cats and even might have killed a couple of them. Soon after, Mom's other four dogs followed Chewy's lead, hopping up on her bed and laying their heads on her body.

More than six hundred people attended a memorial service for Mom at the Pyramid at Long Beach State. Alice printed up the invitations, calling it "Our Farewell Party to Barbara." We asked that people dress casually, wear leis, and bring desserts and photos to share. In lieu of flowers, we suggested that they make donations to cancer charities or to the homeless. That evening I got to see the three different segments of Mom's life—her tennis people, her paddle tennis people, and her volleyball people. I finally got to see all of the faces, and meet all of the characters in my parents' stories, all in one place, all at the same time.

When E.T. stepped to the podium to speak, he shocked a lot of folks in the crowd, who knew my parents once had banished him from our family. Strong, sober, and Mom's loving caregiver until the bitter end, his presence was a powerful testament to love, forgiveness, faith, hope, and moving forward in life. All were qualities Mom embodied. His words were powerful, too.

"We take one deep breath of life, we take one deep breath of love," he recalls saying. "Barbara has passed the torch to Misty. She had pretty big footprints out there, and those footprints will not only be filled, but enlarged, in Barbara's passing the torch to Misty."

As difficult as it was for me to get up in front of everybody, finally being able to read my letter to her out loud, finally being able to let our extended family know exactly what I was feeling, was very important to me. It did wonders for my soul and for Mom's, too. I was so proud of my words, in fact, that I shared copies with many in attendance.

*Saturday, May 4, 2002*

*Dear Mom,*

*I am in San Luis Obispo right now and the time is just after midnight. I really can't sleep, but that is nothing new. Ever since you have been in and out of the hospital I find it difficult for me to stop thinking of you so much. I have a very tough time being away from you. Even in Long Beach I feel light years away.*

*I know that you have been struggling and very restless these past couple of days. Well, to tell you the truth, I don't know how you have stayed so strong throughout this whole ordeal. Mom you are an AMAZING woman, and I only wish that I had half the character that you possess.*

*Well, first off, I want to apologize for getting frustrated on Thursday. I know that you may have not known it, but you are a hard one to please, even when you are sick. I am so sorry, Mom. I just feel like my whole world is slowly falling down around me. After Grandma passed, I never saw these days coming. When she passed away, it was very tough on me. I have never really been the type to easily share my emotions, but I will tell you that even today, I still cry because she is not near. . . .*

*I know that when I was growing up, life wasn't the easiest. We, as a family, had our problems, as well as our ups and downs. I can remember the day that you stopped drinking for the final time. I was so proud of you and still am. That was a big obstacle for you to overcome; at* times, there were bumps in the road, but still you beat that disease. I thank you, not only for me, and Dad, but for yourself as well.

I cry every night because I don't want to see you hurt and in pain. I cry every night because I wish I never grew up, and I could just stay your little girl. I cry every night because I don't want my season to start so that I have to leave. I cry every night, Mom, because I miss you so much.

I often wonder why this had to happen. I blame most of it on the stupid doctors, but the other blame, I just don't know where that lies. I believe that some things happen for a reason, but I am not so sure about this. Why????? It did bring our family closer, and I have had to grow up a lot, knowing that you are not really able to help me with all my stuff. All of your true friends have also pulled together in order to comfort you and take care of you.

My communication with you has never really been the best, but don't feel bad. I really can't communicate with anyone. I keep a lot inside, which really eats me up. I still, to this day, have never really apologized for the way I treated you growing up. You always made sure I was well taken care of and always provided me with everything. At times, I was a brat, and I remember saying things like, "I hate you, and I wish you weren't here." That really kills me because what a little bitch I was. I am so sorry a thousand times. I wish I could make it up to you, but nothing that I would do could ever equal what you did for me. . . .

I often feel like not being here anymore. I just can't see me without you and Dad in my life. It just seems like you two are my whole world, oh, except for Gruden and Boogie. We have always been a close family, and I just can't picture us not together.

I am going to stop rambling on, but the main thing I wanted to let you know is how much I LOVE YOU!!! I know that we don't say it all the time, but I do. I always want you to know how proud I am of you, and I thank you for all the wonderful years and times. I hope that I can make you as proud of me as I am so very proud of you.

I LOVE YOU MOM!

*Misty Elizabeth May*

# 14

# CARRYING ON

After Mom passed away, I experienced a downward spiral. I'm not going to lie, and I'm not going to sugarcoat it. My downward spiral was a result of my grief, and I now realize, grieving in the wrong ways. I just wasn't myself. I didn't get into anything bad, though.

I found different ways to cope with my sadness. For instance, I got a second tattoo.

I'd gotten my first after my Long Beach State number five jersey was retired. I'd had my grandmother's initials tattooed on my lower back—BRG—on either side of a capital V, the Roman numeral for five. It was my favorite number, and I'd worn it since my sophomore year in high school. On an unofficial recruiting trip to UCLA, I attended a men's basketball game against California. I admired the tough, relentless play of Cal's star point guard Jason Kidd. He also wore number five. "Yes, he's a good player, and he's number five, all right!" I thought. That totally solidified it; I'd chosen the perfect number.

After Mom died, on the back of my left shoulder, I tattooed her initials—BGM—a pair of angel's wings, and a halo. That way, whenever I looked over my shoulder, Mom always would be there. My second tattoo helped me cope, too, with the pain of her loss.

To be honest, the first few months after Mom's death, I was severely depressed. I wanted to quit playing volleyball. I couldn't have cared less about it. I contemplated getting off the professional beach volleyball merry-go-round and becoming a college coach. I figured I could give up playing and be fine.

"I don't want to play volleyball," I told myself. "I don't even want to see a volleyball."

I was angry at the sport because Mom had been such a large part of my love for it.

"Why do I want to play, if she can't see my success, be involved, or be a part of this?" I asked myself.

I felt as if my purpose in volleyball, and in life, were gone.

Dad kept trying to convince me that Mom would've wanted me to carry on. On May 29, twenty days after she passed away, I took a big step forward, going through Long Beach State's graduation exercises and finally receiving my bachelor's degree in kinesiology. It took me three years more than my incoming freshman class to complete my course requirements. I'd had to take educational leaves because of the Olympics. The biggest hurdle was completing five hundred internship hours. Between 1998 and 2002, I'd worked at Frogs Fitness in Long Beach and Verizon Wireless's on-site health club facility in Irvine, and I'd also coached Amazon, a local volleyball club, to fulfill those internship hours.

More than six thousand students were honored, including legendary Hollywood movie director Steven Spielberg, who'd re-enrolled at Long Beach State in spring 1998, more than thirty years after he'd dropped out, and picked up his bachelor's degree in film and electronic arts during the College of Arts commencement. It was a day filled with mixed feelings. It was the first major moment of my life since Mom had passed away, and I kept thinking, "I wish Mom were here. She would've loved to have been a part of this." Dad tried to infuse as much happiness into the day as he possibly could. He surprised me with several gorgeous leis, flown in from Hawaii.

Since Mom passed away, Dad had worked overtime trying to make me feel better. He'd been pushing me to get back out on the sand with Kerri and chase the Olympic gold medal Mom had thought was in our reach. He kept telling me that Mom would have wanted me to keep playing, that she never would have wanted her death to keep me from realizing my dreams. Well, that's the strongest argument Dad could have made, that it was Mom's wish. Even today, when Dad wants me to do something, he'll say, "Your mother would have wanted you to . . ." It makes the hair stand up on the back of my neck, and I follow through with whatever it is. Sometimes, the little sneak uses that sentence to manipulate me into doing something he wants me to do, not Mom. But don't worry, I'm on to him.

In this case, though, Dad was right. Mom would've been upset if I'd given up playing beach volleyball. She knew how much I loved it, and I knew how much she'd loved it. When it had come time for me to turn professional, she'd wanted me to play beach over indoor. Eventually, I convinced myself I had to carry on, because, really and truly, I didn't hate volleyball. I just knew that playing volleyball was going to bring up many memories for me, that it always was going to be painfully obvious Mom wasn't there. Sadly, that would never change.

I've always been one of those people who can just move forward. I've always been somebody who closes the door quickly and never looks back. I've never been psychologically traumatized by anything. As a child, I'd learned to cope with my parents' alcoholism. As a college junior, I'd learned to cope with being sexually assaulted.

Physical traumas never have negatively affected me either. Not injuries. Not surgeries. Not even a motor vehicle accident that has left me with a very noticeable tremor in my right hand. When I was three, a car ran a red light at an intersection in Santa Monica, smashing into the driver's side of our van. The impact propelled me toward the windshield, slamming my face into the rearview mirror. Because there were no visible injuries, other than a mark on my lip and lower face, my parents took me home and watched me to make sure I didn't have a concussion. A month later, my teeth turned black.

As I grew, Dad and Mom noticed that my posture changed, with my neck dropping forward and my shoulders beginning to round. Between the ages of five and eight, Dad made me swim, to open up my shoulders. When I turned eight, he made me do exercises on the jungle gym at Muscle Beach, to strengthen my shoulders. When I was ten, Dad noticed my tremor when I was playing volleyball, seeing my right hand shake as I'd reach for the ball, or even as I was holding a sandwich at lunchtime. He just figured I was nervous, playing with older girls. But in high school and college my tremor became quite evident, especially serving the ball. It's a noticeable shake, but once the movement starts, I don't feel it. Away from volleyball, it's more obvious, when I'm doing ordinary things like eating with a fork or sipping from a coffee cup. Drawing a straight line or threading a needle is very difficult for me.

Today, Dad says he still worries about my tremor, mostly because he doesn't want it to get any worse when I get older. However, in the same breath, he'll call me "one of the better cockroaches around," because of my survival skills. I've had my tremor checked by doctors to make absolutely sure it's not the beginning of Parkinson's disease, and I've been assured that it isn't.

Simply put, I'm a survivor. I'm strong inside and out. If I'm subjected to psychological or physical trauma, I'm tough enough to rise above it and move forward in my life. But Mom's death was an entirely different story. I was having a very, very difficult time coping. I'd finally met my match.


As it turned out, volleyball was good therapy for me. It gave me a place to work through my feelings and sweat out my tears. It helped me believe that if there were a heaven, if there were a greater power than ourselves, then Mom was up there, looking down on me, watching me play and loving every minute of it. Training, traveling, and being with Kerri was a real plus, too. She was incredible, a great friend, a strong shoulder to lean on, just a sweetheart of a girl. I never told her when I cried myself to sleep most nights, but somehow, she always sensed when I was sad, and she found ways to pick me up and keep my mind occupied. She distracted me by taking me on tours of cities we were playing in, by discovering restaurants and cafés for us to experience. She also handled the organizational details of our partnership, because my grieving left me scatterbrained. I'm forever grateful to Kerri for keeping me going.

Because I'd spent all of the off-season and most of the preseason rehabilitating from my PCL reconstruction, and because I'd devoted a lot of my free time to being with Mom, I wasn't in the greatest shape heading into the 2002 FIVB season. I'd gained weight due to poor eating habits, more weightlifting and less cardio conditioning, and I knew I'd really have to work hard to get it off.

In early June, Kerri and I set off on a summer-long trip that would take us around the world. We scheduled what turned out to be the most extensive competition schedule of our partnership—eleven tournaments. I knew it would be a physical grind and an emotional roller coaster. So I decided it would be helpful to continue writing letters to Mom. That way, I could take her along with me for the ride. Most important, I could talk to her. I brought along a special journal, with a gray silk cover embroidered with purple and pink flowers. It reminded me of Mom, who was such a nature lover.

We won our first tournament, in Madrid, Spain, June 9, a month to the day after Mom's death. The victory prompted me to talk to her. I couldn't wait to share my life.

*6-11-02*

*Dear Mom,*

*Kerri and I are traveling from Madrid to Barcelona with Lina and Petia Yanchulova, your favorite beach volleyball sister act from Bul-*

*garia. What an experience. I really think that it would be cool with someone I love. At first, we didn't think we would meet our train. Good thing that it was ten minutes late. Well, our friend (not really, but our driver), brought us to the train station and showed us where to get on. The sisters were in a different car than us. They had beds, which now would have been good to have.*

*Kerri and I are seated in first class. You'd think first class would be luxurious and spacious. Forget about it!! There were six seats in our cabin. Good thing it was NO SMOKING! These seats were like those on Southwest Airlines, the ones that are facing each other. . . . We have three Americans and one Spaniard in our cabin. The three Americans have just graduated high school in Pennsylvania. What a great senior trip! The bathrooms are so gross, I would rather pee on myself. We leave our shoes outside because who knows what we are walking in.*

*Kerri and I had been drinking in the bar at the hotel since about 6:00 P.M. We had five Cervezas. Lina had some wine, Petia had a Coke.*

*I am listening to Incubus right now. Kerri is asleep. The three American high school kids are stretched out. I on the other hand prefer the quiet and listening to my music, while writing all my twisted thoughts on paper. I understand that we may have nine hours to sleep, but I would rather write in my book and listen to music. . . .*

*6-17-02*

*Mom,*

*Boy, this traveling has been quite an experience. We have been on two overnight trains. So here we are on our third train ride, five and a half hours from Cannes to Geneva. It is much better to fly, don't let anyone tell you different. Kerri and I were talking just the other day about getting a coach for next year. We couldn't really think of anyone who had that much time. Kerri mentioned Dad, but I know he has to work. Well, when I talked to Dad the other day, he mentioned he would like to retire and join our traveling circus. I got butterflies and goose bumps because I really want that, but didn't think it was possible. I am so excited! I think, too, that Dad is a bit lonely. Well, I am, too. . . .*

The next FIVB tour stop was Gstaad, Switzerland, and we won again, beating Brazil's Shelda Bede and Adriana Behar in the final. Then it was off to Stavanger, Norway. We struggled a bit there, finishing fourth.

7-06-02

*Mom,*

*I miss you so much. I miss calling you for meaningless reasons, I miss seeing you and knowing that when I get home, you will be there to give me a "Hello, Poops" and a hug. It just feels totally weird. I put a family picture by my bed, and I have the picture of us also. I don't leave home without them. I think that you would find my tattoo really neat. I love it just like I love you. I am in a slump, and I know you would know what to tell me or do. So what do I do?? When I dream tonight, please stop by and talk.*

*I REALLY MISS U!!*

Mom's death was a huge turning point in life for me: I finally had to learn to rely on myself. I had to start dealing with a lot of stuff in my life, and quite frankly, so did Dad. We both had rude awakenings. Before that, practically everything had been done for me, for Dad, too, courtesy of Mom. She was a very strong personality, and Dad and I really had to step up.

Throughout the 2002 season, I felt Mom's presence, especially when I was wrestling with life, struggling to handle my grief. I'd hear her whispering in my ear, giving me love, support, and guidance. On the court, I felt her right there with me, too. If the wind was blowing in the wrong direction, and one of my serves trickled to the other side of the net, I'd say to myself, "That's Mom, pushing it over, helping me out."

Our fourth FIVB tour stop was Montreal, Canada, and it was good to be back on North American soil. Dad flew up to see us, and we had an awesome tournament, defeating Holly McPeak and Elaine Youngs in the semifinals, and then Shelda and Adriana in the final.

*7-13-02*

*Mom,*

*We won today! It was a very stressful match. Our match with Holly went three games, and the finals went two. Dad was pretty excited. I didn't have my best match, but it is okay. It is so hard to play because I think about you all the time. I just want to be home. Toni Bowermaster wrote me a nice message, and I wrote her back. I miss you so much, and I can't wait until we are reunited once again. I am so tired, so I will write you later. I love you, Mom. . . .*

Well, no sooner had we gotten to Canada, it seemed, than the day after our victory, we were turning right around and flying back across the Atlantic Ocean for an FIVB tournament in Marseille, France. I had a fleeting thought as I was stepping onto the plane: If only I had a pair of angel's wings like Mom. . . .

*7-15-02*

*Mom,*

*Got into Marseille this afternoon from Montreal. It was so nice having Dad at the tournament with me. We had a talk about you and how much we love you and miss your beautiful face. You know what I always wanted to do but forgot? I wanted to get a cool family portrait done, but we never got around to it. Even one with just you and me would have been awesome.*

*My sinuses were so bad on the plane today. Usually, I would call you and tell you about it, but you were there with me. I thank you so much for teaching me about how important knowing yourself is. You taught me to listen and feel the natural world, but also to cherish time alone. I like being by myself, except when the people I really care about and love are around. I don't need anybody to make me happy.*

*I slept most of the day. We went to our meeting, and we play at 9:50 A.M. You will be there, right? I would pull out the extra bed but we can both fit on my single here. I want to be close to you and feel your arms and love surround me. Mom, I want to play well tomorrow and break out of this offensive slump. Please cheer me on and watch over me. . . .*

*7-19-02*

*Mom,*

*. . . I went to Saint-Tropez yesterday. Boy, the yachts were amazing. It reminded me of somewhere we would have visited on our cruises with Grandma and Grandpa. I watched* Life Is Beautiful *last night. What a great movie. Oh, Dad had told me to watch this movie,* Dragonfly, *and I saw it on one of our flights. It is a story about a grieving doctor being contacted by his late wife through his parents' near-death experience. His wife had a passion for dragonflies, and they're the recurring theme. Anyways, in Saint-Tropez, I bought a dragonfly necklace. You are our dragonfly!*

Kerri and I finished second in Marseille, losing in the final to Holly and E.Y. From there, it was on to Rhodes, Greece, where we were seeded first. Truth be told, I was looking past this tournament because the following week was my birthday, and Dad had promised to meet me at the next FIVB stop in Klagenfurt, Austria. I couldn't wait to see him. I missed him very much. I knew it was going to be an emotional time, my first birthday without Mom, and I didn't want to be alone that day. Dad didn't want me to be alone, either. And, quite frankly, we were so used to celebrating birthdays as a family, as the Three Musketeers, I don't think he wanted to be by himself.

*7-25-02*

*Mom,*

*Sorry I haven't written in a while, but I probably should have. I have just been pretty flat, but there are only four weeks left in the long part of the season. It just isn't the same without you being at home. I wondered today if you were able to hear the letter I wrote to you in San Luis Obispo, the one I read at your memorial service. I hope so! If not, then, I am very upset at myself. I should have told you how sorry I was to ever be a problem and get mad at you. Mom, you were such a giver and only asked for respect and love in return. I think that I took a lot. I did love you, but now I realize I should have given more. Mom, you instilled in me to give. There is so much that I want to do when I get home.*

*I am going to start by going to your favorite thrift store to volunteer a couple hours each week. Mom, I want to make you proud not only on the court, but off as well. I am just at the point where winning is not the same as losing, but the emotions that follow the win are not there. What do I do? Well, this tournament. You have to schedule your time with the thrift shop during my matches, so I can concentrate and play. Or you can sit up in the stands and tease me with a crepe in your hand. Mom, watch over me tomorrow and yell at me to kick butt!*

We laid a big, fat egg in Rhodes, knocked out in four matches. A wave of emotion came over me afterward, and Kerri now says it opened her eyes to my grief. Suddenly, and inexplicably, she recalls, I burst into tears. She says she was confused at first, thinking, "Why is Misty crying over a ninth-place finish?" So she tried comforting me, saying, "Misty, I know we lost, but we'll come back."

When I didn't stop crying, that's when Kerri said something inside her clicked. She's a very smart girl. She began to realize I hadn't been expressing all of my emotions to her that summer, that I'd kept her in the dark about how I was feeling. She started to understand I'd stuffed my grief in the back of my mind. And then, suddenly, all my sadness just came pouring out, like a stream of lava surging from an erupting volcano.

Kerri tried to get me to talk about what was going on inside, but sharing feelings isn't something that has ever come easily to me. I'm sure my being so closed off with Kerri was frustrating to her. And foreign. Kerri was the complete opposite—her emotions were right under the skin. One of the things I didn't have the heart to tell Kerri that night was that I wasn't devastated about finishing ninth. Mom's death had radically changed my perspective on winning and losing.

If I didn't win, it was no big deal. I'd tell myself, "At least I've got my health." If I won, it was no big deal either. I realized that win or lose, I could enjoy life in ways I hadn't before her death.

Mom's passing taught me to appreciate little things like feeling the sun on my face and seeing the stars in the sky, like the ceiling I'd made in my childhood bedroom. It also taught me to appreciate big things like having family and friends who loved me. Most important, Mom's death had brought Dad and me closer together. It had also brought me closer to my half brothers Brack and Scott. The Sydney Olympics had brought them back into my life, thanks in large part to Mom's realizing how sick she was and understanding the importance of including them in that trip. And from that point forward, I'd made an effort to reconnect and stay close to my entire family.

And that's why, several hours after my post-match meltdown, I fell apart again. I had received the news that Dad wasn't going to make the trip to Klagenfurt, Austria. He was en route to the Los Angeles airport when his pal Jim Steele asked which airline he was flying. Dad pulled out his ticket and realized he'd missed his flight. It had departed the day before. He tried to change his ticket at the airport, but it would've cost him thousands of dollars, so he opted not to come to Austria for my birthday. I can't tell you how heartbroken I was. I tried calling Dad at his house, but he already was at the beach, playing volleyball. When I finally reached Dad, he said, "Oh, sorry . . ." And I hung up on him.

*7-30-02*

*Mom,*

*I am very upset. I was so looking forward to seeing Dad here in Klagenfurt. I kept my eyes peeled for him at the airport, and I told everyone he was coming for my birthday. I remember this time last year, you called and made Jodie buy me little knickknacks. Mom, I love you, and you never forgot about me. Dad missed his flight, and so he isn't coming at all. I am very depressed and upset about the whole thing. What is there to say though?*

*I am listening to Andrea Bocelli's "The Prayer" while writing this. I will write more later. I love you!!!*

From that point on, I was hooked on "The Prayer," an Andrea Bocelli and Céline Dion duet. I listened to it over and over. I memorized the lyrics, both in English and in Italian. I always could feel the words pulsating up through my veins from somewhere deep inside. I always could feel Mom's presence surrounding me.

*I pray you'll be our eyes, and watch us where we go
And help us to be wise, in times when we don't know . . .*

The lyrics, by David Foster and Carole Bayer Sager, really spoke to me. Now, I'm not sure I could've gotten through the 2002 FIVB season if I hadn't had "The Prayer" to guide me. It was a great way for me to talk to Mom without having to open my journal. It summoned her up in an effortless way, like waving a magic wand.

*8-01-02*

*Momma,*

*. . . In my last entry, I was really upset with Dad for not making it to Austria. So many people called me early that morning, E.T., Scott, Linda, and Amy. Scott was really upset and wanted to yell at Dad. He said he could understand Dad doing something like that to Brack and him, but not to me. We feel that Dad is just very incompetent without you around because you always did everything. Plus, this is so new to him that he just needs to organize. When I get back in two weeks, I'm going to sit down and organize everything with him. That will make it easier I believe. . . .*

*For my birthday, I got new necklaces, some games, gift certificates. I am really excited because Kerri's mom got me a shorter/thicker gold chain so I can wear your cross when I play. Before I was wearing your gold chain, which I love, but it is very thin and long and it looked like it would break.*

*I talk to Dad every day. Oh, back to that. So I was mad at Dad, but it lasted just a short time. I found out he has been sick, and he also felt really upset about it, too. I let it go, and I told him it was okay. You can't stay upset because it will eat you up, but also life is too short and you don't know what will happen. Dad is all I have, and he has only me, so we have got to stick together.*

*We love you Mom. Dad sent me my China tickets, hot socks, and ice bags, along with a birthday card from you and him. It said:*

*I will love you life after life . . .*

*I will love you age after age . . .*

*I will love you forever . . .*

Kerri and I ended up winning in Klagenfurt. Andrea Bocelli and Céline Dion were huge inspirations. Thanks, Andrea! Thanks, Céline! It was a big win for me because it showed me that, with the help of prayers and talking through my feelings with Mom and Dad, I could pull myself up out of dark moments. Now, it was off to the Far East.

8-07-02

*Mom,*

*I can't stop thinking about you. Dad told me to go out and buy Andrea Bocelli's* Sogno (Dream)—*I bought it in Greece. I am so glad that I did.*

*This is where I wait for you*

*Stealing imaginary kisses as time goes by . . .*

*Your spirit is in his songs, especially "The Prayer." I listen to them every night while going to bed. Now, I am sitting on Austrian Airways, headed for Japan with Yanni in my ears. . . . As we are flying, I have a window seat. I haven't looked out the window at all, but just now I finally did. The sky was pitch black, and I could see so many stars. Then, there you were. You were so bright, wavering just above the tip of the wing. You were by the plane the whole way, weren't you? You always are looking out for me, no matter how high or low I will go. I* wanted to crawl out of the small, double-thickness window and onto the wing. There I would fight the strong forces of wind and start walking away from the plane to the wing's edge. I see your hand reaching out, so I grasp on. Up goes my body. My Nike shoes no longer resting on the metal wing. Away we drift, hand in hand. No fear through the blackness, encircling the other stars, my family. Your energy flows through your touch, and I remember the good times well, and only hold glimpses of the bad ones. We glide, soaring together again!!

We often live life complaining, and reflecting on all of the bad that surrounds us. We often forget to reminisce about the good times. Taking things for granted is an anchor that most of us carry around with us. Life is good!! When we truly are living we have cut away the anchor and allow ourselves to float freely among the stars.

Life is way too short to waste energy on stupid things.

I love you Mom and can't wait to see you in my dreams!

8-08-02

Mom,

. . . I travel with two pictures, one of our family—Dad, you and me—the other is one taken at Long Beach State, and it is just you and me. Your hair is in pigtails. It is cute. You know how I used to make fun of your outfits? Forget it! You looked great, just the way you were. . . . Are you playing volleyball up there?

8-10-02

Momma,

Still in Japan. Only ten more days until I get home! I don't cuss anymore, but GOD DAMN IT! It feels like a dream. I want to get pinched, wake up, and know that you will be home waiting for me . . . I have only half of my heart because you took the other half with you . . . I just want to be hugged by you one more time, lie next to you one more time, kiss you one more time, show my appreciation for you one more time, thank you one more time, and say I LOVE YOU one more time! See you in my dreams!!!

Kerri and I finished third in Osaka. After that, it was off to Maoming, China, where we beat Shelda and Adriana in the semis, and Holly and E.Y. in the final. Both were over in less than an hour. We had a two-week break, and I was looking forward to being home in Long Beach, sleeping in my own bed, getting a bikini wax, indulging myself in Starbucks vanilla lattes, and hanging out with Dad.

*8-26-02*

*Hi, Mama,*

*I am so glad to be back home. Everything is great except you are not physically with us here. I saw Dr. Morrison, he asked how you were. Mom, you touched so many people, I miss you so so so so so much. I just wish that you would come back from your vacation. PLEASE! Well, Dr. Morrison doesn't think the tremor in my hand is Parkinson's disease, which is great!!!*

Our final two FIVB tour stops were in Mallorca, Spain, and Vitoria, Brazil, and we took second in both. We ended up winning five of eleven events, earning $195,140. My share was $97,570, and I racked up 1,535 Olympic qualifying points. We were number one in the world. What were all those so-called beach volleyball experts, who'd questioned why I'd trade Holly for Kerri, saying now? That no two players in U.S. history ever had had a quicker rise to the top!

# 15

# BUILDING OUR RÉSUMÉ

Winning breeds winning, Dad and Mom always taught me.

In 2003, Kerri and I set even higher goals for ourselves. We wanted to be number one on both the FIVB and AVP tours. Lofty aspirations? Perhaps, but we knew we weren't anywhere near our peak.

We hired Dane Selznick to be our coach. He'd taken two U.S. beach volleyball teams to the Olympics—Linda Hanley and Barbra Fontana Harris, fourth in Atlanta in 1996, and Rob Heidger and Kevin Wong, fifth in Sydney in 2000. His father Gene was Holly's and my coach in 2000.

Dane has known my family since before I was born. (He's twenty-one years older than I.) He'd played beach volleyball back in the day, and he was a defensive guru. He grew up playing the game, just like me. When Dane was fifteen, he used to substitute for Dad on Wilt Chamberlain's Big Dippers team. He'd patterned his game after Dad's, and he'd picked up a lot of Dad's nuances.

Dane drilled us hard. We practiced almost every day in the off-season, and two or three days during the season, for at least two hours at a time. Since we already were elite athletes, Dane concentrated on helping us evolve from a somewhat new team into a veteran partnership. He fine-tuned the technical aspects of our game. He got right in there and played with us. We'd often train against male pros, which made all the difference. Dane also gave private lessons, and if he was working with his male clients after our sessions, they'd jump into our drills. One of those guys was Kerri's significant other, Casey. Playing against men greatly improved our skills.

But Dane didn't practice only positive scenarios, those that gave us the best vision of the court, allowed us to stay behind the ball and be as strong as possible for the finish. He'd hammer home his mantra: "The best players are those who can get out of trouble." Therefore, he had us practice negative scenarios. Getting out of trouble has a lot to do with knowing how your partner thinks, plays, and executes certain skills, as well as how well the two of you communicate. I give Dane a lot of credit for developing the early Misty-Kerri chemistry, for getting us to work together in every possible situation. Eventually, Dane got us to the point where the game became totally instinctive every time the ball was in the air. I felt as if we both could play blindfolded, and each of us would still know where the other, and the ball, would be at all times.

Dane kept practice light, pumping out old school rock and roll, 1970s stuff. I'd always protest, and change the station on him, flipping on hip-hop. The music, and the kidding around, helped break the monotony. Having Dane as our coach, not only to train us, but to travel to tournaments and devise game plans, was a huge plus. It was great having somebody else focus on volleyball, so that we didn't have to worry about what we were doing wrong. It was wonderful having Dane videotape practices and games, so we didn't have to rely on Dad or our friends to do that.

Because we were focused on the 2004 Olympics, Kerri and I had played exclusively overseas in 2001 and 2002. The FIVB tour had the toughest competition—all of the world's best female teams played there—plus it was where we'd eventually have to qualify for the Athens Games. We wanted to have as much exposure as possible to the teams we'd likely meet in Greece. But in 2003, we decided to add eight domestic events, sandwiched around the front and back ends of our hectic international schedule. We wanted to get back to the Southern California roots of beach volleyball, and we were looking forward to playing in front of family, friends, and U.S. fans. We won all eight AVP tournaments we entered, the first team to go through an AVP season undefeated. The only 2003 AVP event we didn't win was the one we didn't enter because we were competing in an FIVB event in Rhodes, Greece. But don't draw the conclusion that the AVP tour was easy for us. The top U.S. teams—Holly McPeak and Elaine Youngs, and Annett Davis and Jenny Johnson Jordan—weren't cupcakes. We always seemed to be engaged in three-game battles with them. When all was said and done, we posted a 39–0 match record and won $143,100. Simply put, it was the most dominant season in U.S. women's professional beach volleyball history.

In early June 2003, we headed off to Europe for five weeks. Our FIVB road trip began in Greece, where we were seeded first, but finished a disappointing third. We ran up against an explosive Brazilian team, fifth-seeded Sandra Pires and Ana Paula Connelly, in the semifinals, losing, 14–21, 19–21, in forty-two minutes. Although they were a new partnership, Sandra and Ana Paula had a lot of international experience, and both were veterans of two Olympics. At the 1996 Atlanta Olympics, Sandra teamed with Jackie Silva to win the gold medal in the debut of beach volleyball. In 2000, in Sydney, she teamed with Adriana Samuel to win the bronze. Meanwhile, Ana Paula, one of the most lethal servers in beach volleyball, had come from an indoor background. She participated in the 1992 Barcelona Olympics, then helped Brazil to a bronze in Atlanta four years later.

The following week, in Gstaad, we scored two huge victories, knocking off Holly and E.Y. in the first round of the winners bracket, then defeating Shelda and Adriana in the semifinals. Once again, we faced Sandra and Ana Paula in the final, and this time, we beat them, 23–21, 21–15. Then it was off to Berlin, where we got upended in the semifinals by Sandra and Ana Paula, 17–21, 15–21, in thirty-seven minutes, then lost in the consolation to Shelda and Adriana,

18–21, 19–21, finishing fourth. A week later, in Stavanger, Norway, we finished second, again losing in the final to Sandra and Ana Paula, 19–21, 15–21.

Naturally, beach volleyball experts were lamenting that Brazil was, once again, going to supplant the United States as the world's number one beach volleyball nation. Then Dane came to the rescue. He suggested Kerri and I change our game plan for Sandra and Ana Paula. Instead of serving to the six-foot Ana Paula, Dane said, let's target the five-foot-nine Sandra. He'd done a lot of research into the hot Brazilian team. He'd also scouted all of their matches. He'd learned Sandra was playing on the right side of the court for the first time in her career, and he thought if we bombarded her with serves it might throw off her game. Well, Dane was correct. We completely dominated the Brazilians in the next two Grand Slam tournaments, crushing them in Marseille, France, 21–10, 21–13, in thirty-seven minutes, then walloping them in Klagenfurt, Austria, 21–17, 21–12, in thirty-five minutes.

Five weeks after setting off on our FIVB tour, we arrived back in the United States as the conquering heroines. We'd vaulted from third to first in the world. (Sandra and Ana Paula had been the top-ranked FIVB team.) After winning four straight AVP events, it was back to the FIVB grind. This time, though, I didn't have to jump onto a plane. I just hopped into the car and drove thirty minutes to the Home Depot Center, in Carson, California. Kerri and I defeated Australia's Natalie Cook and Nicole Sanderson in the semifinals, 21–11, 19–21, 15–9, and we were facing a final with—you guessed it—Sandra and Ana Paula.

Predictably, Kerri, ever the type-A-plus personality, was down on herself.

"I'm kind of disappointed with how I played," Kerri told the *Orange County Register.* "Misty carried a little extra weight today. We just picked up on what they were doing, and we won on blocking and digging. I'm overanxious and you're not going to win playing like that all of the time.

"You never want to go to a third game, but we're confident when we get there. This is home, and we want to dominate here. Misty and I don't try to change our style of play. We just step up our game."

Thanks to Dane's new strategy, and our two straight FIVB victories, we felt in control heading into our seventh meeting with Sandra and Ana Paula.

"Usually, when they beat us, it's because they serve us off the court," Kerri told the *Register*. "They get like five aces a game, which is huge. That's how they beat us, so (in the final), it's not going to happen."

What a prophet! It took us an hour and ten minutes, but after losing the first game we battled back to emerge victorious over Sandra and Ana Paula, 22–24, 22–20, 15–12.

Two weeks later, we closed the season with a bang: We beat Shelda and Adriana, 21–19, 21–19, in the FIVB World Beach Volleyball Championship in Rio de Janeiro, the first team from the U.S. ever to do so. We had a perfect 8–0 record, losing only two sets along the way.

Since forming our partnership, we'd won twenty titles in thirty-seven starts, with twenty-nine podium finishes and thirty-one final four finishes. Our $701,999 in career earnings already ranked second all-time behind Shelda and Adriana's $1,610,815. We'd accumulated a career match mark of 198–27 (.875), including 153–27 on the FIVB tour.

With the World Championship check, we finished the FIVB season by winning $252,000 overall. Combined with our AVP play, we won thirteen titles at sixteen events with a 91–4 match win-loss record and $395,100 in combined earnings. We won our last fifty-two matches that season, including twenty-eight straight internationally. We finished the season in second place in FIVB world tour rankings—Sandra and Ana Paula, who played in ten events compared to our eight, were first.

Best of all, we were a lock to represent the United States in the 2004 Olympics.

# 16

## FALLING IN LOVE

A funny thing happened to me on the way to the 2004 Olympics: I met my Prince Charming. I first laid eyes on him, in November 2003, at the Sports Medicine Institute (SMI) in Orange, California. I know what you're thinking. *You met the man of your dreams in physical therapy?* And it gets even more romantic than that. On our first date, we went to a UCLA–University of California–Irvine men's volleyball game. With Dad, no less.

But let me start from the beginning.

I'd been doing my physical therapy at SMI since 2001, rehabilitating my knee after PCL surgery. At eight weeks post-op, I felt I needed a more specialized rehab program. I'd been doing basic physical therapy, and while Dr. Schobert was pleased with my progress, I wanted to pick up the pace so I'd be ready for the 2002 season. PCL rehabs, like PCL surgeries, are tricky: If you go overboard in physical therapy, you can reinjure the ligament and set yourself back. I'd heard a lot of pro baseball players went to SMI for their physical therapy, so I gave it a try. I worked with Matt Stresak, an athletic trainer who spent the first month dialing me back. I'd thrown myself into a high-intensity cycling class, was taking yoga, working with a specialist to improve upper-body flexibility, and lifting upper-body weights.

"Your body is still in the recovery process," Stresak argued. "You're barely two months out of surgery."

I trusted Stresak with my body. He played the same sport (beach volleyball), hung out at the same beach (Huntington), and knew a lot of the same people I did (including Dad). He understood the tremendous pounding beach volleyball gave my body. He knew I had an unorthodox arm swing, which placed a lot of pressure on my shoulder. He knew I threw my core into contorted positions, or as he liked to say, some "big, big trunk twists and big, big flexions." So Stresak became one of my go-to guys for bodywork. In addition, he designed full-body workouts for me, which emphasized strengthening my weaknesses and correcting my imbalances, and I trained, under his watchful eye, at SMI.

So there I was, in November 2003, working out at SMI and minding my own business. Honestly, I didn't notice Matt Treanor at first. He'd recently had arthroscopic knee surgery to repair a torn meniscus. He barely said boo. He blew in, worked out, and blew out. But the more I saw of him, the more interested I became. He resembled Richard Gere in *An Officer and a Gentleman*. As it turned out, Matt already had scoped me out, and he'd asked our mutual SMI colleague Brian Rios, a minor leaguer, to do some espionage work. But subtle isn't in Brian's vocabulary.

"What do you think of Matt Treanor?" Rios asked me one morning.

"He just does his rehab, comes in, and goes out," I replied.

I wasn't looking for a relationship at the time, and as I later learned, neither was Matt. We'd both recently broken up with people. However, if someone wanted to take me to dinner, I wasn't going to say no. But I'd also told myself, "I need to concentrate on myself."

"If Matt asked you out, would you go?" Rios asked.

"Sure, but I don't really know him," I said.

So that night, Brian, Matt, and I met at El Torito for Mexican food and margaritas. I asked my half brother Scott to be my wingman. Brian also invited a friend—a Sharpie pen salesman. And then, he tried to set me up with the guy. Needless to say, Matt and I were perturbed.

A few days later, during our sessions at SMI, Matt and I were chatting, and I sensed he wanted to ask me something, but he couldn't because there were a lot of people around. So I left the building for a few minutes, then came back and announced, "I forgot something in the back room!" Of course, I really hadn't. I dawdled, scribbling on paper, and Matt appeared.

"I know that you're really busy, that you probably don't have the time, but would you like to have dinner?" Matt asked. "I understand you have a busy schedule, and if you can't, you can't. I've got a busy schedule, too. I leave for spring training in a couple of weeks . . ."

"Actually, do you want to go out tonight?" I interrupted.

"What?" he said, startled.

"Do you want to go to a volleyball game with me?" I asked.

"Sure," he said.

Matt picked me up at my Long Beach house. We went to Claim Jumper for happy hour and shared a pizza. We got so caught up in conversation that we were late getting to the volleyball game. Matt was so easy to talk to that I felt I'd known him for a million years. We talked about past relationships, our families, everything. I told him about Mom's cancer battle and how difficult it had been for me to cope after her death. He told me his brother Michael had been murdered (the crime still remains unsolved) and how he'd never gotten over it. He told me another brother, Malachi, had died as an infant. I'd had closure with Mom's death, but, sadly, Matt hadn't had it with either of his brothers.

I felt a strong connection. It just felt natural to be with Matt. He was such a gentleman. He paid for our date. He opened every single door. He endured the UCLA–University of California–Irvine men's volleyball game, hanging on Dad's every word, charming all our family friends. And that was it. I went home that night, opened my day planner, and under January 23, 2004, I wrote: FIRST DATE WITH MATT TREANOR. I knew it was going to be a milestone. From then on, we were inseparable.

Very quickly, Matt got a good dose of my sense of humor. We're both extremely competitive, individually and with each other, in just about everything. Golf. Table tennis. Soccer. Bowling. Surfing. It never starts out that way, then suddenly becomes a competitive mess. And there's always a bet. When we first started dating, Matt and I went bowling. I bet I'd beat him, and he bet he'd beat me. If I won, I told him he'd have to show up at SMI in old school running shorts, tube socks, and a headband, and he'd have to do a dance. If he won, he told me, I'd have to treat everybody at SMI to a song, "You Are My Sunshine," dressed as a ladybug. I beat him the first game, and he beat me the second, so we both paid up.

Nine days after our first date, on February 1, Matt decided it was time for me to meet his family. We drove out to Riverside for a Super Bowl XXXVIII party. I was very nervous, and I instructed Matt to "just give me a gin and tonic." I brought along Tina Bowman, my childhood friend, to help keep me calm. I tried to be myself, but I was very anxious, not only because I wanted Matt's family to like me, but because the Visa commercial "Snowball," starring Kerri and me playing beach volleyball in the ice and snow, in our red USA bikinis, was premiering during the game.

We'd filmed for two days at Westward Beach in Malibu, up against the Pacific Ocean. It was seventy-five degrees. But you'd never know it from seeing the commercial. We were playing on an ice field the size of a volleyball court. Hundreds of gallons of foam were sprayed on a white tarp, along with more than twenty thousand pounds of shaved ice, to create a winter wonderland. It felt like snow cone ice, hard and gravelly, and it was super cold. Icicles were dangling off a stiff volleyball net stretched across the tarp. Then we drove up to Mammoth Lakes, California, and shot for a day and a half, in a snowy, off-road setting. It was a real ice field. When we pulled up to the spot, the thermometer read zero degrees. Then we stripped to our bikinis, and the temperature dipped to five below.

"Theme from *A Summer Place*" by Percy Faith & His Orchestra plays in the background of the commercial, and an announcer says, "Can't wait for this summer's Olympic Games? Neither can we." Kerri and I are grunting and groaning, diving into the ice and snow, embroiled in an intense match against another women's team, professional beach volleyball players Jen Holdren and Sarah Straton. Why are we playing in the dead of winter? Because we are so eager to hit the beach in Athens! Ah, show biz. Kerri and I got ice burns because of the frigid temperatures, and our skin got all cut up because of the jagged ice. At the end of the commercial, the ball goes into the water, and we're both stunned. So who's going in to get it? Kerri calls, "Evens." I call, "Odds." Then, we play rock, paper, scissors for the honor. Kerri loses, sulks off, and I've got a very devilish grin on my face.

Shooting the commercial was great fun, because, obviously, it wasn't something we normally did. Swimmer Michael Phelps came to watch, since he was a Visa-sponsored athlete, so we got to meet him. I was able to take home my behind-the-scenes, down-filled wardrobe—a ski jacket, snow pants, and some really cool boots. We had foot warmers and hand warmers going to try to stay warm. They also gave us piping-hot dressing room trailers. At one point, Kerri stood too close to a free-standing heater, and her gloves caught on fire.

It was our first experience with being treated like Hollywood stars. We even had body doubles.

"May we get you a cup of hot tea?" the crew kept asking.

"No, thanks, we'll walk over to craft services and get some," we'd reply.

"No, no, no," they'd insist, and then they'd call three different people to retrieve cups of tea.

After a while, though, they realized we didn't mind waiting on ourselves, which we later were told was a rarity in Hollywood. Both Kerri and I are easygoing, and we try to keep it simple.

I'm not convinced ice beach volleyball would make a good Winter Olympics sport, though. It definitely would keep doctors and physical therapists in business, thanks to all the sliding around on unpredictable footing. On the other hand, whenever you're injured, the first thing you're told is, "Put some ice on it," so maybe ice beach volleyball is, indeed, a ready-made Winter Olympics sport after all. If I ever got a chance to compete in the Winter Olympics, though, I'd do skeleton or bobsled. (I can't ski, and it's difficult for me to stand on ice.)

To tell you the truth, what I was most concerned about on Super Bowl Sunday was Matt and his family seeing me, in my bikini, on national TV. But they all got into the spirit of the commercial. It, and I, both were big hits. When we first started dating, Matt wasn't keen on my playing in such a skimpy "uniform." He and his family are Catholic and conservative. He didn't like the fact that when I dove around in the sand, my bikini didn't always stay in place, or that when I gave Kerri instructions during matches, flashing hand signals behind my back, just below my waist, the TV cameras showed close-ups of my butt. Eventually, though, he came to grips with my bikini's being functional, not seductive.

When I got home from our Super Bowl date, I pulled out my day planner and wrote down the names of everybody in Matt's family because I knew they'd become important to me and I didn't want to forget them.

Soon afterward, Matt left for spring training, and at the end of March, I flew to Florida for an AVP tournament in Fort Lauderdale. I went a few days early, allegedly so I could do media for the event, but truthfully, I wanted to visit Matt in Miami. When I called home March 31 and announced we were engaged, everybody thought it was an April Fools' joke. When I delivered the news to people at the AVP tournament the following day, April 1, everyone thought the same thing.

Matt called Dad to ask for his permission, and after the phone call, Dad, sobbing uncontrollably, went for a long drive. If ever there was a time he missed Mom, this was it. He had so many regrets that she didn't live to see this milestone in my life. With Dad's blessing, Matt hatched a proposal plan. Before dinner at the River House in Fort Lauderdale, he walked me down to the restaurant's dock and asked me to marry him. We hugged, and I wouldn't let go until Matt finally said, "Do you want to see the ring?"

Our whirlwind courtship was followed by a whirlwind engagement.

"Why don't we have a small wedding?" Matt suggested.

"No, I want to be a princess," I insisted.

Because of my hectic, pre-Olympics schedule, I hired event planner Kathy Jo Peterson to assist us with our special day. Whenever I had a break from the AVP and FIVB tours, and I was home in Long Beach, I got something wedding-related accomplished. Mostly, though, because I was so busy training, and so focused on winning the gold medal, the whole wedding-planning process felt like a nonstop fire drill. If I liked a photographer's work, I'd say, "Book it!" If I liked a florist's work, I'd say, "Book it!" There wasn't time to price-shop, much less overthink things.

Almost immediately, I found a wedding dress, a strapless Eve of Milady ball gown covered with silver embroidery and beading. I also found a pearl-and-crystal tiara. Next, I went shopping for the bridesmaid dresses at Castle for Brides in Huntington Beach, with NBC Sports cameras in tow, shooting footage for an Olympics feature. I tried on the bridesmaid dresses to make sure they were comfortable. I found one in icy pink, floor length, sleeveless, and flowing. I never really liked pink before, but now I love it. It's a very princess color, don't you think?

Together, Peterson and I created another special detail: a watermark with three angels, a tribute to Mom and to Matt's two late brothers, which was printed on every wedding item, from the invitations to the ceremony programs.

We were married on November 13, 2004, at noon, at Holy Family Cathedral in Orange, California, Matt's family's church. The ceremony was followed by a cocktail reception, luncheon, and dancing at the Center Club in Costa Mesa. We had two hundred forty guests.

Jodie Torromeo, an Asics Tigers teammate, was my maid of honor. My six bridesmaids included Kerri; Carol Luber and Liz Martinez (elementary school friends); Tina Bowman and Cara Heads (middle/high school friends); and Marcia Bradbeer (a friend I grew up with at Huntington Beach). They carried pink and white roses and peonies.

My half brothers Brack and Scott, along with Aunt Gen and Uncle John, Dad's sister and brother, offered the communion gifts. Aunt Betty Ann and Uncle Edward represented Mom, walking down the aisle in her place. While I missed Mom deeply, I felt her presence. I'd taken great care to honor her in a multitude of ways. I carried a bouquet of pink peonies, roses, and tropical monkey tails, sprinkled with crystals. Her wedding band was tied to the bouquet. Mom helped me make it through the ceremony without crying, although Dad and Matt certainly shed some tears.

Cards tied to each pew featured words that were meaningful to us: Love, Cherish, Family, Eternity, and finally, on the pew closest to the altar, I Do.

Everyone received a three-tiered program, bordered with a pastel green vine and tied with a sheer pink bow. Titled Misty & Matt, it included the names of the bridal party, an outline of the ceremony, and a message from us:

> To our parents who have guided us, loved us, and given so much to us, we thank you and love you with all of our hearts. To our family and friends for sharing this day with us, your love and support has meant so much. Thank you for enriching our lives in ways that will last forever. Prayers and angels are around us today. We honor all those who have passed on before us . . .

Our cocktail hour had a tropical theme, a nod to my family's Hawaiian heritage and my days on the beach. It was held in an open-air portion of the club, decorated in shells, orchids, and sea-blue linens. We served coconut shrimp, shrimp roll-ups, mushroom puffs, and bruschetta, and we had a steel drum band for background music. A bamboo tray was filled with volleyballs and baseballs for our guests to sign.

Our dinner was held in the ballroom, on tables topped with pink linens, pink and sage satin napkins, and tall candelabra centerpieces bursting with pink and white flowers and crystals. The menu consisted of tossed romaine and baby oak leaf salad with Gorgonzola cheese and toasted pecans, tossed with champagne vinaigrette; a duo of filet of beef and mustard-baked salmon with demi-glace and wild honey chardonnay sauce; garlic whipped potatoes; and seasonal vegetables. Each table was named for something meaningful to us, including SMI, the Florida Marlins, and the 2004 Olympics.

Our first dance was to "When You Say Nothing at All," by Alison Krauss.

*It's amazing how you can speak right to my heart*
*Without saying a word, you can light up the dark . . .*

Throughout the evening, guests toasted us with pink sugar-rimmed champagne glasses.

Our intricate six-tiered wedding cake, designed by Let Them Eat Cake, was the showstopper. A white cake with strawberry and lemon filling, it was covered in pink, white, and sage fondant. I didn't eat it—I shoved it in Matt's face.

Our "Sweet Dreams" table was laden with treats, including chocolate baseballs and gold-wrapped candies that looked like Olympic gold medals, which people could put in beautiful boxes to take home. Our guests also received mini souvenir volleyballs and baseball bats, engraved with our names and the date.

From the anticipation of seeing my soon-to-be husband, to getting ready with all of my girlfriends, to being with Dad and our family, to entering the reception, every moment was amazing. I truly felt like a princess.

Falling in love with Matt helped plant my feet on the ground. I still felt discombobulated by Mom's death. A day didn't go by when I didn't think about her. I missed her very much. Dad did, too, and I felt responsible for him. We both were still a little lost without Mom. I just wanted Dad to be okay. Matt made me feel much more solid in every aspect of my life.

From day one, I felt as if Matt was the missing link in my life. Before I met him, I felt like there was something missing. He has helped me grow as a wife, a daughter, a friend, and a professional athlete. Most important, he has helped me become a better communicator. He'll tell you exactly how he's feeling, whereas I hold it in. Since Matt came into my life, it has been easier for me to explain myself and let out my emotions. Our differences in communication come, in part, from his being one of eight kids and my being an only child. Plus, he's a baseball player, and baseball players just let it fly, whatever it is they're thinking and feeling.

I've added a lot to Matt's life, too. I introduced him to the concept of doing more structured workouts, got him involved with personal trainers, Pilates, and yoga. I inspired him to do whatever it takes to get to the top. He'll tell you it isn't a coincidence that our first date was in January 2004 and that season, at twenty-eight, he broke into the big leagues for the first time in ten years. He credits me with giving him a kick in the pants.

Now, I'd have to say Matt might be the only person in the world more relentless and resilient than I am. Dad and Mom were my role models for a blue-collar work ethic, and Mom taught me never to give up. Matt personifies both of those qualities. He's the son and grandson of firefighters. His mother works for the Catholic Church. He exemplifies dedication, determination, and devotion. He's the first to arrive at the ballpark and the last to leave. He's tough, he plays hurt, and is a great teammate.

"My wife is significantly more famous than I am. I have no problem marrying up," Matt once told *ESPN the Magazine*. (Never mind that Matt knew nothing about volleyball or me when we met. In fact, he asked his little brother Markell if he'd ever heard of "Missy May." "What's with you, man?" Markell said. "You've got problems. She's one of the most famous players in the world.") In California, I often get stopped for autographs. Even in Tahiti, while renting jet skis on our honeymoon, Matt says he heard people on the dock, saying, in broken English, "Olympic volleyball" and pointing to me. Because bikinis are my uniform, Matt's major league baseball teammates regularly razzed him. Before a spring training game, Marlins outfielder Jeff Conine wrote "Matt May" on the blackboard. From that point on, that's how Matt's Marlins teammates referred to him. It takes a secure man to handle ribbing like that.

Joel Wolfe, Matt's agent, once described him as "the anti-Crash Davis," a reference to the minor league catcher played by Kevin Costner in *Bull Durham*. And it's true, Matt's baseball résumé is so mind-boggling, it sounds dreamed up by Hollywood screenwriters.

Matt was drafted out of Mater Dei High School in Santa Ana, California, by the Kansas City Royals in 1994. How's this for a small-world story? Guy Hansen, Aunt Betty Ann's first husband, says he scouted Matt for the Royals. He was selected in the fourth round, the 107th player overall, and he signed for eighty-six thousand dollars. And thus began Matt's unique journey through baseball. He played in about 916 minor league games over 12 seasons, in places like Springfield, Illinois; Lansing, Michigan; Calgary, Canada; Portland, Oregon; and Albuquerque, New Mexico, and for teams named the Sultans, Lugnuts, Manatees, Hammerheads, Sea Dogs, and Isotopes. He didn't get out of Class-A ball until his eighth season.

The Marlins finally called Matt up to the big league club on June 2, 2004. That day, in a game against the Cincinnati Reds, he went one for three with a run scored. I'll never forget getting that call from him. I was headed to practice, and I got so excited, I jumped into the car pool lane (which is reserved for two or more people) and raced to Redondo Beach. Then I phoned DirecTV and ordered the Major League Baseball Extra Innings package, so I could watch him. On June 17, Matt experienced one of the highlights of his career, recording his first RBI on a walk-off single against the Chicago White Sox.

The following season, Matt made the Marlins' 2005 Opening Day roster, and he has been a big leaguer ever since. In his first full season, he played backup to starting catcher Paul Lo Duca, and he recorded a few more career highlights: He threw out all three baserunners who attempted to steal in a game against the Washington Nationals on April 15, and he hit his first major league home run against Baltimore Orioles pitcher Daniel Cabrera June 20. He was released by the Marlins on December 10, 2008, to make room on the team's forty-man roster for the Rule 5 Draft, held the following day. On December 18, he signed with the Detroit Tigers as a backup catcher. After a great spring training, he was sidelined with a hip injury on April 24, limited to just four games that season, subsequently had surgery for a torn labrum, and was put on the disabled list. In December 2009 Matt signed with the Milwaukee Brewers, and in March 2010 he was traded to the Texas Rangers.

People fuss over my Olympic gold medals, but honestly, I'm more impressed by Matt's accomplishments. I wouldn't have had the patience to stick it out. When we met, he was so frustrated he hadn't made the big leagues, he was thinking about quitting. I encouraged him not to. I told Matt that I knew too many athletes who gave up before reaching their dreams, then lived the rest of their lives filled with anger, bitterness, and regret. I told Matt I'd hate for him to get eaten up by the What Ifs? As an example, I told him I felt unfulfilled because I'd left indoor volleyball before reaching my potential. I've encouraged Matt to keep going as long as his body holds up.

Now look at him. He is a big leaguer and a good volleyball player. He passes and sets very well, although all he wants to do is play defense. His vertical, eh; his hitting, eh. But he's learning. I'll pepper with him. We couldn't win a tournament together, but we'd sure have a lot of fun.

As for my baseball, well, I've asked to take batting practice, but Matt doesn't think it's a good idea. We've gone to the batting cages together, and I can't even hit a 40 mph softball. I'm like, "Can't they increase the size of the ball? This is too small!" I've also tossed baseballs to Matt to help him with his catching skills, like blocking.

However, I am batting 1.000 when it comes to throwing out first pitches before major league baseball games. The first one was at a Marlins game at Dolphins Stadium in 2004—I threw it from the mound and put it right over the plate—and Matt caught it. I've also thrown out first pitches before home games for the Los Angeles Dodgers, Arizona Diamondbacks, California Angels, Chicago White Sox (who won it all that season, so I was good luck), and Chicago Cubs. And I've been a guest conductor at Wrigley Field, leading the singing of "Take Me Out to the Ball Game" during the seventh-inning stretch. They gave me a cheat sheet, but I already knew the words. When you're doing something like that, you figure most fans have had a couple of beers, so it doesn't really matter what you sound like.

Throwing out first pitches is nerve-racking. I get nervous because the baseball is so small. I've been in the stands when others have thrown out first pitches and botched them badly, listening as fans boo and yell, "You stink!" Some people actually warm up before getting out there, but I never have. Matt's advice to me: "Don't throw it in the dirt." If I were given a volleyball to throw over the plate, I wouldn't be the least bit nervous. I'd know how hard to throw it, when to release it, and I'd throw a strike every time.

# 17

# FIRST OLYMPIC GOLD MEDAL

I was floating on air.

We were about to kick off our 2004 Olympics run.

We were dominating women's professional beach volleyball.

We were riding a record winning streak on the sand, and away from the beach, we were enjoying our fifteen minutes of fame.

We were scheduling interviews and photo shoots, appearing in cover stories of newspapers and in spreads in magazines, wearing everything from teeny tiny shorts and itsy-bitsy bikinis to togas and Donna Karan white satin, spaghetti-strap gowns.

We were on millions of McDonald's cups and wrappers.

Life was good.

Kerri and I began the 2004 FIVB season in early March in Fortaleza, Brazil, beating Shelda Bede and Adriana Behar in the final. Three weeks later, we opened the AVP season with a victory in Fort Lauderdale. We extended our winning streak to sixty-four worldwide, including forty-four straight on the AVP, defeating Holly McPeak and Elaine Youngs, 21–11, 21–11, in the final.

"They are not only beating up on us, they are beating up on the rest of the world," Holly told the *Los Angeles Times*.

Despite our dominance of the women's pro beach volleyball tour, Kerri was, typically, nervous before the final.

"The first AVP match of the year, there's always a lot of nerves and a lot of jitters," she told the media. "Throughout all of that, we stayed pretty steady, and that's the sign of a really good team."

I, on the other hand, felt as if I were dancing in the sand. I kept showing off my engagement ring to anybody and everybody and pretty much blinding them with it.

Yes, our lives were good. Too good to be true? Perhaps.

While Kerri and I were preparing for our final FIVB Olympic qualifying tournaments, our coach Dane Selznick pushed us through intense training sessions. I was having trouble with my hitting, so he had me hit dozens of balls in a row. I beat the heck out of them, in the wind, again and again. When Dad stopped by the beach to watch practice, he went ballistic.

"Misty, what are you doing?" he bellowed. "That isn't necessary! That isn't good for you!"

Dad's argument was this: Because I've been exposed to so much volleyball, I can visualize, then imitate, anything I'm instructed to do. Some players need things choreographed; not me. To this day, Dad has a certain way of working on skills. He takes a ground-up approach. He breaks them down, then builds them up, piece by piece. Dad was worried I might injure myself. All he could see was me thrusting my body into a violent, crunching, contorted position, dozens of times over. All he could see was me sailing high in the air, swinging my arm across my body, and making contact with the ball just before slamming down hard in the sand. All he could see was my right arm finishing all the way to my left hip, which was incorrect, unnatural, and straining my abdominal muscles. All he could think was, "Misty's making a muscled swing."

Afterward, I sheepishly told Dad, "My stomach hurts." He immediately flashed back to the abdominal tear I had suffered before the 2000 Olympics, and the terrible time I went through, trying to get healthy to compete in Sydney. "Of course it hurts," he screamed.

"You're swinging diagonally across your body." Dad was fuming, and his face was turning bright red. "Misty, you shouldn't be doing this before the final qualifying matches for the Olympics," he barked.

Over the next few days, I didn't feel any further repercussions from the hitting session, so I figured I was out of the woods. Kerri and I flew to Europe for the second FIVB event of the season. We kept our perfect streak going in Rhodes, Greece, defeating Shelda and Adriana in the semifinals, then Holly and E.Y. in the final. All of our matches, except the semis, lasted thirty-four minutes or less. And that was only thirty-eight minutes. We were on quite a roll.

Then, five days later, in the AVP event at Huntington Beach, I felt discomfort in my abdominal muscles. In the final, I dove for the ball, and my body went into complete extension. I heard a crack, and from that moment on, I couldn't get rid of the abdominal pain. Yet, you wouldn't have known anything was wrong by watching my performance on the court. We won the event, cruising past Barbra Fontana and Jennifer Kessy. We were riding a mighty wave of a winning streak that had few, if any, parallels in sports: We now had won eighty-six matches and fifteen tournaments.

"Kerri and Misty are taking the sport to another level," Barbra Fontana told the *Long Beach Press Telegram*.

But the streak was the furthest thing from our minds. We were on a mission to win an Olympic gold medal. All of these tournaments (and the streak) were just the steps along the way.

"I swear to God, we don't think about the streak," Kerri told the *Long Beach Press Telegram*. "I've heard people say that we should lose, so we don't have the pressure of the streak. But we always want to win, and I don't know how we could do that."

We were the talk of professional beach volleyball, around the world. We were being labeled as the spark the struggling AVP tour desperately needed. We were being called the most dominant duo in the history of the sport. We were, undoubtedly, hands down, the gold medal favorite in Athens.

The following week, in the AVP event in Manhattan Beach, my

abdominals flared up again, but this time, the pain affected my performance. We lost to Annett Davis and Jenny Johnson Jordan in the semis, 19–21, 19–21, ending our fifteen-tournament winning streak. One after another, friends and colleagues approached us, saying it was good we'd finally lost. It would alleviate some of the pressure heading into the Olympics, they reasoned. Regardless, the loss still stung. Kerri, who got teary-eyed afterward, kicked herself for not stepping up and carrying a bigger load.

"I felt ineffective," she told *Dig* magazine. "I wish I would have just played crappy, because ineffective is worse. It's like the difference between when my mom says, 'Kerri, I'm pissed off,' and saying, 'I'm disappointed in you.' Pissed off I can handle. Disappointed, that's the worst thing you can hear."

A week later, we won in Gstaad, defeating Shelda and Adriana in the final. My abdominals were screaming, and I fought through the pain. But it wasn't fun. Not one bit. And then the bottom caved in. My abdominal pain was so constant, and so intense that by mid-June we elected not to play in the AVP event in San Diego. A week later, after only one match, we withdrew from an FIVB Grand Slam event in Berlin, which paid more money to the winner ($43,000) than a regular event ($27,000). I tried to gut it out. Big mistake. After forfeiting, Kerri, Dane, and I discussed how we were going to handle the next several weeks. Because we'd already qualified for Athens, our sights were set on the Olympic gold medal. The money wasn't nearly as important. We all decided it would be best for me to take some time off. After not being able to dial it back in 2000, when I suffered an abdominal injury but kept right on playing because Holly McPeak and I were trying to qualify for the Sydney Olympics, I wanted to be smart this time around. Kerri agreed. However, she's not one to sit on the sidelines. She thought it would be best for her to keep playing in tournaments, and I encouraged her.

After returning home from Europe, I immediately went to see Dr. Schobert. He scheduled an MRI of my abdominals. Kerri, meanwhile, joined up with Rachel Wacholder to finish third in the FIVB event in Stavanger, Norway. Two weeks later, Kerri partnered with Jennifer Meredith to finish second in the AVP event in Belmar, New Jersey. And a week after that, she and Rachel won the FIVB event in Marseille, France, defeating Annett and Jenny. It was Rachel's first win, so it was a great moment for both of them. Being on tour without me, though, taught Kerri how deep our bond was. She missed me so much, she must have called me a million times from Europe.

During this stretch of time, Dad received phone calls from Dane and from Kerri's mother, Marge, both expressing concern that I wouldn't be well enough to play in the Olympics. Dad felt pressure to have me withdraw from Athens.

"Butch, it's imperative we know now," Marge said. "Kerri has to pick a partner for Athens. She wants to know if Misty will be ready."

Dad reminded both Dane and Marge that the U.S. Olympic Committee's official deadline to declare its final Athens team roster was several weeks away. He kept reiterating that he wouldn't answer for me, and pointing out that I'd earned the opportunity to decide for myself whether I could play.

Dr. Schobert also began to feel the pressure I was under: The U.S. Olympic Committee phoned his office, requesting a copy of my MRI report. He'd been very relieved with its findings. The MRI showed swelling and some minor disruption of a small number of muscle fibers. He called it a "severe strain," advised me to take five weeks off from competition, and prescribed a rehabilitation program.

For the next two weeks, I did basic physical therapy, gradually expanding my team of healers.

I turned to Dan Rawson, a specialist in Hellerwork Structural Integration, a series of deep-tissue bodywork and movement education designed to realign the body, reorganize muscle and connective tissue, and release chronic tension and stress. I'd first visited Dan in Laguna Beach, California, on January 23, 2004, the day of my first date with Matt. At that time, my posture was my biggest concern. I'd wanted to realign my body. Dan found that my pelvis had a strong anterior tilt, meaning that it was tilted too much forward. My left hip wanted to tilt forward, while my right hip wanted to tilt backward. This created a strong asymmetry. After ten sessions, I looked like a different person. I stood more erect. In fact, I actually measured two inches taller. I also had more flexibility and a better range of motion.

I never told Dan that I played beach volleyball or divulged any of my accomplishments. On the initial informational documents, I listed myself as a "professional athlete." Period. He'd work on me, then I'd head off to practice, and I'd immediately notice a difference—my shoulder didn't hurt, or my serving and digging seemed effortless. After our sessions, he'd leave me in a comfortable place, then the following week, I'd come in, all beaten up, and he'd say, "My God, Misty, what do you do?" Now, he says the only sport more brutal on the body than beach volleyball is competitive motocross.

When I suffered my abdominal strain, I went back to visit Dan. While most physical therapists had been looking at my problem as being in my rectus abdominus, a paired muscle running vertically on each side of the anterior wall of the abdomen, Dan and his colleague Aimee Kolsby believed my problem was coming from the inner thigh on my left leg. Once Dan and Aimee found the shortness in my left adductor muscle, they were able to lengthen it by manual manipulation, which, in turn, took the strain off the rectus abdominus. Aimee and I shared a passion for cupcakes, so Dan's wife, Paige, always had red velvet and banana cupcakes from Sprinkles for my sessions.

I was treated by Dan two or three times a week, for two hours at a time. It was, and still is, the most painful form of bodywork I've ever encountered. It was extremely slow, and very deep, with Dan using his fist, elbow, or flat hands to get into my fascia, malleable tissue that wraps all of the muscles, and all of the individual fibers and bundles of individual fibers that become muscle. In its optimal condition, fascia is a loose, moist tissue. But under continual stress, and lack of movement, fascia becomes rigid and loses its fluidity. Layers of fascia begin to stick to one another, causing "knots." Occasionally, Dan would put a bit of beeswax on his hands, but Hellerwork isn't anything like massage, where the masseur slides his hands over the tissue with oil or lotion. With this form of bodywork, Dan needed traction in order to connect the tissue, and he couldn't do that if his hands were slippery. By adding mechanical energy with his fist, elbow or open hands, Dan generated heat, and in the process, lengthened the fascia where it was short.

Dan's discovery? The fascia of the adductors on my left leg were adhered to the fascia of my quadriceps. The two fascias have different functions, and when they're stuck together, they can't perform individually. That was why I wasn't healing from my abdominal injury. To treat me, he'd place my left leg, and the tissue, in the place he wanted them, then call for movement in the area of the inner thigh.

"Misty, flex your foot . . . bend your knee forward . . . step through the heel," he instruct. He'd ask me to make a small movement, mimicking the motion I made when I walked, and as I did that, it helped create independent function between the various muscle groups.

In addition to Dan, I added another amazing guru to my team of healers: Gail Wetzler, the owner of Wetzler Integrated Physical Therapy Center in Newport Beach. I was referred to her by some of my professional beach volleyball buddies, who thought she was a miracle worker. I was extremely interested in one of Gail's passions, visceral manipulation, which was developed by Dr. Jean-Pierre Barral, a French osteopathic physician and registered physical therapist.

In our first visit, I told Gail my abdominal strain was manifesting itself in several ways. I had headaches. I was having trouble sleeping. I was experiencing pain during daily activities, exercise, and prolonged standing. I was feeling a constant cramping, burning, and knifelike sensation in my stomach. I had inconsistent menstrual cycles.

Gail did a complete assessment and found numerous issues throughout my upper and lower back. She said that my right shoulder girdle maintained a line of tension down to my left abdomen via abdominal obliques and intercostal muscles. She said that I had fascial lines of tension in my left pelvis and abdominal muscles from my previous left knee injury. She said that I had a lack of motion in my sacrum and ilium. In addition, her palpitation of my stomach revealed my abdominal muscle layers were pulling in different directions. The most internal layer pulled completely to the back tissues that surrounded my left kidney.

One of her major findings: My left diaphragm was protecting the area of pain, but it was adapted into a contraction position, making it difficult to breathe deeply. Her palpitation revealed constriction in the connective tissue behind the left kidney. This strain was pulling on the twelfth intercostal nerve in my thoracic region, and the ilioinguinal and iliohypogastric nerves that travel behind the kidneys. This area produced the main source of my pain, she said.

Gail's therapy consisted of an integrated approach of soft-tissue release techniques. The primary ones were organ-specific fascial mobilization (also known as visceral manipulation); functional orthopedics with musculo-skeletal release techniques; and laser therapy.

After a two-week hiatus from training, and a month off from competition, I was feeling a lot better. In late July, I rejoined Kerri at the AVP event in Hermosa Beach. All systems were go. We met at Hermosa for practice, the day before the start of the tournament, and it was very windy. Still, I decided I needed to work on my hitting. Nothing too radical, of course. However, several minutes into my hitting session, I tweaked my abdominal muscles.

For extra support I played wearing a brace around my midsection. Then, in the semifinals, my abdominals acted up, once again, but we ended up rallying to beat Barbra Fontana and Jennifer Kessy, 16–21, 21–12, 17–15. After the match, I told Kerri that, for precautionary reasons, I didn't want to play in the final. I'd made progress in rehab, and I wanted to stop before, God forbid, I made the injury any worse. So we forfeited the nationally televised final to Holly and E.Y.

With three weeks until the Olympics, I was confident I had enough time to completely heal. In the past, I'd recovered in less time. Now, I was older and wiser. I had an excellent team of healers. I knew my body, and I knew me. Frankly, I was more worried about Kerri being stressed out over my health than I was about not being ready for Athens. The more time I'd spent off the AVP and FIVB tours, the more success she'd had without me, and the more the media hounded her about my health. Will Misty be ready for Athens? Who will you play with, Kerri, if she can't go? How long will you wait, Kerri, before you make a decision on your partner? I felt bad for Kerri. I sensed she was beginning to doubt me. I sensed others were, too.

My health had become a major topic on tour, with everyone weighing in on what they thought I would, and should, do. I knew I didn't have to get healthy overnight. I'd qualified for Athens, and a decision on playing did not have to be made until two days before Olympic play would begin on August 15.

Kerri's words to the media after our forfeiture in Hermosa Beach hurt me deeply.

"I don't want to have to think about it," Kerri told the *Long Beach Press Telegram*, when asked about her options should I not recover. Although she and Rachel had played well together internationally, including in the Hermosa Beach exhibition final, Kerri went on to tell the media that, in the worst-case scenario, she would likely ask Annett Davis to be her Olympic partner. Annett and her partner Jenny Johnson Jordan were the number-three-ranked team in the United States, and only two teams per country qualified for Athens.

I called Kerri and spoke to her about her comments.

"Kerri, I'm going to be fine," I told her.

"I know, they were just pressuring me," she replied.

Two days after our forfeiture in Hermosa Beach, the U.S. Olympic Committee's website front page reported my injury could knock me out of the Olympics.

"I'm fine," I told the *Long Beach Press Telegram*. "I just felt a pull and had to decide whether I wanted to continue to play or play it safe."

Then came the crowning blow. A week after our forfeiture in Hermosa Beach, Kerri and Rachel won the FIVB tournament in Klagenfurt, Austria, beating Shelda and Adriana in the final. The exaggerated reports about my health reached Kerri in Europe, and she wrote me a nervous email. She told me how concerned she was about me, and said she was worried about whether I'd truly be ready for Athens. I replied succinctly: "Kerri, don't worry. I will be there. We're going to win this gold medal."

All of this speculation, all of this drama, made me mad. So mad, in fact, that I wanted to prove them all wrong. All of the doubters. And I especially wanted to prove Kerri wrong. She doubted me, even though she told me she didn't. I just wished she'd focus on herself and not worry about me. When she showed up in Athens, I wanted her to be ready to go, so there were no question marks.

Bottom line, I wanted the privilege of saying, "I'm not healthy enough to play in the Olympics." I wanted to be the one to make the decision. I didn't want anybody making it for me. I'd earned the right to make the final call. Who knows my body better than I do? Besides, I never would've gotten on a plane and flown to Athens if I weren't healthy enough to play.

It was hard for me to sit out. But because I was older, and I'd had experience with injuries, especially an abdominal tear, I knew there was no problem with my being back for Athens. I stopped because I wanted to heal. That was my goal. In college, I would've reacted differently. It always was, "I don't care if I'm hurt. I just want to play." As you get older, though, you have to do what's best for the team, and what's best for you.

On August 4, Gail re-evaluated me. She deemed my body ready to play competitive beach volleyball again. I also saw Dan and Dr. Schobert, who both cleared me as well.

Now, it was time to rely on my two secret weapons: Dad and fitness coach Mike Rangel, the owner of PlyoCity and a huge proponent of plyometric training. First known simply as "jump training," plyometrics links strength with speed of movement to produce power. Several years before, Dad had seen Karch playing in a tournament and marveled at how much quicker, faster, and more explosive he was.

"You've turned back the clock five or six years! What are you doing differently?" Dad asked.

Only one thing—he was training with Mike. So Dad got in touch with Mike to inquire about the possibility of my training with him. And thus began one of the most important partnerships in my professional beach volleyball career. I've trained with Mike twice a week, seven or eight months a year, typically at Huntington Beach, since June 2002. Dad has been there, observing and participating, at almost every workout. We've trained on my birthday, Mike's birthday, holidays, on the road before tournaments, and the day after winning events. Why? Because that was the hellacious training schedule Karch was committed to, and I wanted to do everything he did because, in my mind, he was the best ever to play the sport. (Karch, who retired from competitive volleyball in September 2007, at forty-six, still trains with Mike, doing virtually the same routine he did when he was competing.)

Our workouts were just me, the sand, the sun, and medicine balls weighing between twelve and sixteen pounds. After stretching, I'd do about forty-five minutes of plyometrics—a series of hops, skips, and jumps. Mike gave me a short water break, then we went right back at it, working on volleyball drills for forty-five to ninety minutes. Passing. Setting. Hitting. Digging. From both sides of the court. We'd finish every workout with Mike's "suicide drills." He'd stand on a box on one side of the net, and I'd be on the other side. He'd toss a ball anywhere on the other side, even outside the court. I'd have to touch ten balls. It was a killer. Just imagine running back and forth across the court, twenty yards here, thirty yards there. As soon as I touched the ball, I'd have to stand up where I was, and he'd toss another ball. After "suicide drills," I'd take a break, and I'd practice serving. Or Dad and I'd work on some kind of individual stuff.

After two weeks off, per my healers' orders, I'd gone back to working with Mike to keep my conditioning and my volleyball skills on target for Athens. I exercised all of my skills without putting my body into full extension. I never hit a ball, never dove for a ball. I kept everything below my shoulders. Mike, Dad, and I devised a program that kept me aerobically fit, as well as retained my volleyball quickness, strength, stamina, and power, without aggravating my abdominals.

Sure enough, when I boarded that plane to Greece, I felt confident, healed, and ready to go. Kerri and Dane could tell, just by looking at me, that I was in great shape. Frankly, I think I surprised them both, because we hadn't seen each other in five weeks.

We arrived in Athens, wide-eyed and eager. We were like two kids in a candy store. We were staying aboard the *Queen Mary 2,* the magnificent ocean liner, which was exciting and glamorous. She was docked in Piraeus and used for two weeks as a hotel ship. British prime minister Tony Blair, President George H. W. Bush, and French president Jacques Chirac were among those aboard. The U.S. Olympic men's and women's basketball teams were living there, too. And it was just so much fun.

Three days before our first match, I hadn't taken a swing at a ball in practice in five weeks. Not one swing. Now, everybody on the outside began buzzing around, saying, "Uh-oh, Kerri and Misty are done!" No way. As Dad kept telling me, "Misty May at 80 percent would be as good as most players at 100 percent." Or to use the phrase Dad used to motivate me throughout the weeks leading up to the Games: "Just because you cut the rattle off a rattlesnake doesn't mean it's not a rattlesnake."


Just as in Atlanta and Sydney, the beach volleyball venue was the place to be in Athens. Raucous crowds packed the ten-thousand-seat stadium, located not far from Piraeus, and they were whipped into frenzies by energetic DJs, loud, pulsating rock music, and dancing girls from the Canary Islands dressed in silver hot pants. Van Halen, Tina Turner, the Monkees, with songs from *Zorba the Greek* mixed in.

It was inspiring.

We were seeded number one in the Olympic tournament. Twenty-four teams were split equally into six pools of four, with each team playing each other in a best-of-three match. We opened Pool A match play on the second day of competition, with a 21–9, 21–16 win over Chiaki Kusuhara and Ryo Tokuno of Japan in just thirty-five minutes. We looked as if we hadn't missed a beat.

At the beginning of the match, I dove on the back line for a dig, hopped up, and kept right on going. Like the Energizer Bunny. Throughout the match, I played very well, diving for balls, blocking at the net, even slamming some balls straight down off some great sets by Kerri. The victory was the perfect birthday gift for Kerri, who'd turned twenty-six that day.

Right from the start, it was clear to us that Athens might be more of a mental test than a physical one for our team. It had nothing to do with the expectations heaped upon us, but rather the large amount of time off between matches during pool play. The schedule was great for me because it gave me time to keep my abdominal strain in check. But it wasn't great for Kerri. A racehorse, she's always chomping at the bit.

We won our second match, two days later, posting a 21–11, 21–13 victory over Netherlands' number-thirteen-seeded Rebekka Kadijk and Marrit Leenstra. As a comparison, in winning an AVP tournament, Kerri and I would've played three matches Saturday and three Sunday, tipping off at 8:00 A.M., 11:00 A.M., and 2:00 P.M. In other words, we'd have finished our second match about four hours into the first day—not four days into the tournament, as we did in Athens.

"I was telling Misty this morning, I think this is going to be a test more of emotional and mental strength," Kerri said afterward. "When you have thirty-six hours to think about your next match, you can get a little headsy."

"Headsy" was Kerri's term for having too much pent-up energy.

We defeated Sona Novakova and Eva Celbova of the Czech Republic, 21–17, 21–17, in forty minutes to advance from pool play with a 3–0 record. We secured our top seed in the Round of Sixteen, the sixteen-team women's elimination bracket, which would begin the next day. The maddening, every-other-day match schedule was over.

Now, it was a single-elimination tournament—one loss and you're done—and the Olympic medals were within sight.

We opened the Round of Sixteen by defeating Wang Fei and Tian Jia of China, 21–11, 21–18. Next, in the quarterfinals, we defeated Guylaine Dumont and Annie Martin of Canada, 21–19, 21–14. And that set up a semifinal match between the two U.S. women's teams. We'd be facing the fourth-seeded Holly and E.Y. This meant that the U.S. women would be guaranteed at least a silver medal, after having failed to reach the medals podium in Atlanta and Sydney.

We were feeling confident about the matchup. We'd won sixteen of the previous nineteen meetings with Holly and E.Y. I knew Monday's semifinal match would be an emotional one for me and my family. Especially for Dad, who was the only person who'd accompanied me to Athens. My parents both had hoped, prayed, and believed that Holly and I'd get into the medal round in Sydney. It would've been such a sweet moment if Mom could've experienced my winning an Olympic medal before she'd passed away. But it wasn't meant to be. We'd finished a disappointing fifth. Mom had suffered through Holly's and my loss, so sick that she couldn't sit on top of the action in the stands, but instead had to find a seat, off to the side, in the shade. However, that didn't mean Mom was going to miss out on this Olympics. In fact, I was going to make sure she had the best seat in the house.

I was very nervous before the semifinals, which was very uncharacteristic for me. We'd gotten a manicure, and we'd asked that our nails be painted red, white, and blue. I'd tried to calm myself down by visualizing our match, as I did as a high jumper in high school, by listening to music on my iPod, including the Beatles and relaxing instrumentals you'd hear in a spa, and by reading a chapter from *The Da Vinci Code*. Worst of all, I couldn't eat, which is very unlike me.

We defeated Holly and E.Y., 21–18, 21–15, in forty-one minutes. I played like an absolute maniac: I raced around the court, chasing down wild shots and thrusting my hands, fists, and forearms in position to save rallies. They fought off two match points before Kerri chipped a left-side angle shot that rolled across the top of the net and dropped in the front corner, too far out of reach for Holly.

Afterward, Holly and E.Y. gave us hugs.

"Bring home the gold," E.Y. said. "We're expecting it."

"You deserve it. Go get it!" Holly said.

I really hated having to play another U.S. team, and especially Holly and E.Y., whom Kerri and I both liked and respected very much. I'd much rather have faced them in the gold medal game, not the semifinals. Of course, in the final, if there's one team you want to win, it's you.

After our semifinal victory, I sprinkled some of Mom's ashes on the court, then mixed them into the sand that Kerri and I had owned throughout the tournament. The ashes were in one of Mom's old prescription pill bottles—in fact, the label bore a prescription for medicine taken by cancer patients for nausea—and they'd been given to me by Dad. The whole tournament he'd been trying to get me to do it, but I kept saying, "Not yet, not yet." Finally, the moment felt right. I'd been waiting for it since she'd passed away in May 2002. Everyone else's family was there to watch them compete at the Olympics, why couldn't my Mom be, too?

We would play for the gold the following day, Tuesday, against Shelda and Adriana, who'd dominated Australians Natalie Cook and Nicole Sanderson, 21–17, 21–16, in an earlier Monday match. The Brazilians had won the silver in 2000.

"I am happy, but it isn't finished yet," Shelda said after their match.

Shelda and Adriana were the all-time winningest pair on the FIVB tour, with thirty-one victories. They were a team I'd looked up to since my days with Holly. They were the Peles of volleyball in Brazil. Kerri and I always had admired their style of play; we patterned ourselves after them. However, we led the series between the two teams, 13–7, and we'd won the last six straight matches after losing to them in the bronze medal match in Berlin last season. But they were looking to redeem their disappointment at winning silver in Sydney. They were very experienced, and they knew how to prepare for the big game. They'd played for an Olympic gold medal before, so they knew how to handle the pressure. We were certain they weren't going to fall easily.

Meanwhile, Holly and E.Y. would play Natalie and Nicole for the bronze.

From the beginning of the gold medal match, Kerri and I were in complete control. It was as if somebody (Mom?) had put wings on our feet. I was everywhere on the court, coming up with fifteen digs, never botching a serve, and repeatedly setting up Kerri well at the net. We won the first four points of the first game and were never threatened throughout, winning 21–17. Then, we trailed 3–4 in the second game before outscoring the former five-time world champions, 18–7, en route to a 21–11 victory. It took just forty-two minutes.

We'd worked perfectly together, in perfect harmony like Fred Astaire and Ginger Rogers. Kerri was the windmill at the net; I was the deceptive one, with the ability to look one way and tap the ball crosscourt to an open spot. When she backpedaled from the net, I slid forward to split the court in half. Kerri set the tone in the first game, shoving the ball down the Brazilians' throats. When Shelda and Adriana tried to work the back of the court, I retaliated by pulverizing them with kills or crosscourt winners.

We'd become the first U.S. women's team to win gold in beach volleyball, and along with Holly and E.Y., who'd won the bronze, became the first American women to medal in the sport. We were the most dominating team on the AVP and FIVB beach volleyball tours, and we were the most dominating team at the Athens Olympics, never losing a game in seven matches. Since forming our partnership in 2001, Kerri and I had gone 179–27 internationally with fifteen titles, and we had a 75–3 mark on the AVP tour, with thirteen titles.

Kerri fell to her knees, and I ran to embrace her. We both fell backward in the sand. I'd tackled the hell out of her, and I didn't care if I'd broken both of her knees in the celebration. After this, she was going to have lots of time to rest. Interestingly, the picture of us tackling each other in our bikinis raised quite a few eyebrows, and it became as talked about and as iconic as the photo of soccer star Brandi Chastain whipping off her shirt and exposing her sports bra to celebrate the USA winning the 1999 Women's World Cup. Ours was the photo of the Athens Olympics. It stunned people to see two women rolling around in bikinis, skin touching skin. But hey, when the U.S. softball players struck gold, they piled all over each other. We'd just won an Olympic gold medal! How should we have expressed our elation? By standing across the court from each other and giving the thumbs-up sign? By high-fiving each other? I don't think so. Get over it!

I found Dad in the packed stadium, and I darted toward him. I was so excited that I realized if I connected with him using our special version of a high five, a gentle, loving Buddhist forehead touch, I would have split our heads wide open. So I threw my arms around him instead. Then, it was Mom's turn to share in the gold medal celebration. I pulled out the prescription pill bottle and joyously sprinkled her all over the sand. Now, everybody in my family was there. My dad was there. My mom was there. That meant a lot to me. I don't think I would have ever gone to practice when I was a kid if it hadn't been for my mom. She worked with me a lot. She and Dad always made sure I had the best stuff, even though we couldn't afford it. They always brought out the best in me.

Suddenly, I felt a huge hole in my heart. I missed Mom very much at that moment. She had been a catalyst for Kerri and me becoming partners, and now she wasn't there to see her dreams become reality. She would have been so proud of me. She would have loved to put my Olympic gold medal around her neck. And she especially would have been excited to meet Matt. My heart ached. I felt sorry she'd never had the chance to share these things with me. At that instant, I would've traded everything, including the Olympic gold medal, if I could've touched her one more time.

Since she'd passed away, I felt as if she'd influenced my matches from heaven. There'd be no wind, or anything, and I'd hit a bad shot, and the ball would go over the net. It was very weird. I'd have no clue how I pulled it off. And then, I'd whisper, "Mom?" She loved playing volleyball so much that I figured she was still at it, batting the ball back and forth up above—and pulling strings for me down below. Throughout the Olympics, I felt as if she were the angel on my right shoulder. (I already had her initials, a pair of angel's wings, and a halo tattooed on my left shoulder.) I think she even had a hand in the performance of my tennis-playing cousin Taylor Dent, who's three years younger than I am. He'd won four Association of Tennis Professionals (ATP) singles titles during his career, but his most memorable performance occurred at the 2004 Olympics. He'd made a run all the way to the semifinals, losing to eventual gold medalist Nicolas Massu of Chile. Even more memorable was his bronze medal match against Chile's Fernando González, which he lost, 16–14, in the third set.

Mom, it seemed to me, was everywhere.

Dad was completely spent after the gold medal match. He was a big, mushy puddle of emotions. He'd reminisced often during the Olympics about how he and Mom had selected Kerri to be my partner. He'd talked about Mom a lot, he'd thought about her constantly. And he was so superstitious that once we started winning, he never took off his green Florida Marlins T-shirt. Dad had missed Mom deeply in Athens, even though he'd kept trying to argue that she wouldn't have totally enjoyed being there. Mom and I had stopped in Athens on a world cruise with my grandparents, when I was about eight years old, and it wasn't one of her favorite cities back then. There were (and still are) stray dogs and cats everywhere. Before the Olympics, to beautify Athens for the world stage, officials rounded up tens of thousands of strays and relocated them, and the thought of that would've driven Mom crazy.

Matt was pretty wiped out, too. He'd cried hysterically in his Colorado Springs hotel room, while receiving a play-by-play of the gold medal match from a reporter in Athens via telephone before preparing for a Pacific Coast League game between his Albuquerque Isotopes and the Colorado Springs Sky Sox. He estimated he'd cried for at least twenty minutes. Even when he watched the replay later, already knowing the outcome, he said his palms sweated profusely.

I kissed our engagement photo after the gold medal match, then I called Matt. And wouldn't you know it? He started tearing up again. The Isotopes had been on a twelve-game road trip during the Olympics, which meant Matt had to cheer me on from a variety of minor league baseball outposts. We'd phoned each other every day, at least once, just to stay, "I love you." But even if Matt could've somehow finagled a trip to Greece, he told me later he wouldn't have wanted to go. He said he'd wanted me to be able to concentrate on one thing, and one thing only, winning the Olympic gold medal.

Was I the only person who wasn't exhausted after the gold medal match? Was I the only one who wasn't blubbering away? Sheesh. For once, I bet I was more amped up than Kerri. I was flying high, floating on a cloud, living life at 310 percent, with an angel on my right shoulder. After Prince Albert of Monaco, a member of the International Olympic Committee, put the Olympic gold medal around my neck, I kissed it, and then I studied it. There was an angel on it, an image of "Winged Nike," the ancient goddess of victory. I decided it was a sign from Mom.

# 18

# Gold Medal Aftermath

One of our family friends, Rafer Johnson, the 1960 Olympic gold medalist in the decathlon, told Dad that winning a world championship changes your life, but that winning an Olympic gold medal means your life is never the same. I didn't truly comprehend what Johnson meant until I arrived home from Athens.

You know those TV commercials, with athletes at their moment of triumph answering that famous question, "You've just won the Super Bowl! What are you going to do next?" Well, my first stop after winning the Olympic gold medal wasn't Disneyland (although that is one of my favorite places on earth). Instead, I took a trip to Albuquerque, New Mexico, to see my future husband. Matt showered me with bouquets of flowers and balloons. I threw out the ceremonial first pitch in his Albuquerque Isotopes' 10–2 loss to the Colorado Springs Sky Sox in Isotopes Park. That was more nerve-racking than any of our matches in Athens.

After that, I had gigs scheduled on *The Tonight Show with Jay Leno, MTV Video Music Awards, Daytime Emmys, Today,* and a handful of other TV shows. And, every chance I got, I mentioned I was waiting for an invitation to host *Saturday Night Live.*

And then there was the rousing welcome-home surprise party,

attended by my family, friends, neighbors, and kids from down the block. Taped across my two-car garage was a big brown paper sign, with WE LOVE YOU MISTY! in red, white, and blue. The driveway was packed with people, including my Long Beach State head volleyball coach Brian Gimmillaro, my Newport Harbor High volleyball teammate Jeanette Hecker, and former Olympians Susie Atwood and Joan Lind Van Blom. Atwood, a swimmer, won a silver in the 200-meter backstroke and a bronze in the 100-meter backstroke in 1972. She's my insurance agent. Van Blom, a rower, won a silver in 1976 in single sculls and a silver in the coxed quad sculls in 1984. She's a member of the Long Beach Century Club.

I felt as if I were on that old TV show, *This Is Your Life.*

"What I say is that it takes a village to raise a child," Dad told the *Long Beach Press Telegram.* "Let the child do the work and have the village give her support. There are many people responsible for this."

It was a prelude of what my life was about to become, because in the first month after Athens, I wasn't home in Long Beach for more than three days total.

Believe it or not, before I could catch my breath, I was back out on the AVP tour. That's right, just nine days after we'd won the Olympic gold medal, Kerri and I played in a tournament in Chicago. We still had a domestic pro beach volleyball season to complete. Fueled by adrenaline, Kerri and I won the event, as well as the AVP's Las Vegas tournament a week later.


Our next trip, to Honolulu, Hawaii, two weeks later, for the AVP Best of the Beach Championships in Waikiki, was a homecoming for us Mays. It was the first time in twelve years the AVP tour had had a stop in Hawaii. It also was the first time Dad's extended family would get to see me play in person.

Only the 2004 AVP season's top men and women were invited. Unfortunately, my Hawaiian relatives weren't going to get a chance to see me and Kerri play together. The Best of the Beach event separates regular partners, with each player having a different teammate every match. It gives volleyball fans a chance to experience never-before teams and matchups, and it's also a lot of fun for us athletes to mix it up a bit.

Besides playing in the Best of the Beach, Dad and I had come to Hawaii for a more important reason, to fulfill Mom's dying wish that her ashes be scattered in various places she loved. Dad had waited two years to bring Mom home with him to Hawaii because he just couldn't bring himself to believe she was truly gone. It took him even longer than that to go through all of her belongings, give them to me, donate them to charity, or pitch them into the trash. Even today, her bedroom sanctuary has barely been touched. A part of him still thinks she's going to come waltzing through the door.

Sunday, the day after the tournament, our dearest friends and family members met in St. Louis Heights for a ceremony overseen by David Lyman, at the home of Gordon Pi'ianaia. Both were Dad's longtime friends. We scattered Mom's ashes in a beautiful spot overlooking Manoa Valley. Mom had loved it from the moment she saw it. As we threw the ashes out, they blew right back at us.

"Maybe Barbara doesn't want to leave," Lyman said.

We laughed, all covered in gray ashes, feeling Mom's presence.

From that moment on, we knew that whenever we were visiting the Hawaiian Islands, or we looked out over the Manoa Valley, it was just another peaceful way of saying, "Although we can't physically touch you, Mom, we know that you're spiritually present."

Three weeks later, in mid-October in Santa Barbara, we beat Holly and E.Y. in the final and wrapped up the AVP season. Despite the barrage of commitments away from the beach, and a lot of helter-skelter travel around the country, Kerri and I still were able to post a 14–1 match won-loss record and win three AVP tournaments post-Athens. I was proud of the way we were handling our new stature as Olympic gold medalists. Living in a fishbowl, being recognized everywhere, and having crazy, crammed schedules, was all very new to us. It took a lot of patience, smiling, and sleeping standing up to cope with it all, but it was well worth it.

In addition to all the perks, Kerri and I also had been thrust into the role of iconic figures in beach volleyball, and along with that lofty stature came great responsibility as role models and ambassadors. The day after winning in Santa Barbara, Kerri and I were in New York to accept the Women's Sports Foundation's Sportswomen of the Year award in team sports. Nine days after that, I was inducted into Long Beach State's 49er Athletic Hall of Fame. I squeezed in a stint as the celebrity grand marshal of the City of Bellflower Liberty Day Parade, and a few weeks later, it was announced I would be the grand marshal for the Belmont Shore twenty-second Christmas Parade in Long Beach.

When we first met, Matt and I had made a pact that we'd never morph into "star cravers." He hadn't changed, from the day he first was promoted to the majors by the Florida Marlins, June 2, 2004. I'd promised him then, and I'd promised him again after winning the 2004 Olympic gold medal, that I wouldn't ever change either. Not even if *Saturday Night Live* called. Hint. Hint.

# 19

## What's Next?

After we'd won the Olympic gold medal in Athens, we knew one wasn't going to be enough. Kerri and I were on such a high that we made the commitment to each other, right then and there, on the court in Greece, that, yes, we were going to try for a second gold medal at the 2008 Beijing Olympics. The decision was a no-brainer. We knew we could become the first beach volleyball team in history, male or female, to win back-to-back Olympic gold medals. And, after winning in Athens, we knew with absolute certainty that we had something very, very special, something that only comes around once in a lifetime. We'd captured lightning in a bottle, and we weren't about to let it go.

What we didn't know at our moment of triumph in Athens, though, was just how many different ways being the reigning Olympic gold medalists would affect, and change, our lives.

After Matt and I were married in November 2004, we tried for a couple of months to get pregnant, but nothing happened. In early 2005, I had to make a choice: "Do I, or do I not, push myself for four more years?" We had several discussions about our lives together, our goals for our family, and our dreams for our careers. We both realized we had a lot left to accomplish as athletes.

"Matt, since both of our careers are doing well right now, why don't we make the commitment to them?" I said. "I'll make the commitment for four more years, and then I'll be happy to step away for a little bit."

When you have children, one of the parents has to have his or her feet on the ground. Dragging kids all over the place isn't any fun. When you become a parent, your children should be your top priority. So Matt and I made the decision I'd try for the 2008 Olympics. That became our goal, and we stuck to it. We focused on making ourselves financially secure, so that after Beijing, I could afford to take time off.

Throughout 2005 and 2006, the addictive, post-Olympics rush kept Kerri and me going. We were more focused on perfection those first two years after we won the Olympic gold medal than at any other time in our partnership, because, now, instead of having to live up to expectations, we'd arrived.

Now, we were America's Golden Girls.

Now, we were beach volleyball's iconic team.

Now, we were simply Misty and Kerri.

Now, instead of being talked about in terms of promise and potential, we were being held to the highest standards possible.

At every tournament, domestically and internationally, we were the team to watch, and most important, we were the team to beat. The moment we stepped onto the sand, we had huge targets on our backs. As a result, we had to be at our peak all the time. We couldn't ever cruise. Because of that, we trained harder than ever, elevating our game to astronomical levels. We lived in an intense, demanding atmosphere, which at times became physically, mentally, and emotionally exhausting.

In 2005 and 2006, Kerri and I had extremely full competitive schedules, domestically and internationally, because every tournament wanted us in the field for media, marketing and sponsorship opportunities, and ticket sales. We thought of ourselves as ambassadors of the sport, and we believed it was important to compete in as many different cities and countries as possible, to best represent the United States. To prepare for our wild ride, I added new wrinkles to my training regimen, and almost instantly, I underwent a physical and emotional transformation. I became really happy and really passionate, about Matt, about our marriage, about volleyball, about my career, and I completely dedicated myself from a fitness standpoint.

In hindsight, I'd have to say Matt inspired those changes inside me. With him, I'd found my soul mate. Being more removed, time-wise, from Mom's death also helped buoy me. And, on top of all that, I was maturing beyond the athletic field.

First, I began working two or three times a week with Miriam Richter, the owner of Pilates Bodyworks in Coral Springs, Florida, where Matt and I had a home. I'd never tried Pilates before. With my past abdominal issues, I knew that I had to strengthen my core and increase my flexibility. I'd heard great things about Pilates. The program focuses on the muscles that keep the body balanced; they're essential to providing support for the spine. Each movement in Pilates incorporates six basic principles: control, concentration, centering, focus, precision, and breathing.

I discovered Miriam on the Internet and quickly realized I'd struck gold. Her résumé blew me away: She's a registered nurse from Johns Hopkins School of Nursing. She also has two degrees in psychology. She's a certified personal trainer with the National Strength and Conditioning Association, and she's a certified instructor with All-American Pilates. She teaches exercises that are designed to restore the natural curves of the spine ("neutral spine") and rebalance the muscles around the joints.

When I went in for my initial consultation, I explained to Miriam, in great detail, my abdominal injuries, as well as my body's strengths and weaknesses. Miriam asked me to demonstrate the various positions I put my body in when playing beach volleyball. Before our second session, she went online and studied photographs and videos of me, and other beach volleyball players, to get a better idea of movement patterns. With all of that information, Miriam then designed a Pilates program for me.

For example, to balance the strength and flexibility in my legs, so that I landed on both feet when I jumped (I tended to favor one

leg over the other), I lay on my back on the Pilates reformer, a platform that moves back and forth along a carriage. Resistance was provided by my body weight and by the springs attached to the carriage
and platform. I jumped up and off a padded footplate. It mimicked
jumping in the sand, but was much easier on my joints. To strengthen
my rotational muscles, she used specific Pilates exercises for me, plus
I invented a new move. On the reformer, I did side rotation, holding
cords in both hands, with specific spring resistance. On the Cadillac,
a six-foot-tall machine with leg and arm springs, fuzzy loops to hang
from, a push-through bar to stretch you out, and a trapeze, we did
lying flexion. I added some rotation to that exercise. Now Miriam
calls it "Misty's move," and she makes Matt do it, too.

Today, Miriam remains a vital member of my team, as well as a
close friend. Pilates has made me a better beach volleyball player. It
has helped stabilize my shoulders, correct my back issues, and given
me better posture. In long, grueling games on the beach, my body
doesn't disintegrate as much. All the rotational exercises I do really
help prevent abdominal muscle strain, especially when I dive in the
sand. Overall, my body's not as fatigued, not just after weekend tournaments, but as the seasons roll on.

I've even coaxed Dad into doing Pilates, reminding him that an
old dog like him can learn new tricks. I'll never forget the day we
trained at the beach, then went by Miriam's studio for our Pilates
sessions. I worked out with her first. Dad said he'd be next up. Then
he proceeded to lie down on a Pilates mat and fall asleep.

In addition to trying Pilates, I decided I needed to improve my
speed, acceleration and deceleration, explosive power, strength, and
sports specific movements. Next, I joined Cris Carter's FAST Program in Coral Springs, Florida, which trains top pro, college, and
Olympic athletes. I was assigned to Eddie Winslow, one of three staff
trainers. Carter, the former NFL wide receiver and current ESPN
commentator, eventually closed his business. Now, Eddie owns My
Speed Trainer (MST) Sports Performance in Margate, Florida.

From 2005 forward, from November until March, I've trained with

Eddie three or four days a week, two or three hours at a time. He says the progress I've made in just about every category is "above and beyond what the normal high-level athlete would achieve." In the beginning, Matt and I trained together, but Eddie quickly realized that, for domestic tranquility, it would be better for us to train separately. Next, he trained me with high-level male athletes, but I kicked their butts, too, and finally, he figured it was better just to train me individually.

Among high-level beach volleyball players, Eddie says, my training program is one of the most comprehensive ever. Case in point: I do full Olympic lifting, and my strength has greatly increased. At one point in 2008, I was squatting with 225 pounds. That's a lot for a woman, but that particular Olympic lift has helped tremendously with my jumping ability and my movements in the sand. Also, I feel faster and more explosive, thanks to Eddie's breaking down my running technique, then completely rebuilding it.

To supervise my training on the West Coast, I turned to Anya Tronson, who worked at the American Sports Center (ASC) in Anaheim, California. She was part of the facility's Competitive Athlete Training Zone (CATZ). She also was a performance trainer for the U.S. national men's indoor volleyball team. I happened to meet her when Matt and I were at ASC watching our niece Ashley Young-Treanor play basketball. Anya introduced herself and said, "Why don't you check us out the next time you're in town? We'd love your feedback." A few months later, I treated myself to one of Anya's hour-long "fitness sessions." I almost puked and died. How's that for feedback?

A former college soccer player and javelin thrower, Anya worked out right beside me, which made our sessions much more intense because she never stopped pushing. She's a five-foot-four dynamo, whose nickname is Teenage Mutant Ninja Turtle. She packs a big wallop, moving from one exercise to the next, mixing cardio, sprints, core, agility, and strength. Starting in 2005, we worked out three times a week in the preseason and twice a week during the season. Every workout was different, so my body never adapted. She estimated I burned a thousand calories per session, similar to an advanced cross-country skier.

From the get-go, Anya focused on improving my change of direction, flexibility, and core strength. She concentrated on movements that helped prevent injuries. I worked with medicine balls, core balls, Swiss balls, dumbbells, ladders, and rings. And oh, yes, "dollies," those flat little discs with wheels on the bottom. They were an ASC creation, great for core strength, but my least favorite piece of equipment.

Even Matt gave Anya's workouts a try. He was leery at first, but soon, he came into the facility, a cup of coffee in hand, and yelled, "Anya, let's get after this beast!" Typically, he got to the point in her workout where he was bent over, sweating profusely, and breathing heavily, and he shook his head and said, "Anya, I don't know about this." Of course, it was even more intense when Matt and I worked out together with Anya. It always turned competitive. Matt would try to beat me or Anya, or both of us—and he could, but only if he tried really, really hard.

Today, Anya says she's blown away by my work ethic, as well as my ability to understand my body.

Besides adding new trainers after Athens, I also added a new sport to my résumé—auto racing. In early April 2005, I participated in the Pro/Celebrity Race portion of the 30th Toyota Grand Prix of Long Beach, the city's biggest event, featuring Indy cars roaring through downtown at 200 mph. The ten-lap race through a 1.97-mile street circuit featured celebrities racing against pro drivers, as well as a few "buy-in" drivers. Everybody raced an identically prepped Toyota Celica vehicle. The pros spotted the celebrities thirty seconds at the start; after that, it was every driver for himself or herself.

I prepared for the event by spending three days at Danny McKeever's FAST LANE, in Willow Springs, California, the official racing school of Toyota Motorsports. The thing I loved most about racing cars was the discipline. It was much more mentally and physically demanding than volleyball. I'd recommend racing school for every teenager. If you missed a turn by the slightest of margins, you'd end up hitting the wall. I always was exhausted after a day at FAST LANE.

I realized I've got what it takes to race cars—I ended up finishing fifth overall, the top woman. I've got great reflexes and timing, thanks to Mom, and as Dad proudly says, I've got "a set of balls" (his contribution). The qualifying and the racing were super exciting for the spectators, but nerve-racking for us drivers, because both events were filled with chills, thrills, spills, and crashes. However, there were plenty of lighter moments, like when the organizers gave me a blowup doll with a Marlins cap because, they said, I was a "baseball widow." I shot back, "Don't say that! Matt's not dead!" I brought the doll back to my hotel, but in the middle of the night I saw it propped up against the wall, and it totally freaked me out. I jumped out of bed, punched the air out of it, stuffed it in a corner, and left it there.

Singer/actor Meat Loaf, who finished seventh, was good for a lot of laughs, quite the larger-than-life character, always trying so hard, but forever wildly grinding his gears. Of course, Dad and I instantly bonded with Meat. He stood up in the drivers' meeting before the start of race weekend and announced, "My name is Meat Loaf, and I'm the one to beat." So Dad, through Spadooza, an apparel company he owns, designed T-shirts for the forty staff members and twenty racers. On the front of everybody's shirt were the words BEAT THE MEAT. But on the back of Meat Loaf's T-shirt, Dad had written I AM THE MEAT TO BEAT. Meat loved that T-shirt. In the future, I'd like to race cars. I'm not sure what kind of cars, but I know I'd be good at it. In the meantime, in a charity auction, I won sessions at a NASCAR racing school for Matt and me.

Thank goodness I fortified myself with a strong team of trainers, a total body training regimen, and yes, even the challenge and discipline of auto racing, because the post-Athens Olympic gold medal onslaught was brutal. Over the course of 2005 and 2006, Kerri and I played in forty-five tournaments, which turned out to be the largest number of events over a two-year span in our careers. In 2005, we won eleven of fourteen AVP tournaments and six of seven FIVB tournaments. And although neither of us has ever paid much attention to streaks or statistics, on May 22, 2005, we became the second women's team to surpass the $1 million mark in combined earnings. In 2006, we won thirteen of sixteen AVP tournaments and three of eight FIVB tournaments. We were on the road, often for weeks at a time, from April to October.

After marrying Matt, who was playing for the Marlins, I split my time between our homes in Long Beach and Coral Springs. Because our beach volleyball and baseball seasons overlapped, we didn't see each other often or for very long. In the summers of 2005 and 2006, we were together about twenty days total during each of those periods. If I had a few weeks off between events, and the Marlins were playing in Florida, I'd fly there to be with him. That meant I wasn't in Southern California to practice with Kerri. So she'd practice with Dane, while Dad often flew to Florida to put me through my paces. Kerri, meanwhile, married Casey Jennings on December 4, 2005. I was one of her bridesmaids. They were luckier than us because their careers coincided. They always were together, at their Hermosa Beach home and on the AVP and FIVB circuits.

For all of our hard work and our hectic schedules, in 2005 and 2006, I earned $407,400 on the AVP tour and $232,200 on the FIVB tour, my two most lucrative seasons ever, prize-money-wise. In 2005 and 2006, I won the three biggest AVP awards: Best Offensive Player, Best Defensive Player, and Most Valuable Player. Plus, Kerri and I won Team of the Year, both years.

Because of the dramatic changes in our lives due to having won the 2004 Olympic gold medal, because of the stress and strain that came along with living in the spotlight and being on the front burner of the stove all of the time, success came at a cost: Midway through the 2006 season, Kerri and I began experiencing friction in our relationship and our partnership. It wasn't just one thing that caused the rub. It felt more like a hundred. The pressure of being America's Golden Girls, and the pressure of being Misty and Kerri, was starting to get to us.

Now, we were outdrawing the men's final at some AVP events.

Now, we were so well known that we were recognized when we

practiced at the beach, which often meant distractions in our workouts.

Now, whenever I went somewhere, to the grocery store, to Starbucks, to the gas station, I always got, "Where's Kerri?" And she heard, "Where's Misty?" People expected us to be joined at the hip. Kerri, who's admittedly more high-strung than I am, had trouble decompressing after tournaments because she couldn't get away from the crowds to find some inner peace.

"It's night and day different," Kerri told *Dig* magazine. "I don't think it's anything you can relate to until it happens to you. I never expected this. It's a great side effect of what we've done, and the fans are awesome. It's just that when you have a bad day, it gets tough, because they can be relentless. They'll follow you into the bathroom, follow you into the players' tent. People are so kind, but sometimes you have to say, 'No,' which is unfortunate. But you've got to take care of yourself. You've got to take care of number one, which is winning."

And I told *Dig*: "There are a lot of people out there who would love to trade spots, so I have nothing to complain about. But we are spread pretty thin. People don't see that. Sometimes they think we just come out here and play volleyball."

Adding to our pressure was the fact that we weren't winning as regularly on the international circuit. It was the sixth year of our partnership, and it wasn't an Olympic qualifying year, so quite honestly, we both were a bit bored. More than any other season, 2006 was a grind for the top men's and women's teams because, between domestic and international competitions, there were twenty-four weekend tournaments from March 31 through November 5. There were stretches where I saw Matt only two and a half days over the course of three months. Losing, plus being mentally and physically fried, opened up all kinds of cracks and fissures in Kerri's and my relationship. We weren't communicating well, on or off the court. We constantly seemed to be on each other's nerves. We weren't spending much time together, outside practices and competitions. We had reached a crossroad.

It's very unusual for professional beach volleyball teams, especially female teams, to stay together for long periods. More often than not, what breaks up a partnership is the fact that there's another team that's doing a lot of winning. Most of the teams Kerri and I have seen throughout our partnership have broken up because they've tried so hard to beat us and they've failed, perhaps even just once, so it was, "Uh-oh, this isn't working." And poof, somebody gets dumped.

Besides the frustration of not winning tournaments, another major factor in the breakup of teams is the inordinate amount of time the two players spend together. Being part of a professional beach volleyball duo is a little like a marriage. Day after day, week after week, month after month, season after season, you're together 24/7. It's difficult to be that close to someone who isn't your spouse.

Interestingly, men and women professional beach volleyball players handle their partnerships very differently. For men, it's performance first, earning a partner's acceptance second. For women, it's all about feeling the connection with your teammate, then it's about performing. There have been great men's teams that have played together for years but couldn't stand each other. For instance, there was a team of brothers at the 2000 and 2004 Olympics, Switzerland's Paul and Martin Laciga, who hadn't spoken to each other in years. Because every time one made a suggestion to the other, they'd imploded, they figured it was best not to say anything. Zilch. I can't see that happening with a top women's team. Female athletes need to feel a connection with every single athlete on their team. They need to have interpersonal relationships in order to feel more free to go out and perform.

Karch had a great partnership with Ken Steffes, and they won seventy-five tournaments together, and the first men's Olympic beach volleyball tournament in 1996, but they were very different and spent little time socializing off the court. When Karch did TV commentary for beach volleyball events, he says the things he heard the most, in talking to women players, were, "This year, the chemistry is so great," or "This year, we're such great friends." Karch says he "never gave a crap about chemistry." All he cared about was whether he and his partner were committed to being the best team they could be.

Rumors became rampant on the AVP and FIVB tours that Kerri and I were going to break up our partnership. None of them came from us. We heard all of the talk. "I think they should split up." "Kerri should play with Rachel [Wacholder]." Misty should play with E.Y." Never mind that there were strong rumors that Rachel and E.Y., clearly the number two U.S. team heading into Beijing, were breaking up, too. (They eventually did in August.) In the meantime, we had other female beach volleyball pros putting bugs in our ears. "If you break up, I'm available." And we got all sorts of critiques about our play, especially when we weren't winning as much on the 2006 FIVB tour.

In addition to all the rumors and behind-the-scenes chatter, E.Y. began putting some pressure on me to play with her. Being a friend of mine, she sensed the tension between Kerri and me. Clearly, E.Y. wanted to win an Olympic gold medal and she saw an opportunity for that. I told Dad that E.Y. had spoken to me about becoming my partner, and Dad, wise to the Kerri-Misty breakup talk, became involved in the drama, too. He's a driving force in the success I've had, but he often loses perspective when it comes to me. He's very close to it, wrapped up in it, and emotional about it. Instinctively, Dad knew how unhappy and unsettled I was. My aunt Bonnie says Dad has a sixth sense about me, that he can feel my emotions.

"You have to face your demons," Dad said. "You have to tell Kerri everything you're feeling."

"But I don't want to make waves," I replied.

"Misty, I like Kerri, I like Dane, I like Kerri's family, but this isn't about making friends," Dad said. "You're not out there to make friends. You're out there to win Olympic gold medals. We all want the same thing.

"You can't keep making the same mistakes as a team and expect to get over the hump. That's the definition of an F.A., a future alcoholic: Doing the same thing and expecting different results."

Meanwhile, Dad was thinking through all the scenarios, as well as studying the calendar and recognizing that Beijing Olympic qualifying was only a year away. At times, he'd told me that he thought E.Y.

was the best blocker on the beach, and he said it actually might be a good decision to partner with her. So he was in my head, saying, "If you change partners, you need to do it now. If you change coaches, you need to do it now. You've got to make something happen, Misty, if you want to win another Olympic gold medal."

And if all of that drama wasn't enough, in the early spring, Kerri suffered a miscarriage, and for months afterward, she was in a fragile state. She'd had her heart set on being pregnant the entire 2006 season, and I'd even told her, "Just let me know, we'll play together until you can't play anymore." When the miscarriage occurred, in March or April, Kerri was devastated. Over the course of several months, she'd endured a roller coaster of emotions. First, she'd had to make the difficult decision to put her successful career on hold to have a baby. Then she'd been excited to learn she was pregnant. Finally, she'd suffered a huge letdown when she miscarried. She was confused about why she'd lost the baby. She was angry that she now would have to wait until after the 2006 season, six months to a year, to get pregnant again, and she realized that that couldn't happen, if we wanted to go for our second Olympic gold medal in Beijing. She'd missed her current window of opportunity for having a baby.

Now, Kerri admits that, at that point, she "resented" her job. When she miscarried, she says, "everything changed" for her. Her attitude became: "If I'm out here, and I'm not having a baby, and I'm putting all of this on hold, then I need to win. I don't want to waste my time." She became incorrigible. In Huntington Beach, for instance, she was overly irritated by a 19–21, 21–12, 15–13 victory over Holly and Nicole Branagh in the third match of the tournament. She'd thought the win was much too tight, and afterward told the media, "This match won't be out of my head for two weeks."

Never mind that we ended up winning the tournament over E.Y. and Rachel. The victory also made me only the second woman to go over the $1 million mark in earnings. (Holly was the first to do it.)

Today, Kerri says her resentment toward her job and her over-the-top drive for the perfect victory was "a terrible mind-set by me."

Truth be told, her mind-set put a lot of stress on our partnership, and especially on me.

All of these elements came together to cause the perfect storm, two weekends later, June 9 to 11, at the AVP tournament in Hermosa Beach. I'll never forget the moment of convergence. We were struggling in the third match, against Tyra Turner and Makare Wilson. I was playing defense, and I asked Kerri to respond a certain way on the court. I don't express my feelings very much, on or off the court, so I had asked, "Can you just wait on your block a little longer?" Instead of responding with a yes, she snapped at me, saying, "Well, why don't you just worry about your defense?"

I wasn't being critical or accusatory. I just asked her to make a change to help me out. After her response, I shut down completely. I thought, "I'm not going to say anything." That wasn't very mature of me, but that was in keeping with my lack of communication skills. Overall, partnering with Kerri had helped teach me to better communicate in real life, but expressing my feelings is still difficult for me. I'm a people pleaser; I go with the flow. Nothing seems to irritate me, and then it builds up and builds up, and all of a sudden, something sets me off, and I'll lose it. Which is exactly what happened: I exploded on the court. And I kept right on simmering through our match, which we ended up winning, 22–24, 21–19, 15–8, in just under an hour.

In this instance, my mistake with Kerri was that I'd kept my feelings bottled up inside, for weeks and weeks at a time. Throughout our partnership, I'd never blown up at Kerri. I'd never even come close. This was the first, and only, time. It was a learning experience for me, for a couple of reasons. It taught me to always let Kerri know how I'm feeling, to communicate earlier rather than let it fester. It taught me nobody, not Kerri, not Matt, not Dad, not even my friends, can read my mind. Kerri always asks me, "What do you want to say, Misty?" She tries to pull things out of me. Sometimes, I just don't know how to say things. I don't want them to come out wrong. Most important, it also taught me that Kerri needs to be talked to differently from me. I respond to constructive criticism in a very different way from Kerri.

She's much more like a woman, in that her feelings can get hurt. I, on the other hand, am much more like a man, thanks to how Dad always has spoken so frankly to me. I have always been talked to as an athlete, and honest, blunt criticism has always been normal to me.

That day, things came out the wrong way: I cursed at Kerri, and there were some F— Yous in the box after the game. I know people sitting in the stands heard my tirade. It wasn't my proudest moment. I was wrong for losing it. When the match was over, Kerri and I sat in the shade, and we talked it all out. What we learned was that, underneath all the rumors and behind-the-scenes chatter about us, our partnership, our playing, and our training, underneath all of the different emotions we'd both been experiencing over recent weeks, she and I both were frustrated with Dane. But we'd been too afraid to say anything about him to each other. In talking about our feelings, we discovered that we both were worried that we weren't evolving as a team, and that we were fearful we wouldn't stay on top, or be in the position to win a second Olympic gold medal, if we didn't continue to grow.

At various times, Dad had tried to talk to Dane about changing things, but he was very resistant, which caused friction and flare-ups between them.

"Why do I need to change things?" he'd say to Dad. "They're the best team in the world."

"Because if other coaches take a look at this, they're going to pick on this thing and that thing, and they're going to exploit it," Dad would argue with him. "You've always got to make adjustments."

In fact, Dad got so fed up with Dane's inability to grow as a coach and take us to new levels that after my blowup with Kerri at Hermosa Beach, he actually told Liz Masakayan, who coached E.Y. and Rachel, the best way to beat us.

"Why would you tell me something like this, Butch?" Liz asked.

"Because otherwise we'll never see a change, Liz, until they see their noses rubbed in it," Dad replied.

"This is what I would do if I were coaching against them," Dad began, and then he spilled the beans. Afterward, he told me what he'd done.

Dad recounted: "I told Liz, 'Serve Kerri twice on her left and then serve Misty. Because Kerri is used to Misty getting served, on the contact of the serve, Kerri always moves to her right. She was an opposite hitter indoors. So if you serve Kerri to her left, she'll be a step away from it. And only give Kerri two serves in a row each time, because she always thinks they were errant serves, that boy were you lucky. Then, wait a couple balls and go back to Kerri's left.'"

I just shook my head at my nutty father.

"Bring it on!" I replied.

Sure enough, E.Y. and Rachel beat us in the final.

Having that blowup in Hermosa Beach and then sitting down together and pouring out our hearts was an important step in the growth of our partnership. It was a big deal for me to finally admit to Kerri that I wasn't getting what I needed from Dane. In fact, I told her if we were going to continue playing together, we needed to change our coach. She was a lot closer to him than I was, and all along I'd thought if I told her what I was feeling, she might become defensive. Most teams are too quick to break up, but we decided we were going to work through this rough patch together.

Why would you ever want to break up a team that was on its way to being the greatest combination in the history of the game? With Kerri and me, it was very special. So we recommitted to Beijing, to each other, and to winning a second gold medal. We'd needed to reconfirm our goals, our dreams, and our friendship. We'd realized it was us, just us, together. And we'd recognized we were stronger together than we were apart. At the end of the 2006 season, we agreed, we'd have to let Dane go.

While Kerri and I might have had different personalities on the court, it was clear, the more we talked it out, that we had the same dreams and aspirations. While we might have had different likes and dislikes off the court, we had the same goals and values. We loved and respected each other. And, there were, and still are, no two better business partners in all of professional sports. From that moment forward, it was: Beijing, till death do us part!

# 20

# STARTING OVER

I n the beach volleyball world, every major decision goes through Karch. He is the Obi-Wan Kenobi of the sport, the Jedi Master of the sand, reminiscent of the wise, exalted character in the *Star Wars* universe who teaches Luke Skywalker the ways of the Force. He's all-knowing, all-seeing.

Yet, instead of approaching Karch and asking for his thoughts about who we should hire as our new coach, Kerri and I took the bold step of asking him if he'd coach us. We'd been chasing the Legend, so why not learn from him? After all, he was the best ever in the sport. Unfortunately, he had too many family and TV commitments, but luckily he turned us on to Troy Tanner.

Troy was a member of the U.S. men's national indoor volleyball team that won the gold medal at the 1988 Summer Olympics in Seoul, South Korea. After the Olympics, he played in an international pro indoor league (Rome, Italy; Zagreb, Croatia; and Osaka, Japan). From 1992 through 1998, he competed in pro beach volleyball, domestically and internationally. While earning his master's in mass communications at Brigham Young University, he was an assistant coach for the Cougars' men's volleyball team for five years and part of two NCAA Championships. Then he spent four years on the coaching staff of the U.S. national men's indoor team and had been named an assistant coach for that team at the Beijing Olympics. He also was head volleyball coach at Junipero Serra High School in San Juan Capistrano, California.

Kerri contacted Troy and asked if the three of us could meet when I returned to Southern California for training. Troy was floored by the call—he'd been out of beach volleyball for years—but he agreed to get together, and to better prepare for our meeting, he asked Kerri to send video of us in competition over the past few years.

In January 2007, Kerri and I met Troy at Huntington Beach, and we talked about our goals, our concerns, and most important, what we wanted from a coach. Troy made the observation that while we were still dominant domestically, we were dipping internationally because the women on the international tour were getting better. He told us we'd have to improve in order to keep beating them, and he said he'd studied a lot of video and had found areas in which we could get markedly better. He proceeded to show us video clips of those female players he thought were the best in the world at using various skills. Then he showed us clips of us using those same skills. Surprisingly, we were inconsistent in many aspects of the game.

On day one, it was all business, which set the tone of our relationship going forward. Immediately, Troy began working on revamping our game. He wanted to simplify our skills, break them down to the most basic level, and work at a slower pace to make sure that later, at competition speed, they'd be as crisp as could be. I felt comfortable with his coaching technique because Dad always has trained me that way.

"Here are the mechanics of volleyball," Troy said, starting with fundamentals. "We can tighten up all of this stuff and become better."

Troy thought we were in great physical shape and we had the strongest minds in the game. However, he felt our confidence had been shaken in 2006 by our international losses. He believed that by refining our skills and changing some of our mechanics, as well as having him give us detailed scouting reports of our opponents, we wouldn't just grow and improve as a team, but once again we'd be in the driver's seat on the way to a 2008 Olympic gold medal.

How could we have gotten so lackadaisical about our skills? Maybe because we hadn't practiced the right things. Maybe because we hadn't broken down the game as much as we needed. Maybe because we hadn't analyzed ourselves to see what skills we could improve. In 2004, as we were one of the younger teams, our training sessions had included a lot of playing time. Nothing was slowed down. It was all at competition speed. We didn't back off and break down each skill. For us, at that time in our careers, that's what worked. When I was in college, I was used to the same practice warm-up routine every day. It was a progression. You'd start out passing. Then you'd get into team passing. You'd build one skill onto another. Then you'd add a little more, and add a little more to that. That's what you should be doing on the beach, too.

Over the next several days, we met with Troy at the beach, studied video, then put his suggestions into action in training sessions. We already saw ourselves making improvement. Having a new perspective on our game, Kerri and I both recognized, was doing us good. Troy, too, said he was happy with how well we were responding to him. I'm a visual learner. I can make adjustments through audio cues, but not as successfully, because I can't see it or feel it. That was the beauty of Troy's style: He slowed us down so much that we were able to feel what we were doing. We could watch each other grow and redevelop—not only our game but our team chemistry. Just by slowing things down, by challenging ourselves to develop our skills again, so we each had to focus on the other. It was, "I need to do this in order to make Kerri better, and she needs to do this in order to help me out and make me better."

So as we evolved, so did our coaching. At different times, different coaches are the right fit for you.

"Let's go forward with this," we told Troy, a week into the trial period.

"Okay, we've got to put a contract in place because I have to quit my job," Troy said. "I have to leave the U.S. national team. I have to leave my high school, where I'm still coaching and teaching physical education."

We hammered out a two-year deal for Troy that would take the three of us from early January 2007 through the 2008 Olympics. From that point forward, we trained with him four or five days a week in the preseason, and then, because our AVP and FIVB tour schedules were daunting, we trained twice a week during the season. Most of the time, we'd meet Troy at Emerald Bay, a private community in Laguna Beach. There, we had privacy, nobody coming by and asking for autographs during our training. We'd stretch on the sand while watching dolphins jumping in the Pacific Ocean. Once, we even saw a whale. The locals brought their dogs down to the sand and ran along the water's edge. It was just a nice setting.

We'd get going around 8:00 A.M., often practicing against guys, including Karch, Steve Obradovich, Tom Pestolesi, and Jay Hosack. We'd finish up about 10:30 or 11:00 A.M., and at that point, Kerri and I would head off in different directions, to other workouts (Pilates, weightlifting and core training, cardio work, Mike Rangel's plyometrics, and so on), bodywork (massage, Hellerwork, chiropractic, and so on), or media interviews, photo shoots, or marketing and sponsorship commitments. Most days, I was in my car, driving all over Southern California, from 7:00 A.M. until 7:00 P.M.

Because Troy had heard our partnership was strained in 2006, he also emphasized improving the emotional side of our game. He talked about our having common goals, about our winning a second Olympic gold medal, about our dominating the sport, and about our setting records that would never be broken. He talked about what all of that would mean to us in terms of our legacy, not fame- and fortunewise, but personally. He talked about what it would mean to us in our hearts and souls.

Troy said that he felt our families, especially my father and Kerri's mother, both of whom were driven, demanding, and opinionated, were adding more stress to an already pressure-packed situation. He was right. Truthfully, in many ways, they were more consumed with our winning a second gold medal than we were: Dad wanted it for me; Marge wanted it for Kerri. Troy instructed us to tone down our families' expectations.

"Despite our differences, and no matter what our fathers, our mothers, or our groups are saying, they are getting in the way," Troy told us. "Everybody must be united in a common goal."

Now, I realize that Troy spent a portion of the beginning of each practice helping us bond with each other. We'd sit off to the side, stretching and chit-chatting, talking about what we had planned for that day (and what we'd done the night before), laughing and giggling, and often we'd start practice ten or fifteen minutes late. To an outsider, I'm sure it looked like an utter waste of time, but I really believe it was the best-spent time of our workouts. Those ten or fifteen minutes helped us get back our team chemistry. Although we were the best team in the world, Troy understood we still needed our time to bond, we still needed our social time, and he built that right into our warm-up.

When I first began training with Troy, a couple of flaws really stood out, the most obvious being that I was an inconsistent passer. He harped on it from the first video session. He showed me over and over on video, "Here's what you're doing," and the video was a real eye-opener. I'm very open to listening to input; I'm always trying to pick up new things.

In addition, Troy worked extremely hard to find my favorite approach angle, because, he pointed out, at times I was approaching with my right foot, or what is called being "goofy footed." Footedness in sports refers to an athlete's preference for putting the left or right foot forward, and most often is used in skateboarding, snowboarding, and wakeboarding. Regular stance, regular foot, or simply "reg" refers to a boarder for whom it feels natural to ride with the left foot in front. This stance is called "regular" because it is found more commonly among participants of these board sports. The opposite is called "goofy foot," which refers to athletes who prefer to lead with the right foot.

Troy wanted me to approach the same way every time. He wanted me to approach from the right side, always planting my left foot forward—left, right, left—even though I might get a little bit crossed up. He wanted a standard approach because, he believed, doing it differently every time threw me off. The normal indoor approach is to take the big stride with the right leg and close with the left. If you're right-handed like me, the order of your last three steps should be left-right-left. If you're left-handed, the order of steps is exactly the opposite, right-left-right. When a right-handed hitter approaches right-left-right, that's referred to as "goofy footed." That's what I used on the beach (so did Karch), because I felt it helped me attack the line better. Troy said my goofy footedness meant extra ground contact, albeit very slight, which cost me in the height and force I got in my vertical leap. Goofy footers, he said, took longer to get up in the air and hit the ball less hard.

Troy did plenty of tweaking with our other skills. Take setting, for example. He showed Kerri and me video of how we were setting when we were in control of our game. Then he pointed out the inconsistencies. Again, he said he wanted to define how we were going to set the ball, time and time again. Was it going to be left foot forward? Was it going to be right foot forward? Troy and I decided that I'd do it right foot forward every time, unless I couldn't get my right foot forward.

While Troy and I were refining my skills, I solidified my goals in my mind. Not only did I want to be the most physically dominant player in the sport, but mentally I always wanted to be a second or two ahead of my opponents. I'm already a step ahead, I believe, thanks to my unique ability to see and feel what my opponent might do. But now, I wanted to be a step ahead of everybody in the sand, too. I never, ever wanted to be caught off guard.

To achieve that goal, after working out with Troy, later in the day, Dad and I would meet Mike Rangel at Huntington Beach and go through his killer plyometric beach volleyball boot camp. When Kerri and I were going through the rocky period in our relationship, one of the things that helped me get through all of the emotions was focusing on Mike's conditioning sessions.

Every time Mike mentioned he'd given Karch a new drill, I had to do it, too. When I changed my passing in 2006, I went to Karch's workouts with Mike and watched him pass for hours. I mastered the brutal "Twenty Drill," because Karch had mastered it. Mike stood on one side of the net, serving the ball to Karch on the other side. Karch had to pass twenty balls out of twenty serves. He has done twenty out of twenty a couple of times. The best I've ever done is eighteen out of twenty. Mike says the average elite player gets nine, maybe ten.

After every practice, I always thanked Mike for his hard work, and of course, I teased him about being a dead ringer for *Baywatch* actor David Hasselhoff. One season, there were seven AVP tournaments in a row where I gave Mike the business, tacking up a sign on a bulletinboardnearthetournamentschedule: COME MEET DAVID HASSELHOFF SIGNING AUTOGRAPHS IN FRONT OF THE LADIES ROOM.


Kerri and I approached the 2007 season as a work in progress. New coach. New skills. New attitude. That mind-set served us well in Miami, Florida, when we lost in the semifinal of the season's debut event on the AVP tour to number two team E.Y. and Nicole in just forty-three minutes. We didn't panic. We just stuck to our game plan and knuckled down. We went on to win the next two AVP events, beating E.Y. and Nicole in both, first in Dallas, then in Huntington Beach.

In addition to refining our skills, Kerri and I believed that the other aspect of our partnership that could improve was our communication, both on and off the court. After a rough 2006 season, and just three tournaments into the 2007 campaign, we were beginning to see the fruits of our labor in that arena, too.

"It was a tough year," Kerri told *USA Today,* referring to the challenges our partnership endured in 2006. "It was the first time it really felt like a business. We never saw each other off the court. We didn't have that friendship or intimacy going."

Although I was notorious for not being a great communicator, Kerri also admitted to *Dig* magazine that she'd had to work on her own communication skills.

"Casey [Jennings, her husband] and I have talked a lot about Misty and my personality on the court," she told the magazine. "I'm the cheerleader, and Misty is very quiet, and I sometimes go agro and overcompensate. Casey has pointed out that I may not be helping Misty by doing that, and it's definitely not helping me. He's very tactful. I'm a sensitive girl."

After that, we went on a tear, winning eight consecutive AVP tournaments, including the Hermosa Beach event in mid-May, where our victory over Tyra Turner and Rachel in the final added another credential to my résumé—the winningest female player in beach volleyball history. The victory in Hermosa Beach was my seventy-third, which surpassed the previous record held by Holly. After the record-breaker, I told the fans who hung around for our victory ceremony that while records were great, I preferred keeping a low profile.

"I don't like to be the center of attention, unless I'm on the dance floor," I joked.

Our victory in the AVP event in Louisville, Kentucky, a week later, provided us motivation for the rest of the 2007 season, thanks to E.Y.'s comments to the *Louisville Courier-Journal*.

"They've been my rivals for several years," E.Y. told the newspaper. "We want to win tournaments. In order to do that, we have to beat them. . . . It's not like anyone is afraid of them anymore."

Oh, yeah? I saved that sports section—I still have it in my archives—because it was such great bulletin board fodder. All told, in 2007, we won thirteen of fifteen AVP tournaments.

In the meantime, internationally, we re-established our dominance. We won seven of eight tournaments, including the 2007 FIVB World Championship in Gstaad.

Because our main goal was to qualify for Beijing, as in the two years leading up to Athens, we wanted to concentrate on playing in FIVB rather than AVP tournaments, because that's where the qualification points from our eight best finishes were earned. We also wanted to accumulate our qualification points as quickly as possible. Word got out that we planned to skip the AVP event in Charleston, South Carolina, in mid-June, to play in the FIVB event in Korea. We thought it was important to play overseas to see and get a feel for our competition before playing in the Grand Slam in Paris, the following weekend. Grand Slams were worth double qualification points, and we didn't want to blow that opportunity. However, the AVP put pressure on us to play domestically, threatening legal action against us if we didn't live up to our contractual obligations. So because we didn't want to get sued, we grudgingly played in Charleston, then jetted off to Paris. We won both tournaments, by the way. And I indulged myself with my Parisian favorites: coffee and Nutella crepes, every day after I was done playing. Oh, that creamy chocolate hazelnut spread. Decadent and divine.

Just as in the years leading up to Sydney and Athens, the Olympic qualifying schedule was outrageous and exhausting.

Kerri and I had very different ways of keeping ourselves grounded. She loved to read. Or should I say speed read? She had an ability to go through books like no other. She'd often get up early in the morning, walk around whatever city we were in, find a little café, and pull out a book. She also loved to go shopping. I can't believe how she was able to fit into the types of clothes she did—I don't think I've ever been that skinny, not even at birth. She always looked amazing; I could never see myself wearing what she can.

Meanwhile, I'd keep myself entertained by watching complete DVD collections of Showtime's *Weeds*, ABC's *Desperate Housewives*, and HBO's *Carnivale*. I loved to stay at the tournament site all day—I couldn't tell you what I did because I have no clue—and I enjoyed hanging out with our medical staff. I also got a kick out of recording video travelogues of our trips, creating skits complete with characters and accents from the countries in which we happened to be playing. I especially enjoyed recording running gags about going in search of my favorite Starbucks nonfat vanilla lattes in all corners of the globe. Nicole Branagh was my coproducer.

There never was a time we didn't come to play. The best example of our keen mind-set occurred at the 2007 World Championships in Gstaad. We were in the throes of a long, grueling stretch of tournaments. We'd already played thirteen weeks in a row, in a combination of AVP and FIVB events. We'd just won in Montreal, Berlin, and Long Beach, where I was so whipped I'd told the *Long Beach Press Telegram,* "I could use a personal time-out," before running to catch another plane. Now, here we were, in the final at Gstaad, getting ready to face the number one Chinese team Tian Jia and Wang Jie. A month earlier, we'd beaten them in an FIVB event in Paris. Then, the following week, they'd beaten us, in the rain, in the semifinals in Stavanger, Norway, in what would turn out to be our only loss on the FIVB tour in the 2007 season.

When he awakened the morning of the Gstaad final, Troy wondered if, after more than three months of running around the world and always raising our performance to the highest levels, we'd be sharp enough to pull out another victory. He recalls saying to himself, "After all these weekends in a row, and these two tough FIVB Grand Slam wins, now they're going into the final against the best China has to offer. It would be so easy for them to be tired and out of it."

Sure enough, we crushed Tian and Wang, 21–16, 21–10, in thirty-nine minutes for our third straight FIVB World Championship. It was a victory to savor, not just at that moment, but later when we were in Beijing.

It also was a weekend to savor, because of our American sweep, with Phil Dalhausser and Todd Rogers, the top U.S. men's team, capturing the men's gold medal. It was the first time in history a Brazilian men's team wasn't on the world championship medals podium. And there was another reason it was a beach volleyball event unlike any other. More than a hundred thousand spectators had converged upon Gstaad to witness the most important international tournament in the qualification process for Beijing.

In addition to $1 million in prize money, the tour stop also offered double qualification points. Plus, Gstaad boasted a twelve-thousand-plus-seat stadium, which rivaled the Chaoyang Park Beach Volleyball Stadium, the Olympics venue in Beijing.

Our 2007 season statistics were mind-boggling. We'd compiled a match record (international and domestic) of 129–4 and a set record of 258–25. Kerri and I were named Sportspersons of the Year by the FIVB. The AVP named us Team of the Year, and we won the Crocs Cup Championship, given to the most outstanding team on the AVP circuit. And of course, we'd also reached our ultimate goal: We'd qualified as one of the United States' two women's beach volleyball teams for Beijing—the other was E.Y. and Nicole—leading all women's teams in qualifying points.

# 21

# Second Olympic Gold Medal

As soon as the 2008 calendar year began, we felt the Olympic gold medal pressure mounting. It was much more intense than four years before, because, this time around, we were one of the best beach volleyball teams in history, male or female, and we were heavily favored to win. The demands, the expectations, the opportunities, the aspirations, all were ratcheted up a hundred times. This time around, we were simply Misty and Kerri. This time around, we were trying to make history.

Adding to the pressure we were feeling was the fact that Kerri still was struggling to regain strength in her right shoulder, after having had rotator cuff surgery in November 2007. Dr. Schobert also had removed bone spurs, bone chips, and scar tissue. She hadn't taken any hard-driven balls in practice in January, February, or March, and so as we neared the beginning of the AVP and FIVB tours, she wasn't ready. In my opinion, we didn't have to play any 2008 regular-season tournaments, at home or abroad. We could wait until Beijing to step onto the sand, if that's what Kerri's shoulder dictated. After having struggled with abdominal problems before the 2000 and 2004 Olympics, I knew full well that if we wanted to win the gold medal, we both had to be 100 percent healthy.

But Kerri, being Kerri, wanted to push it. I relented a bit, suggesting we use the first AVP event in Miami in mid-April as a test run for her shoulder. If that tournament taught us it would be better for Kerri's shoulder to play every other weekend, then that's what we'd do. But she had to promise to be honest with me. I told her she had to promise to tell me if she needed a break.

"Our success in Beijing is dependent upon your pacing yourself," I impressed upon Kerri.

Well, we bolted right out of the starting gate, coming on like gangbusters and winning three straight AVP tournaments. But what's that old saying about the best-laid plans? On Sunday, May 4, the day after we'd won our third title, in Huntington Beach, Kerri's shoulder flared up in the twenty-five-thousand-dollar Cuervo Gold Crown series winner-take-all event, a playoff of the top four teams in the points standings. We withdrew after beating Annett Davis and Jenny Johnson Jordan in a morning semifinal, sending shock waves through the beach volleyball world.

"If she needs to pull out, pull out," I told the Associated Press. "If we're going to do this, we're going to do this together. . . . She needs to take the appropriate measures and make sure she's okay because there's a bigger goal in mind."

Kerri proclaimed she'd be ready to play the following weekend, in Charleston, South Carolina, going so far as to predict she'd be "good to go" by Thursday. However, the day before her self-imposed deadline, her shoulder wasn't any better, so we withdrew. Then we skipped an FIVB event in Seoul, South Korea.

When we finally returned to the AVP tour, May 24, in Louisville, Kentucky, Kerri's shoulder was good to go. We sailed through the tournament. And from there, we kept right on going, winning six straight AVP events and three consecutive FIVB Grand Slams over the next two months, including a victory over China's number one team, Tian and Wang, in the final in Berlin, 21–18, 22–20, in forty-five minutes. While we'd been called the greatest female beach volleyball team of all time, now we had another title to prove it: By winning the Berlin

Grand Slam, we'd earned our thirty-second career FIVB World Tour gold medal, surpassing legendary Brazilian tandems Shelda Bede and Adriana Behar and Emanuel Rego and Ricardo Santos.

Most professional athletes look at the Olympics, the Super Bowl, the World Series, the NBA Finals, or any other major championship in their particular sport as one of the goals they've set for themselves, and they'll check it off their list when they reach it, then keep moving forward in their career. They don't take the time to enjoy the entire experience, or understand its full meaning, because they're so focused on winning. They don't see the beauty and the majesty that surrounds them because they've got blinders on. They forget to open their eyes and ears, their hearts and souls; they forget to be in the moment, to drink it all in, to embrace every last ounce.

Since I'd already won an Olympic gold medal, I decided to approach Beijing as one of life's blessings. I was going to revel in the experience. If Kerri and I ended up winning a second gold medal, that'd be great. If we tried our best, but came up short, that'd be fine, too. For me, the 2008 Olympics were about creating lifetime memories.

A few weeks before leaving for Beijing, Kerri and I were among a dozen or so Olympic and Paralympic athletes invited to the White House, July 21, for a send-off party hosted by President George W. Bush and his wife, Laura. It began with a reception in the Rose Garden, and we looked like such all-American kids, decked out in USA polo shirts and blue jeans. He urged us to "compete swifter, higher, stronger," but also to be mindful that we would be "ambassadors of liberty" to the people of China and elsewhere. Afterward, we separated into groups for media interviews.

"Follow me this way!" President Bush said.

"But we have an interview to go to," we replied.

"I want to see you in the Oval Office!" he insisted.

Seriously, how can you argue with the leader of the free world?

So several of us followed the president to the Oval Office, where he happily gave us a personal tour, telling us about his desk, saying that President Roosevelt had installed a front panel, so nobody knew he was sitting behind it in a wheelchair. He told us every president is allowed to decorate the Oval Office in his own style, then proceeded to talk about interior design from the carpeting up.

Eventually, we got around to formal introductions. We'd been instructed to say our name and our sport, then step aside so we could have our pictures taken with the president. Well, I was the last athlete in the group to meet him.

Kerri went before me.

"Hi, Mr. President, thank you for inviting us to the White House. I'm Kerri Walsh," she said.

President Bush smiled and mimicked hitting a volleyball.

Kerri nodded that, yes, he'd gotten it exactly right.

"Hi, Mr. Bush, thank you for having us, my name is Misty May-Treanor," I said.

"What do you do?" he asked.

"Oh, I play beach volleyball," I said. "I play with Kerri Walsh. I play defense."

And then, to help remind him of who I was and what I look like on the court, I gave him a good example of the camera shots the TV guys always take of me in my defensive stance: my backside. I bent over in front of him, put my hands on my knees, and stuck out my butt, ever so slightly.

"Doesn't this look familiar?" I joked.

"Oh, I know who you are," he said, chuckling, "You're the one with the tattoos."

From that point on, the Prez and I were buddies.

I couldn't help thinking, as I was waiting in the receiving line to shake his hand, about Forrest Gump's presidential moment. When Forrest shakes President Kennedy's hand, he says, "I've gotta pee." After I'd stuck out my butt, I thought, "Who in their right mind bends over in front of the president of the United States and asks, 'Doesn't this look familiar?' What was I thinking?" Oh, well. That's just me.

It was a day to remember, no ifs, ands or butts. I'd never been to the White House before. I'd always been competing when presidents had hosted the Olympians after the Games. The celebratory homecoming event hadn't ever fit into my schedule. So it was very nice. We toured the White House, complete with all the history lessons. It's a lot bigger than you think.

As Kerri and I were leaving to go back to the hotel to change into dressy clothes for the dinner event that evening, we spotted a ball on the East Lawn. We simultaneously gasped: "A volleyball!" We grabbed it and started peppering on the lawn. What a thrill. A couple of Secret Service agents told us the volleyball actually belonged to Barney, President and Mrs. Bush's beloved Scottish Terrier. We learned later that the First Dog was quite fanatical about sports, that he loved playing with volleyballs and golf balls, as well as observing horseshoe matches.

That evening, before we were seated for dinner, the president and the First Lady argued over whose table I was going to sit at. The First Lady won, but the president still managed to finagle a table full of tall, gorgeous, female Olympians. I guess that's an unwritten presidential perk.

The menu, printed on an off-white card, with the presidential seal and the Olympic rings at the top, included pea soup with duck pastrami cheese puffs; crispy black sea bass with butter beans, tomatoes, and corn; and summer greens with cucumber and carrot ribbons, dressed with a roasted artichoke vinaigrette. Each course was accompanied by a special glass of wine. And to top it all off, there was a fabulous dessert called the Olympic Torch, a dark chocolate tart with raspberries and a brown sugar Olympic flame, which was served with a glass of Chandon Blanc de Noirs. Music was provided by Seldom Scene, one of the most influential bluegrass bands of the last thirty years. It was one of those nights I'll never forget.

It's important that you have a little history about my Forrest Gump moment in the Oval Office because it foreshadowed what has come to be known in Olympic and beach volleyball lore as "the Bush slap." President Bush traveled to Beijing for the Olympics, meeting with U.S. athletes before we walked in the Opening Ceremony. The next day, after taking a brisk mountain bike ride—he described his workout as "unbelievably difficult; that's why they call it an Olympic Course"—the president checked out various venues. And he tried his hand, so to speak, at beach volleyball.

On the Chaoyang Park practice courts, on Saturday, August 9, about an hour before the beach volleyball competition was scheduled to begin, the president bumped the ball around with Kerri and me.

It was clear President Bush was a very good athlete and very competitive. But truth be told, his passing needed a lot of work: He hit a pair of balls straight, but off his knuckles, then he opted not to dive after one of the balls I returned. Thank God. Kerri and I held our collective breaths for several seconds, thinking he might actually try to save it from hitting the beach, and we weren't the only ones who had that thought. His Secret Service agents perked up, ready to spring into action. The photographers surged forward, ready to snap the perfect shot. His entourage watched nervously, envisioning him in a face plant in the sand. Suddenly, the president began waving his arms in large, looping circles, pretending to fight to keep himself upright.

"I think if he'd take his shoes off, he'd be a stud," Kerri told the media.

"We've got to get him some shorts and a tank top," I added. "Give him a little more time, and he'll be good."

As he was leaving, I had another Forrest Gump moment.

"Next time, I'll come back and bring my tattoos," the president joked.

"Like that one?" I kidded, turning my back and sticking out my butt. Again.

The president brushed his hand across the small of my back, giving me a friendly slap on my large tattoo, and he joked about getting a tattoo of his own one day. And thus, "the Bush slap" was born. Before he left, he posed for a photograph standing between us, and as he put his arms around us, he proclaimed, "I'm with the champs right here!" Oh, how I hoped the Prez was prophetic.

The following day, Kerri and I were poised to begin our quest for back-to-back gold medals. There were twenty-four teams each in the men's and women's brackets. The teams were broken into six groups of four for pool play—we were in Pool B—with sixteen teams advancing to the single-elimination round. We'd moved out of the Olympic Village, and into the Hilton hotel, which was closer to our venue.

In the four years between Athens and Beijing, the popularity of Olympic beach volleyball had grown enormously; everybody wanted to join in the party. It's not a regimented sport for spectators. If you want to stand up the whole time until somebody yells at you to sit down, you can. If you want to dress in costume, you can. You can wear a bathing suit. You can get out of your work clothes. It's a loose environment.

Announcer Chris (Geeter) McGee, who travels with us on the AVP tour, kept fans stoked, whipping the crowd into a frenzy with his charged-up play-by-play. A DJ got everybody's blood pumping, blaring music throughout the match, mixing oldies, Southern California beach tunes, and current hits. Scantily clad, bikinied dancing girls elevated the temperatures of the male fans, shaking their booties during breaks in the action. And on top of that, there were cheerleaders. No wonder U.S. Olympic basketball teammates Kobe Bryant, LeBron James, and Jason Kidd came to watch us at various points throughout the tournament. Tennis star Lindsay Davenport, a friend of the family, stopped by, too.

Before the tournament began, Karch, NBC's beach volleyball color commentator, raved about how big, enthusiastic crowds had been drawn to the sport since it was added to the Olympics in 1996. But, he noted, there would be one big difference in Beijing: The sport was going to be a centerpiece of NBC's coverage. Kerri and I were to be featured as one of the network's top five story lines of the Games, along with swimmer Michael Phelps, the U.S. women's gymnastics team, the U.S. men's basketball team, and the U.S. track and field athletes. All of our matches were scheduled to be televised in prime time.

"I don't think it has anything to do with bikinis or not bikinis," Karch told the Associated Press. "The sport has a sex appeal that track and field and some others don't. But this is not tennis and it's not golf. You can make noise any time you want."

I, too, believed our sport was about more than sex appeal.

"People used to think, 'You guys are just a bunch of girls in bathing suits, running around,'" I told the Associated Press. "But when people come to an event, they see the athleticism. Then they get caught up in everything. The venue will be hopping."

While I'm on the subject, let me say a quick word about my "uniform." I grew up on the beach, so wearing a bikini is normal for me. When I watch "old school" videos from the 1960s, some of the girls Dad played with were wearing string bikinis. He says they'd dive around the court, and their tops would come flying off. I've only had one incident, back in high school. I went up to hit a ball, and my top snapped. No wardrobe malfunctions since then, though. Kerri hasn't been as lucky: Her top broke in the middle of a game.

Look, bikinis are functional for what we do. You'd get too hot and too full of sand if you played in shorts and tank tops. Quite honestly, when most girls first start playing beach volleyball, they feel very pale and very exposed. I'm so used to it now I don't even think twice about it. I cherish my bikinis. I've saved every single one. I'm even superstitious about them. You know how Tiger Woods always wears a red shirt to play his final rounds in tournaments? Well, Kerri and I always wear black bikinis in the finals. That's our power color. The only time I'm overly modest on the beach is during warm-ups, when I'll cover up because that's when random people snap my picture. If I'm stretching, especially if my legs are split apart, I feel very vulnerable. And the only time any of us girls are overly sensitive about wearing our bikinis is when we're feeling heavy or bloated. Bikinis tell all, especially when you're the slightest bit out of shape.

When it came to the 2008 Olympics, though, I was just happy to have any bathing suit to play in. We'd arrived in China bikiniless. Speedo was supposed to have provided our suits, and somebody, somewhere had dropped the ball. The scenario was almost comical: You're on the biggest stage in the world, and you could potentially be performing naked. Fortunately, Nike stepped in, and we finally got our suits the day before the FIVB technical meeting. But there only were two of them—we usually have at least three—and they fit terribly. If we bent over, our chests showed. Kerri and I made some changes, and a Chinese seamstress did the alterations. Eventually, we had three suits—red, white, and blue. If we hadn't had suits to show the FIVB technical committee, which checks such things as the size of sponsor emblems and the placement of numbers, we might've been sanctioned and not allowed to play.

When we opened pool play on August 10, we were the number one team in the world, but the number two seed in the tournament. That's because, in the Olympics, there's a "homer rule." China's Tian and Wang were the number one seed since they hailed from the host country. The media was calling us the "prohibitive favorites." We were taking a record winning streak of eighteen consecutive tournaments into Beijing—we'd won 101 straight matches—and Kerri, with a gold medal victory, would join me as the only two women in the sport's history with a hundred career victories. Only five others in beach volleyball had won a hundred or more matches, and all of them were men.

Of course, I planned to drink it all in. Marching in the Opening Ceremony with Kerri. Attending other Olympic events, especially men's and women's table tennis, which China had dominated since the 1960s. Sightseeing with Misty's Misfits. Learning a little Chinese. (I wasn't going to eat Chinese food, though, because I didn't want to chance getting sick.) This Olympics would be very different from Athens, where my only tourist highlight was a quick peek at the Acropolis. This Olympics, I told myself, might very well be my last, so I'd better do it right.

In our first match, we defeated Japan's Mika Teru Saiki and Chiaki Kusuhara, 21–12, 21–15, in thirty-six minutes. It was the first time we'd seen center court. We treated it as a warm-up, something to get our rhythm going. We'd never played the Japanese team before—at five feet eight and five feet nine, they were the second-shortest team in the tournament—so, when we won, we were like, "Okay, that was good . . ." We got a break from the heat blanketing Beijing—it was eighty-two degrees at game time with 87 percent humidity—and light showers fell throughout the match. But the rain didn't slow us down, and it certainly didn't dampen our enthusiasm.

The Japanese women had come out strong in the second game, running up a 7–4 lead, until we scored six of the next seven points to take control of the game and match. I had ten match digs; Kerri was excellent at the net, with three intimidating blocks. She played with black "kinesio" tape on her surgically repaired right shoulder to help increase circulation and lymph node drainage, and to help keep her joint in line. Our favorite physiotherapist, Pericles, who'd treated us in Athens through the FIVB, but whom we'd paid to join us in Beijing, had turned her on to the tape. She said its impact was like taking some Advil. With or without the tape, Kerri looked sharp. I think her shoulder surgery actually had improved her finesse game.

With our victory over the Japanese, we were off and running. Well, except for one hiccup. When Kerri went up for a block against the Japanese, her gold wedding ring flew off. She actually handled the incident quite well. She was like, "Uh-oh," and then she said, "Okay, we'll just deal with it later." It was the Olympics, and she wanted to win. Her focus was pretty good, but I could tell between rallies her wedding band was on her mind because she'd look down at the sand, trying to spot it. When it happened, I thought, "Why are you wearing it in the first place?" In just the past year alone, at least three professional men's players had lost their wedding rings. It's just the nature of the sport: Your hands get sweaty, and your rings fall off. And that's why I don't wear mine.

After the match, Kerri was so bummed out about losing her wedding band that she phoned her husband, Casey, and asked him to have another made so he could bring it to China when he flew out later in the week. She was extremely sentimental about it: He'd given it to her when he'd proposed in 2004 beside a river on Molokai, Hawaii. Inside, he'd engraved "SIX FEET OF SUNSHINE," her nickname.

More than seventeen thousand tons of sand had been brought into Chaoyang Park to create the beach volleyball venue, and the venue volunteers regularly raked it throughout the day's competition, so trying to pinpoint her ring would be comparable to finding a needle in a haystack. With the help of NBC's broadcast of our match, and the network's ability to reduce the moment to super-slow motion, volunteers figured out when and where it had flown off. Most important, metal detectors were on the FIVB's checklist for equipment for international play, since many of the events are on beaches and foreign objects are common.

Several hours after our match, a volunteer named Song Zhendong dug up the ring. Kerri learned Sunday night that her wedding ring had been recovered, but she didn't have it back on until the following day. She met with the volunteer Monday, presenting him with some Olympic pins as a thank-you gift. She said she had not taken off the ring since Casey presented it to her years before.

I understood about superstitions and sentimentality when it came to jewelry. I'd invited Debbie Green, my setting coach at Long Beach State, to come watch me play in Beijing, but she'd declined because she didn't have a current passport and she couldn't miss the start of practice for college volleyball season. So unbeknownst to me, she gave a box to our family friend Jim Steele to bring with him to Beijing. Inside the box, she'd put a gold necklace with a symbol of a volleyball player and the five Olympic rings. It had been given to her before the 1984 Olympics by the mother of one of her teammates, Linda Chisholm. Debbie had worn it as she'd helped lead her U.S. indoor teammates to the silver medal. She'd worn it for years, without taking it off, but she hadn't worn it for the past decade. She'd always thought she'd pass it down to her daughters, Nicole and Dana, but then she felt she wanted me to have it. So she'd talked to her kids, and they'd said, absolutely! It was the only piece of jewelry I wore throughout our competition in Beijing.

Two days later, in our second match in pool play, we knocked off Cuba's Dalixia Fernandez Grasset and Tamara Larrea Peraza, 21–15,

21–16, in thirty-seven minutes. They were the only women's team to have competed together in three Olympics. They'd finished ninth in Sydney and Athens. Kerri wore her wedding ring, but covered it with flesh-colored athletic tape to make sure it wouldn't fly off. We were playing what Karch described as "May-Walsh volleyball," the two of us on cruise control, and I was getting a lot of pop on the ball.

Two days later, we beat Norway's Ingrid Torlen and Nila Ann Hakedal, 21–12, 21–15, in thirty-seven minutes, finishing pool play with a 3–0 mark and advancing to the Round of Sixteen, while holding our number two seed overall. We'd made it through pool play without losing a set and without allowing any team more than sixteen points in a game. Kerri was dominant at the net, finishing with sixteen kills and seven blocks. Hers were the only blocks of any player in the match. She also had three aces. I finished with eight kills, two aces, and three digs.

However, the match had exposed one of our weaknesses. For years, teams had served me because I was the shorter player. But the Norwegians had decided to serve Kerri. She'd had trouble with her serve receive. (When you aren't served very often, it's hard to get in a rhythm. So it was a good strategy.) At one point in the match, nineteen serves had gone to Kerri, only three to me. She'd been aced a handful of times and had committed an error on another.

As in Athens, Kerri admitted it was difficult adjusting to the slow-paced Olympic schedule, competing every two days during pool play. She was used to playing every day on the professional beach volleyball tours—sometimes as many as three matches a day.

"Three matches in six days, that's mentally wearing on me," she told the Associated Press. "That's one of the challenges of the Olympics. We're so eager when we get on the court. You have to bottle up the energy and make sure you don't wear out."

To counteract that, Troy suggested we emulate an AVP schedule, practicing the morning after our matches. That way, we always were playing; we never took a day off. We kept ourselves busy, we kept ourselves playing, which I think made the time go by faster.

In the meantime, I was enjoying the pace of the Olympics, especially the fact that we were practicing or playing in the mornings, which gave us the bulk of the day free to hang out with family and friends and embrace the culture. Thinking about it now, my China experience was unlike any other I'd had while competing in the sport. Many athletes feel enormous pressure being in the Olympics. Kerri said she certainly did, but that's what makes her such a great athlete. She pours her entire being into competing. However, as the Games unfolded, I felt less and less pressure. The Olympics felt more like a playground to me, in every way imaginable. I was everywhere, doing everything. I was on the Great Wall, decked out in a huge Chinese straw hat, bumping a volleyball. One minute, I was sledding over the Great Wall's slopes on a toboggan; the next, I was dancing down its dozens and dozens of steps. Sandy Malpee also brought along an official Misty May bobblehead doll to photograph on the Great Wall. And, oh, yes. Mom was right there with us, her ashes traveling in a little bottle.

Most athletes would've trained, eaten, and slept, and then, perhaps, spent a little of their remaining free time with their immediate family. Most athletes would've focused on the task at hand and not gotten distracted by the outside world. But I was determined to win a gold medal in experiencing the Olympics. I went to every single event I possibly could go to. And it wasn't like I was taking limos to the venues, or I had tickets in private suites, where I could sit in air-conditioning with my feet up. No, I was part of the crowd, and I loved it.

For me, for my journeys through volleyball and life, it has always been, and it always will be, all about people. The people I touch, the people who touch me. That's who I am. I'm not one to sit and worry about myself, and how it's all going to affect me. For me, it's all about living life and being there for others.

You need to have an element of selfishness in order to be great at what you do, for the most part. At least most athletes feel that way. Athletes have to be selfish about what they eat, about what they drink, about when they sleep, about how they spend their time away from the court, in order to be great at what they do. You have to take care of yourself first, in order to be great on the field.

I'm the antithesis of that. Yes, I work my tail off. At the height of my Olympic training, I was in my car from 7:00 A.M. until 7:00 P.M., running from workout to workout, bodywork session to bodywork session. I'm prepared. I'm fit. I'm ready. However, I always make sure to have an extra minute for somebody. I always make sure I'm able to do things away from the court and the venue. I'm always prepared to be completely selfless with my time. That's something I learned from Dad and Mom. They taught me it's possible to be an elite athlete, but at the same time, to be loving and generous with yourself, your time, and your athletic gifts.

Our biggest scare of the tournament occurred on August 15, Kerri's thirtieth birthday. We overcame five set points in the first set to beat Belgium's Liesbeth Mouha and Liesbet van Breedam, 24–22, 21–10, to advance to the quarterfinals. At six feet four, 195 pounds, Mouha was the second tallest player in the tournament, and it was the first time in Beijing Kerri had played against somebody taller than she was. Women's beach volleyball nets are seven feet four and one eighth inches high, and Kerri's reach is eight feet one. However, she really had to stretch to get the ball over the higher blocker, which gave van Breedam time to chase the ball down behind Mouha, which wasn't good for us.

After we'd finally kicked it into gear at the end of the first game, we played much more like ourselves. We won the clinching second game in only fifteen minutes, in characteristic Misty-Kerri fashion. We'd jumped to a 6–2 lead. Then we went up 9–5; Kerri got the serve and went on a 7–0 run, putting away the match.

Next up, the number three seed, Brazilians Ana Paula Connelly and Larissa Franca. We approached our quarterfinal match against them with trepidation. They'd formed their team a day before the Olympic competition began. Larissa's usual partner, Juliana Felisberta Silva, had been forced to withdraw from the tournament due to a knee injury. It's always a challenge to play a new partnership. Although our two teams seemed well matched, talentwise, it was clear from the outset that Ana Paula and Larissa had not yet found their rhythm as a team. Kerri scored on five blocks against them. She also had eleven kills. I finished with ten digs, thirteen kills, and an ace. We won, 21–18, 21–15, to advance to the semifinals.

"We came in expecting the unexpected," I told the media. "Our coach gave us a great game plan."

On the AVP tour, coaches are allowed to sit courtside, but for FIVB tournaments, they can't. They have to sit in the stands, and they're not supposed to talk or make any noise for fear of cheating. They can't even clap. But they can videotape. When we weren't competing, Troy would be at the venue, shooting video of our competitors. The night before our matches, we'd meet to watch videotape, and then we'd all go our separate ways. In the mornings, we'd get worked on by Pericles, our physiotherapist, then we'd head over to the venue. We'd run a little bit. Then Troy would stop us, and we'd go back over the scouting report. After that, we'd get into our warm-up, and then it was game on.

From the outset in the semifinals, against Brazil's number six seed Talita Antunes and Renata Ribeiro, we were on fire. We jumped out to a 5–1 lead and increased it to 12–5 as the Brazilian errors started to mount. We reached set point at 20–11, and a serving error made it 20–12, before my kill won the set. The second set was closer, as the score was tied at 6–6 and 10–10. Two Brazilian errors increased our lead to 12–10. After two errors (one by us, one by them), plus a Brazilian point, the score was 13–12. But then we went on a 6–0 run, making it 19–12. Renata and Talita held off the loss for two serves before eventually making an error to end the match. We won, 21–12, 21–14, in just thirty-eight minutes.

The Brazilians were the best team we'd played, and this was the best we'd played. I'd come down with a cold and a fever, but you wouldn't have known it just by looking at me. I'd practiced the morning before, then had seen the team and IOC doctors. They'd prescribed antibiotics, and I'd spent the remainder of the day resting. I'll let you in on a little secret: I've always played better when I was sick. It makes me concentrate harder.

Before the match, we'd had an interesting discussion with Troy. He'd thought serving Renata, who was on the right side, was the best strategy for beating the Brazilians. We'd disagreed, saying we preferred to serve Talita on the left. We ended up winning the debate, which gave us a little extra motivation. (As far as the Brazilians' serving went, they were encouraged to serve Kerri because they'd gotten points off her at the end of the first set.) Meanwhile, the Brazilian team also contributed to our motivation. We'd arrived on the practice court sixty-six minutes before the start of our match. Brazil pulled rank, kicking us off the practice court and banishing us to an outer court. Talk about waking up a sleeping bear.

We were one step closer to our goal, and NBC's Heather Cox asked us afterward if the reality of these Games was beginning to sink in.

"We just beat a great Brazilian team, and we're going to the Finals," Kerri said, her voice cracking with emotion. "It is what we wanted to do. We've been fighting so hard since Athens, and now it's going to be China. This is what I'd hoped for, USA versus China in the final, and it's going to be tough, so we made it, and that's the first step."

We weren't sure yet which Chinese team we were going to face, but we did know that the venue would be packed with Chinese fans, and that they'd have the home-court advantage in the final step in our quest for history.

"We feed off that," I told Heather. "We love the energy. We love the crowds. And as I've been joking around all year, 'We don't know what they're saying, but they're cheering for us.' They're saying, 'USA,' even though they're saying, 'China, China.'"

Before I left the court, I pulled out a black film canister and sprinkled Mom's ashes on the court. I saved half of the canister's contents for the gold medal match.

"You can't leave home without her," I said, tapping the film canister. "But she'll stay here."

Just one match away from history, I wanted to summon up all of the love, support, and good vibes I could get—from those around me, as well as from up above. My entourage had expanded as the Games went on, with Anya flying in for the last week of competition after having been in Japan on a soccer mission, and Debbie jetting in to surprise me for the semifinals.

The day before the gold medal match, we met with Troy in Kerri's hotel room to discuss our game plan against China's Tian and Wang, who'd beaten the number two Chinese team to reach the final.

"We don't need to play the match of our lives," Troy told us. "We know what these girls are going to do. We know what we're capable of doing. Let's just get out there and play the way we can play. Don't let it become anything more than that."

We talked about my partner being better than Tian's partner; we talked about Kerri's partner being better than Wang's partner. We talked about all of the little things in the Chinese team's game, then compared them to all of the little things in our game. We talked about how we were better at every facet, not by a ton, but by enough. He reminded us that we had an hour to prove that we were better, so if we made an error, we must just keep pushing.

"Let your skills be better than theirs over the course of an hour," he told us.

Then we watched videotape of Tian and Wang. It was a good, calm meeting, but it wasn't anything special. It wasn't Troy trying to bombard us with lots of video. It wasn't his trying to fire us up with a "Win One for the Gipper" pep talk. We didn't need him to do that.

The night before our gold medal match, I became unusually reflective about my career, thinking about how grateful I was to all of those people who'd helped me get to this moment in time. Dad. Mom. Matt. Kerri and her family. My grandparents. My parents' Muscle Beach crew. My coaches. My teammates. My trainers. My healers. The list was endless.

President Bush tried to call us at about 10:30 P.M. to wish us well, but Al Lau, our team leader, had told the White House secretary that we were asleep and refused to put the call through. (We both were still awake, and we gave Al a hard time about it the next day.)

Between 12:30 and 1:00 A.M., I called Mike Rangel's cell phone and left him a message. He still has it, and it went like this:

> Hi, Mike, it's Misty. Just getting ready to go to bed. Wanted to say hi before we play tomorrow. Thank you for all that you've done for us. I know why you're not answering. You're in either one of two places, either you're playing poker at the casino, or you're meeting with your agent about your book signing about the autobiography of David Hasselhoff.

When I woke up in the morning, I discovered Dad's text message: "No matter what happens, we all came here because we love and support you. Win or lose, we still love you."

It made me feel very good, until I looked out the window and saw a torrential downpour. The rain was coming down violently, and there was electricity in the air. But none of us were worried. Not me. Not Kerri. Not Troy. And we weren't the least bit concerned we'd selected white bikinis to play in. (Our power color, black, wasn't an option.) If the water made them see-through, well, so what? We'd practiced and played in crummy weather throughout our eight years together. We'd never, ever run from a day at the beach. We'd beaten this Chinese team, in the rain, in 2007, in an FIVB event in Norway. We'd played in 120 degree temperatures in the sand in Phoenix, and we'd played when there was frost on the court in Northern Europe. We'd addressed difficult situations early in our career, and no matter what the conditions were, it always was to our advantage. If we're in deep sand, we jump better. If we're in hard-packed sand, we're going to be faster. If it's raining, our ball control will come through.

How could the rain change our game? Well, rain does make the ball heavier, so your strategy may change a little bit because of that. Also, you can't wear sunglasses, so sometimes when you're hitting the ball, your eyes can telegraph where you're going to go with it.

Although she was nicknamed "Six Feet of Sunshine," Kerri loves playing in the rain, and she'd actually had a dream the night before that we'd won the gold medal in a downpour. Meanwhile, I thought the rain was fitting: We could get right into the jungle and play, just battle it out, just be fierce, relentless warriors, just be ourselves.

I'm superstitious, so I went through the same routine that morning as I had for all our other matches. I'd be up and eating breakfast by 5:45 A.M., then I'd get physical therapy. I wore my hair the same way, the same hairpins and hair tie, same headband. I had to put on five strokes of deodorant under each arm, because five is my lucky number.

Kerri, Troy, and I met on the bus and rode to the venue in dead silence. Kerri and I both were listening to our iPods. Every day, throughout the Games, I made sure to listen to Kanye West's "Stronger." Then I put my iPod on scramble, and I listened to Michael Jackson, Prince, and anyone else who could pump me up. Troy didn't say a word; he knew we understood what we had to do. At one point during the ride, I started crying, overwhelmed we were about to realize our dream of playing for our second Olympic gold medal, and incredibly sad Mom wasn't there to witness it. When we got to the venue, we went straight to the practice court and went through our regular warm-up routine. Troy steered clear of us. About thirty minutes later, he reiterated a few key points. He finished with what he'd told us before every match since he'd begun to coach us: Remember the three Bs. Battling. Believing. Breathing. And with that, we all knew nothing more needed to be said.

Meanwhile, Dad and my Misty's Misfits crew had arrived at the venue at the crack of dawn. They'd all awakened by 5:00 A.M., they were so anxious about my gold medal match. Ever since I'd begun playing professional beach volleyball, Dad and his pal Jim Steele had had a ritual, where they'd get to the beach by 6:00 A.M., so they could get all settled in. They'd planned to watch the bronze medal match, which was held before ours.

Venue volunteers passed out pastel-colored rain ponchos to the crowd. Folks huddled under umbrellas, clutching Chinese and U.S. flags. Not that any of those things kept anybody dry. Half an hour before we were to start, I called Eileen Clancy McClintock on her cell phone and asked where Dad was. I told her I wanted to see him. Eileen understood it was important for me to be with Dad before I went onto the court, just as it was important for him to be with me. This was a once-in-a-lifetime moment, and I needed to share it with him. We're all little girls when it comes to our dads, and I needed to hear him say, "Win or lose, we love you. Just go out and play." He always senses exactly what I'm feeling. It's uncanny.

"What do you think?" I asked Dad, making a reference to the torrential rain.

"It's a good day to win an Olympic gold medal," he replied.

And then we gently touched foreheads. Dad says he read somewhere that it's a tradition of Buddhists in the Himalayas, that touching foreheads is their way of honoring another person. So he'd started doing it with me several years before. Now, we don't hug or kiss before matches, we lovingly bump foreheads.

Right from the start, the match was tight, but the rain wasn't a factor, the relentless play of the Chinese women was.

"I think it's harder being a fan, sitting out in the rain, than being a player," I told the media. "This is just another reason why we play in bathing suits."

The Chinese women took the lead at 6–4 in the first set before we came back to tie it at 6–6. We ran the score to 12–10, but then they rallied to even it again at 13–13. Finally, with the score tied at 17–17, my three straight kills gave us a 20–17 cushion. At that point, China called time-out to slow our momentum. Then a kill by Wang made it 20–18. The Chinese saved one set point on brilliant teamwork—Wang dropped the ball down the line off a set from Tian on her knees—but I followed with a kill to close out the first set.

We jumped out to a 6–3 lead in the second set, but thanks to a couple of Tian aces, the Chinese women fought back to go ahead, 9–8. The set was nip and tuck from there—tied at 11, 12, 13, 14, and 15. Kerri crushed the ball or slipped a line shot past the left arm of Wang, who jammed the ball down the line, hit a devastating serve that just bounced right off me, or blocked a Kerri shot. We scored the next two points, making it 17–15, and then Tian called a five-minute medical time-out, which lasted closer to ten minutes. We knew that Tian had a reputation for creating drama in her matches, in the hope of distracting her opponents. She'd asked a trainer to come out onto the court and rub her left forearm and elbow. But her tricks didn't affect us: We were like two sharks, smelling blood in the water.

When play resumed, Tian hit a dink shot, from right to left, to cut the lead to 17–16. On the next point, Wang tried muscling the ball over on the second touch while falling backward, and the ball fell into the net. We were up, 18–16. The Chinese women weren't fazed, and they went on to score the next two. Now, the score was knotted at 18–18. A kill by me put us up by one, and it demoralized the Chinese women. An attack error by them made the score 20–18. And finally, I served the ball, China passed and set it, and their attack went over Kerri's block. I passed it, and Kerri slammed it straight down the center, putting an exclamation point on our victory, on our careers, and on history.

# 22

# DANCING WITH THE STARS

Y ou never know what doors an Olympic gold medal will open.
Never in a million years did I think I'd get asked to be on
ABC's hit TV show *Dancing with the Stars*. I'd interviewed with the
show's producers a few months before the 2008 Olympics, but I hadn't
heard back until halfway through our competition in Beijing. When
they finally called and asked if I'd be interested, I jumped at the chance.

I've always loved to dance. I've hammed it up on the AVP tour,
dancing my way onto the court during introductions or gyrating my
hips after emotional points. I've also made my grand entrance by
dancing my own creation, "The Turtle," crawling onto the court on
my hands and knees, wearing a turtle costume.

After Athens, I was hit with the typical onslaught of media
opportunities, awards show appearances, corporate sponsorship
gigs, and speaking engagements, but this time around, I wanted to
take advantage of post-Olympics experiences that took me out of
my normal setting, experiences that challenged me and stretched my
limits. *Dancing with the Stars* was an opportunity that might only
come around once in a lifetime. It was something I could tell my kids
about one day. So I made the decision to participate in the show and
turn down the usual post-Olympic stuff.

Little did I know how time-consuming it would become.

When I flew home from Beijing, the moment I stepped off the plane in Los Angeles, I was introduced to my dance partner, Maksim (Maks) Chmerkovskiy. ABC's cameras were rolling to capture my reaction. I'd made sure to put on my big Chinese hat and my new Olympic gold medal for the occasion. I'd heard rumors Maks was going to be my partner, but I hadn't known if they were true. I'd been a huge fan of the show since it had started, and he'd always been my favorite dancer, so I was thrilled when I finally met him. However, I was sorry that I'd flown a million hours, that I had bags under my eyes, that my hair was messy, that my teeth needed to be brushed, and that I desperately needed a shower.

Then the camera crew asked us to do some reshoots.

"Misty, can you come back out again?" they said. "And can you look surprised again?"

That's show biz.

I rushed home to Long Beach, packed a little bag, and flew to Phoenix, where Matt and the Marlins were playing the Diamondbacks. I threw out the first pitch, wearing my new Olympic gold medal and a Diamondbacks jersey, and Matt, dressed in his Marlins uniform, caught me. I met Senator John McCain, the Republican presidential candidate.

Twenty-four hours later, I raced back to Los Angeles to start training with Maks. I immersed myself in dance practice, six to eight hours a day, over the next three days. Then, I was off to the AVP tournament in Cincinnati. Maks went along, too, so we could practice in our free time. He was a huge hit with the ladies. Nobody cared about Kerri and me. All we heard all weekend long was, "Is Maks here?" Well, Kerri and I ended up losing in the final to E.Y. and Nicole Branagh, 19-21, 21-10, 23-25, in an hour and forty-five minutes, the second-longest match in AVP history—our record-winning streak was stopped at 112 matches and 19 titles—and Maks blamed himself for our loss. He thought he'd tired me out with all the hours of dancing. He worried he was bad luck.

I tried to explain to Maks that nobody can understand how physically, mentally, and emotionally fatigued you are after competing in an Olympics, not even a professional dancer. I told Maks if he'd asked me before the Cincinnati tournament if I thought Kerri and I were going to win, I would've answered, "Probably not." We'd just been through one of the most emotional tournaments of our lives, and we hadn't had a whole lot left to give, on the court or off it. And that wasn't even taking into account all the training, qualifying, and competing in our two-year buildup to Beijing. Sure, I went into Cincinnati hoping to win, but in the back of my mind, I knew if we lost, it really wasn't a big deal in the scheme of my volleyball career or my life. You can't be on top forever. You move on. Or in the prophetic words of Tiger Woods, who texted me after the loss: "START ANOTHER STREAK."

Now that I've got the benefit of hindsight, I know Kerri was already pregnant by the Cincinnati tournament. At various points during that trip, and at other points that fall, I remember her saying to me, "I don't feel well." Or, "I'm tired, I'm going back to the hotel." It just didn't register that she might be pregnant, that she and Casey already had started working on their gold medal baby in Beijing. (Joseph Michael Jennings was born May 22, 2009.) However, her pregnancy wasn't the reason we lost.

There are two questions people always ask me about *Dancing with the Stars.* How much weight did you lose? None. I went into the show in great shape. Although I did get leaner, which I didn't think was possible. What was the hardest part of the show? Maintaining perfect posture and being light on my feet, especially in high heels.

On second thought, maybe just the high heels, period, were the biggest challenge. I've never been someone who lives for fashion or is addicted to shoes, like *Sex and the City*'s Carrie Bradshaw, or even Kerri, who loves to shop. Unlike Carrie and Kerri, I don't have an affinity for expensive designer shoes like Manolo Blahnik, Christian Louboutin, or Jimmy Choo. In fact, my closet looks more like Foot Locker than Neiman Marcus. Having to walk, much less dance, in high heels, day after day, hour after hour, was a huge challenge for me. There's no way around it: You've got to train in high heels, in order for you and your partner to get all of your dance steps down.

At times, I had such nasty blisters, I was wearing Band-Aids, as well as gauze patches and adhesive tape, seemingly all over my feet. The balls of my feet hurt the worst. My knees throbbed. My calves were tight. I was working so many different muscles. It was such a switch, training in high heels rather than in bare feet in the sand or in athletic shoes in the gym. When we started the show, Maks instructed me not to get pedicures because, he said, he wanted my feet to callus. He also told me that professional dancers were notorious for having ugly feet, that the better the dancer, the more beaten up their feet were.

Right from the start, I had a total blast. I loved Oscar-winning actress and comedian Cloris Leachman and her shtick. I hope I'm moving that well at her age—she was eighty-two when we did the show together—or, for that matter, that I'm even alive. Seven-time NFL Pro Bowler and Super Bowl champion Warren Sapp was a crack-up, too. The media kept calling him "a diva," but I didn't see it. He was a big teddy bear.

I got the footwork down quickly. However, not thinking about my feet was a true challenge. So was learning to express myself through my face and my arms. Segmenting my body wasn't a snap either. As an athlete, I move forward for the ball with my entire body. But as a dancer, I might have to step forward, without moving my entire body forward, so I can begin my next move.

All of our practice sessions were filmed. We had four weeks to learn two dances for the show's season seven premiere. We learned our first mambo in three days. Then, we learned the fox-trot in three days.

Maks is a very gifted choreographer, and he worked hard to create routines that made me look my best. He's also a very tough coach, at times even tougher than Dad. Maks saw something in me that I didn't, and he drove me hard to get it out of me. He hammered home the basics. In some of the video clips of our practices, he looked like an absolute beast, but he pushed because he knew I could be good.

The biggest issue I encountered on *Dancing with the Stars* was time management. Practice time is based on each contestant's real-life schedules. Maks and I were working six to eight hours a day, sometimes more, but as far as everybody else, I'm not so sure they were putting in that kind of time. I think some contestants were working two and a half hours a day. As an athlete, if your coach tells you that you have to be in the gym for six, eight, or ten hours a day, you're going to be in the gym for that amount of time. You're geared toward putting in a lot of practice time, as well as having somebody tell you what to do. Do I regret the amount of time we put in each day? Absolutely not. Although there never seemed to be enough hours in the day left to eat, sleep, get bodywork, and walk my two dogs. I would have liked to schedule massages and Pilates sessions, but it was impossible. I'd get into the studio in the morning and wouldn't leave until night time, so it was tough.

The first week of the show, because it was the premiere, we performed Monday and Tuesday. We did the fox-trot to "This Will Be (An Everlasting Love)," and we scored twenty-one points out of thirty overall. Then, we did the mambo to "Black Mambo," and again scored twenty-one. However, once the show got rolling, we'd perform Monday, with the results show on Tuesday. That night, we were given our dance to learn for the following week. Then, we had Wednesday through Sunday to work on it. Wednesdays, we discussed our costumes, and later in the week, we had fittings. Sundays, we had an hour blocked out to dance on the stage. We also had tanning sessions that day. Mondays, we had our dress rehearsal, and then the show was shot live, at 5:00 P.M., Pacific time.

Costumes are an integral part of *Dancing with the Stars,* and the designers never put me in an outfit I didn't like. I was very open to their ideas. They'd always ask me which colors I liked wearing, whether there was a particular style or cut I wouldn't be caught dead in. I really admired the costume designers, and the hair and makeup artists. They're incredibly creative. I wasn't used to wearing a lot of makeup, fake eyelashes, or rhinestones on my eyelids. They've got one of the most difficult jobs on the show: They have to re-create your look, right down to the most minute detail, for the awards show the night after your performance. They take lots of pictures of you after you're all dolled up, so they can do just that. Although I must admit there were many times I looked at myself in the mirror after getting all decked out, and having spent hours in hair and makeup, and I thought, "Wow, I look like a drag queen!"

For those of you who think ballroom dancing is a skill, I can attest to the fact that it really is a sport. It's athletic. It takes aerobic fitness, power, quickness, stamina, balance, plus discipline, determination, and drive. Professional ballroom dancers put in just as much time as professional athletes. It's no wonder that in five of the eight seasons of *Dancing with the Stars* Olympic or professional athletes have won the coveted mirrored ball trophy: Emmitt Smith, Apolo Anton Ohno, Helio Castroneves, Kristi Yamaguchi, and Shawn Johnson. There are three reasons for that. One, obviously, there's a tremendous amount of footwork involved. As athletes, we have to know, at all times, what our feet are doing. Two, we're trained to perform, physically, under pressure. Three, we're relentless. Like I said, athletes are among the few people who, when we're told to do something, we'll do it. If you tell us it's going to take six or eight hours, we're going to be there for six or eight hours. I just kept going and going and going.

Which is probably why I ended up rupturing my left Achilles tendon the third week of the season. It happened on a Friday evening. All day long we'd been practicing that week's dance, the jive, an American dance that evolved from the jitterbug by removing the lifts and acrobatic elements. It's very fast, full of bouncy movement, using the balls of the feet a lot and tons of kicks. We were in the middle of our second run-through in front of the cameras, and I was doing a move where I hopped backward from a jump on my left leg. For the first time in the contest, I was wearing flat tennis shoes instead of high heels, but my calves had felt tight all day. I thought, "Oh, they just need to warm up, and I'll be ready to go." I jumped back on my left foot, and I heard a pop, which was loud enough to be picked up by the microphones recording our practice. I asked pro dancer Karina Smirnoff, who'd just come out to the side of the stage with her partner Rocco DiSpirito, if I'd kicked the bottom stair up to the judges' table.

"No, you're five feet from it," Karina said.

I tried to put down my foot, and the floor wasn't there. I didn't have an ankle. I didn't have a foot. I knew instantly I'd torn my Achilles. Karina and Rocco, and the production crew, rushed to elevate my foot and put ice on my Achilles. It didn't hurt when I did it; my foot went numb. However, once I elevated it, and the blood started pumping, it became really sore. The producers called an ambulance, and I was carted out on a stretcher, for the first time ever in my career. I was transported to the emergency room at Cedars-Sinai Medical Center in Los Angeles. Maks insisted on going with me. He felt terrible, but I felt more terrible for him. The show was over for him.

Several minutes after rupturing my Achilles, I text-messaged Dr. Schobert: I HURT MYSELF, DOC.

In all this commotion, though, I held off calling Matt. It was about 9:00 P.M. Pacific time—midnight in Philadelphia, where he was, having had double hernia surgery two days before. I didn't want to bother him, plus he's a worrywart anyway. But I eventually broke down and called.

Then I phoned Dad because I didn't have a ride home from the hospital.

"What are you doing?" I said, matter-of-factly.

"Nothing," he replied.

"Can you come to the hospital and pick me up?" I asked.

"No, pal, I'm in St. Louis at a wedding," he said.

"Okay, peace," I said.

So the show hired a sedan to take me home.

Saturday morning, Dr. Schobert came over to my house, unwrapped my bandage, and examined my Achilles. He ordered an

MRI—the MRI facility is closed on Saturdays, but he was able to roust out some of the technicians, as well as a radiologist, all of whom were very accommodating. I know a lot of people think it was my high heels that caused the rupture, that practicing in those shoes had shortened my calf muscles, but Dr. Schobert says my Achilles could've gone at any time. He says I could've stepped off a curb and kaboom.

Sunday, Dad and Matt both arrived back in Long Beach. Dad recalls the comical scene when they came through the front door to greet me: me on my crutches, Matt bent over due to his double hernia surgery. When we tried to kiss each other, we looked like two old people about ready to fall over into each other.

"I've seen dogs kiss windows better than that," Dad joked.

Two days later, after I appeared on Monday night's show on crutches to publicly disclose my injury—I vowed to come back in the future and do the jive with Maks—Dr. Schobert performed my surgery, which took about seventy-five minutes. "You really trashed the hell out of it," Dr. Schobert said afterward. The tendon was stripped from the muscle, he told me, making it difficult to suture. Normally, Achilles tendon repair is tendon-to-tendon.

Of all the injuries I've suffered in my lifetime, my ruptured Achilles tendon was the most difficult to rehabilitate. It takes a solid year to get back into competitive form. The first eight weeks after surgery it's completely non-weight-bearing on that foot. I felt for Matt because there he was, hunched over, trying to recover from hernia surgery, having to wait on me hand and foot. Our household was the walking wounded. He'd make breakfast and bring it to me on a tray. He'd make me lunch, too. He was able to get around, but when he coughed and sneezed, he was in a lot of pain. But I gave him time off every day, when I swallowed my pain pills and floated off to La-La Land for five or six hours.

For the first eight weeks, I was on crutches, or in a wheelchair or a motorized scooter. The scooter allowed me to be mobile, because there was only so much lying in bed that I could take. That way, when Matt walked the dogs, I could go with them. One day, while

I was in a local nail salon having a pedicure, getting half of my toes done—you get a discount when it's only one leg—a customer sitting at the station behind me recognized me from *Dancing with the Stars*. Her name was Carla, and she asked me for my autograph. We got to talking about my scooter, and she offered me her Hoveround power chair, a wheelchair that can do 360s in one spot. She'd bought it for her father, but he'd passed away. It was brand new, just sitting in Carla's garage. It just goes to show you: You never know who you're going to meet.

While I was in the hard and then the soft cast, I created a little game to distract myself. How long could I grow the hair on my leg before I was forced to shave it? The longest I went was three weeks. It would itch too much. I don't recommend that game to anybody. The soft cast (a plastic boot that went up to just below my knee) was no picnic either. It had a foam sock inside, which was so hot it made my leg and foot sweat. After a while, it really smelled.

Ah, but there was an upside to my ruptured Achilles tendon: It got me to the front of the lines at Disneyland, my favorite place on earth. I took my goddaughter Mariah Clausen and her sister Sarah right before Christmas. Matt pushed me around in a wheelchair. I couldn't walk long distances in my boot, but I sure could get onto all of the rides, and my ruptured Achilles tendon was my ticket to the front of the lines. Disneyland was a breeze. However, I'm here to report I did see a lot of people who were using wheelchairs but didn't need them. What's up with that? I wanted to make a citizen's arrest of all those cheaters.

Throughout my career, I've received a lot of fan mail, and I've always tried to read and answer every letter. When I got home from Beijing, I received one from two women who were very angry I was going on *Dancing with the Stars*. They pointed out that I was a professional athlete, not a professional dancer, and they said I was going to be dancing with has-beens. Their letter bashed everything about the show. Above all else, I'll never forget the last sentence, which predicted I was going to get hurt and never play volleyball again. And don't think that letter didn't pop into my head when I ruptured my Achilles.

After I got hurt, I was barraged with get-well cards, as well as all sorts of designs of crutches and wheelchairs. A lot of people wrote and said that they'd never watched the show before, that they'd only tuned in because of me, and now that I was no longer a contestant, they wouldn't watch it anymore. I'm saving those cards and letters as ammunition, when I approach the producers of *Dancing with the Stars* in the future and ask, "May I please come back on the show?" And I got a lot of letters from people, too, who'd torn their Achilles tendons, and assured me that I'd be back, playing beach volleyball and dancing up a storm, no problem, in a year or so.

I've never feared that my Achilles tendon injury would be career ending, but even if it were to turn out that way, I'd be okay with it. There are so many other things I'd like to do in life, like coach, for example. I'd be fine with stepping away from competition. My goal is, and always has been, to win. Once I got it through my head I was talented enough to go to the Olympics, then my goal became, "Okay, I want to win a gold medal." Well, that happened in Athens in 2004. If I'd gotten hit by a bus the next day, and I'd been told I couldn't play again, I'd have said, "That's okay. I've accomplished everything I wanted to do." Even winning back-to-back gold medals was nice, but 2008 was just more icing on the cake.

After we'd won in Beijing, Dad says Kerri's mom, Marge, tried to get him to commit to my playing with Kerri in the 2012 Olympics in London. She kept prodding Dad into saying "Three-peat," but he told Marge that he just wanted to savor this moment for a while before he started thinking about the future. Dad also told her that he couldn't speak for me. I know Kerri has said that she hopes to play in 2012, that she wants to win a third Olympic gold medal and that she doesn't want to play with anybody but me. Her favorite line is this: "I've loved that girl since I was fourteen." Would I like to continue?

Yes. At the same speed as before? I don't know about the traveling and whatnot. Am I driven to win a third Olympic gold medal? No. Could I be? Yes. But is the need there? Not really.

I'm sure I'd feel different if we hadn't won in Athens and Beijing. I'm also sure I'd feel different if Mom were still around. Before she died, volleyball was my life. After her death, my life became about now. When people ask me, "Are you going to play in the 2012 Olympics?"—and believe me, not a day goes by when somebody doesn't ask—I always tell them, "I'm just worried about today. Who knows what's going to happen tomorrow?" I'm not going to live or die depending on whether I make the 2012 Olympics. If it happens, it happens. Look at what I've already accomplished!

Truthfully, if I could give back my Olympic gold medals for the chance to spend a day with my Mom, I'd do it in a heartbeat. Her death taught me a valuable lesson: Life is short and precious. You're not guaranteed tomorrow. Unfortunately, she had to die for me to learn that.

Over the years, I've made many sacrifices to win two Olympic gold medals and put together winning streaks that will never be broken, and now I want to experience life.

I want to kick back and enjoy.

I want to breathe.

I want to experience something as simple as summer.

My family never took summer vacations. Dad never took us anywhere, unless it involved volleyball. For him, it was always about volleyball, but there are other things that I wanted to do. Like my half brother Brack says, "We all love Dad, but it would be nice if we could just say, 'Hey, let's go to France and eat some croissants.'"

It's time for me to eat some croissants.

What are some of the other things I'd like to do? Spend more time with my husband. Start a family. Hang out in Hawaii. See some national parks. Go camping. Ride my bike to the beach. Get my master's degree. Become a coach. Put on volleyball clinics with Dad. Do the jive with Maks on *Dancing with the Stars*.

Of course, there are also many things I'd like to do for others. Matt and I have created the May-Treanor O'hana Foundation in an effort to support the causes closest to our hearts. *O'hana* is Hawaiian for family. We'd like to give away financial grants—or better yet, give away ourselves—to support the two areas dearest to us: children and animals. We are passionate about giving all children the chance to be successful in sports and in school. We also are interested in protecting those who cannot protect themselves, animals and the environment.

I'd also like to spend time giving back to volleyball, indoors and beach, helping kids learn the sport and the values I did. I'd like everybody to have the same emotional support I had.

I feel a responsibility to share myself, and my sport, the way so many of Misty's Misfits have done for me over the years, and continue to do.

Most important, though, my biggest goal for the future is motherhood. I'll tell you right now, becoming a mother would rank as my greatest accomplishment of all.

## 23

---

# PRECIOUS GIFTS

There's a lot of responsibility that goes along with being an Olympic gold medalist.

Several months after winning my first, when I was finally able to reflect on what I'd accomplished in Athens, I had a major awakening. It became very clear to me, from the cities I'd visited, the tournaments I'd played in, and the people I'd come in contact with, that there was a power in an Olympic gold medal.

It was strong.

It was special.

It was genuine.

It was magical.

Once I came to this realization, my perspective as an Olympic gold medalist forever changed. No longer did it signify winning. No longer did it belong only to me. The Olympic gold medal became much more valuable, and it took on a deeper meaning when I shared it with others. I discovered that when I gave it to other people, especially those facing difficult challenges in life, it motivated and inspired them. It gave them joy and hope. In the process, I realized it made me feel better than the day I stood on the medals podium in Athens and Beijing.

I realized that, with the help of Olympic gold medals, I could change lives.

From that moment on, I embarked on a new journey through volleyball and life, traveling an important and intimate road that continues to make me a better human being.

The Olympic gold medals have connected me to many wonderful people. Like the kids who've attended the Special Olympics luncheons I've hosted at the Cincinnati AVP tour stop. Like the teenager who was battling a life-threatening illness and spent the day with me in Southern California, thanks to the Make-A-Wish Foundation. Like the athletes on the 2008 U.S. Paralympic Sitting Volleyball Team, who taught me how to play the game the way they do—crab crawling on the floor, scooting around with your hands—then kicked my butt. And, oh, my butt hurt so much.

Like Steve Lewis, whose daughter Robin was my Ichiban teammate. Years later, he developed liver cancer, and his family and friends organized an event to help inspire him to keep fighting. I brought along the Olympic gold medal I'd won in Athens. When I slipped the medal around his neck, he just beamed. It brought tears to our eyes.

My two Olympic gold medals have taught me we are all tied together on this planet, that each of our lives somehow affects others. They've taught me we constantly are touching others and constantly are being touched by others. They've taught me we don't live singular, isolated lives. If I can influence one person, then I've done my job. If I can be a mentor, a confidante, or a shoulder to lean on, then I'll feel complete. I don't want to be known only as Misty May, the two-time Olympic gold medalist volleyball player. No, I'd rather people feel they can call me their friend.

One of the best things about professional beach volleyball is that fans can come up to us any time they want. If I'm just coming off the court after a match and somebody wants an autograph, I can give it to them, or I can say, "I'm going to be doing a signing over at the booth, if you want to meet me there in ten minutes." Heck, I've even snapped myself with fans with my own cell phone camera, then emailed them the photos. You'll never find me hiding out in the players' tent. I'll be sitting in the stands, in the middle of all the fun. I like interacting, having a good time, meeting new people.

I'll always remember a trip I took to Honolulu, Hawaii, a few months after Beijing. I met the commander of the Pacific Fleet, and I gave an impromptu motivational speech to the entire group. I noticed all these military guys getting all bug-eyed about my new Olympic gold medal. So I said, "Do you want to hold it?" They all started posing with it and taking pictures like a bunch of little kids. It made me giggle. Then, I asked, "Do you want to put it on?" And they said, "Oh, yeah!" When they put it around their necks, they all said the same thing: "This is heavy!"

Let me introduce you to some of the special people I've met, thanks to the power of Olympic gold medals.

In August 2005, Amber Peters, a talented twelve-year-old volleyball player from Loveland, Ohio, was involved in a horrific car accident and suffered a major brain injury. She was placed in a medically induced coma for three weeks. Doctors told her parents she might not make it. While she was fighting for her life, somebody emailed me and shared Amber's story. On September 14, I logged on to Amber's Care Page on the Internet, and I wrote her a message of hope and support.

After that, I'd check in on Amber through her Care Page, and I'd leave her more messages in hopes of cheering her on. Then, one day, the Internet just wasn't enough for me. I thought, "Why don't I go visit her?" In February 2006, I flew in from Florida to visit Amber for a day, and the Peters family picked me up at the Cincinnati airport. I went to their house, and Amber showed me her room, where she'd put up an autographed poster I'd sent her, along with some of my wristbands and headbands. Her parents had hung it to help motivate her, because she'd had to relearn to walk, talk, eat, everything.

Since that visit, my relationship with Amber and her family has grown immeasurably. We exchange Christmas cards and presents (they like to buy me toys for my dogs Gruden and Boogie). When the AVP tour stops in Cincinnati and Louisville. I include them in all the AVP functions, supply them with VIP tickets and passes, the whole nine yards. They always spend the weekend with me and Dad. One year, I asked Amber to come to the pre-AVP dinner, and I introduced her to the other pro beach players and snapped her picture with them. As I was about to take a picture of her with Holly, Holly looked at me and said, in all seriousness, "Wow, Amber, your mom really looks a lot like Misty May." Then Holly did a double take and realized it was indeed me.

In summer 2007, I met another talented teenage volleyball player, Jenna Pilipovich, at the AVP tournament in Cincinnati. Jenna had been diagnosed with bone cancer in December 2006. She'd had a tumor in her right lower leg, and in March 2007, she'd undergone a thirteen-hour surgery at the Mayo Clinic in Rochester, Minnesota, to save her limb. She'd endured ten months of chemotherapy. Her father, George, had gotten in touch with Dan Levy, my agent. I wrote her an email. I told her I'd heard what she was going through, that I just wanted to write to tell her to hang in there, and that one day I'd love to meet her.

Jenna and I traded emails back and forth, and we texted and phoned each other, and now we've got a nice friendship going. She calls me her big sister. Jenna and I, along with her family, have spent time together at the AVP events in Cincinnati and Louisville.

In late August 2008, shortly after we'd lost in the finals of the Cincinnati AVP event to E.Y. and Nicole, stopping our record-setting victory streak at 112 matches, Jenna and I did an interview about our friendship with a local television station. Jenna felt bad about agreeing to the story, as if she were imposing on me after the loss. I assured her I wasn't fazed by the end of the streak, and I told the TV reporter, "It's a tough loss, but look at what Jenna's done. This is not a big deal. What Jenna's done is so much bigger." I kept trying to impress upon Jenna and the TV reporter, "Hey, let's look at the big picture. It's just volleyball. It's just a sport. Jenna has battled cancer. She's a survivor. Let's not forget that there are so many bigger things in life."

Like the moment that occurred three weeks later. After two years of surgeries, chemotherapy, wheelchairs, and crutches, Jenna stepped back onto the volleyball court at Mount Notre Dame High School's "Ace Out Cancer" game on September 18. Although she had yet to be cleared to run or jump, Coach Joe Burke put her in to serve a point against Ursuline Academy. The gym erupted. What she said afterward still gives me strength: "Stepping onto the court again was like shoving it back in cancer's face, saying, 'Look, I beat you. I'm done with you. I've got my life to live now.' Cancer's put life in a whole new perspective for me, and I now know I can do anything."

The first time I met Jenna, I brought along my Olympic gold medal. I hung it around her neck. I told her about having just put it around the necks of several Special Olympians, a group I've devoted time to at the Cincinnati AVP stop. I told her that one of the Special Olympics kids happened to make a black mark on the medal with a Sharpie pen and that some of the adults were freaking out about it. It was not a big deal to me. I told Jenna, "Whatever. It doesn't matter." I explained that the more people it touched, and the more people who touched it, why, the more likely it was to get a little beaten up. It was, and always will be, perfect to me. That black mark, and any other scratches or dents, only adds to its power.

In August 2006, I met Nicholas Rydzynski, who was just four at the time, but he made quite a big impression on me. He was born with cerebral palsy, and he couldn't move very well, so he lived vicariously through others by watching sports on TV. When he was three and a half, his parents, Kirk and Christy, had discovered a tumor on his adrenal gland. He had stage-four neuroblastoma, and according to the doctors, only about a 30 percent chance of survival. When he was hospitalized for five or six weeks at a time while receiving treatment, he'd lie in his hospital bed and watch AVP events.

Six weeks before he died, Kirk and Christy stopped treatments because the cancer was spreading everywhere. Instead of sitting home and crying about the fact that their son was going to die, they decided to give Nicholas something they called his "Best Days Ever Tour." Every day, Kirk and Christy would take off in the morning, or in the afternoon, and they'd do things as a family. They went to a NASCAR race. They went back to Buffalo, where Nicholas was born. They went to the beach. They did the things they would've wanted Nicholas to do, if he could've lived another five or ten years. In those six weeks, they packed in as much excitement as his little body could handle. The Rydzynskis were determined to send Nicholas out with a big bang.

One day, during his "Best Days Ever Tour," Nicholas and his parents were at Huntington Beach, watching the volleyball players. Christy noticed four women on the beach, and when there was a break in the action, she walked up and said, "If you come over and just give my son a high five, he's going to think you're the girls from TV. He's going to think you're Misty May and Kerri Walsh." Ironically, the group of women included Stacy Bonomi, one of Mom's former teammates and closest friends. Stacy and her buddies were flattered anybody, even a four-year-old, would mistake them for pros. After they'd high-fived Nicholas, Stacy told Christy she knew me.

"I'd like to have Misty call you, since Nicholas is such a huge fan," Stacy said.

Thirty minutes after leaving the beach, the Rydzynskis' phone was ringing.

"I hear you bumped into a friend of mine and that you have a little boy who thought I was at the beach today," I said to Christy.

I was touched that Nicholas was enamored of me. Christy suggested they all come up to Huntington Beach to watch me practice a few weeks later. When they arrived, I had a special goodie bag for Nicholas—an autographed volleyball, some Misty May posters, a bunch of wristbands and headbands. I pulled my Olympic gold medal out of my workout bag and hung it around his neck. The look on his face was priceless. Then he gave me the best gift of all—a big kiss on the cheek.

In mid-August, I invited Nicholas and his family to the AVP Manhattan Beach tournament. Dad and I made sure the Rydzynskis had tickets, VIP passes to the sponsors tent, and up-front parking. We all had a blast that weekend. I just loved hanging out with Nick.

Three weeks later, on September 11, Nicholas died. I called the Rydzynskis to offer my condolences and to tell them what an honor it was to have met their son. I told them he really touched my life. He couldn't walk, he couldn't talk, but he was very, very smart. He never got upset about anything ever, he just tried his hardest. He was just a wonderful, inspirational little boy.

When they were at Huntington Beach, watching our practice, I remember seeing his parents hold him underneath his armpits and let his little feet dangle on the ground. He scissor kicked them, trying hard to walk. I have a degree in kinesiology, the study of the body's movement. I just stood there in complete amazement. I could see how hard it was for him to coordinate those muscles to do those little things. If that doesn't inspire you to take what you have been given in life and do the very best you can with it, then nothing will.

The Rydzynskis were able to bury Nicholas with his favorite things, things that were his and his alone. They placed the autographed volleyball I'd given him in his casket, along with my wristbands and headbands. They also put in videotapes of my AVP tournaments, the ones where I'd given him shout-outs during the broadcasts. And they slipped in his favorite poster of me, too. Sweet dreams, Nicholas. On the poster, I'd written the sentiment that I've always lived by, words that always have guided me, and will continue to guide me, on my journey through volleyball and life: "Dream in Gold!"

Amber, Jenna, Nicholas, the Special Olympians, and all of the other special people that I've met, thanks to my two Olympic gold medals, fill my heart and feed my soul. They've inspired me, and they'll continue to inspire me. They've taught me the most important life lesson of all: Olympic gold medals aren't about the awards; instead, they're all about the rewards. I want to spend the rest of my time on earth experiencing the gifts of my Olympic gold medals, connecting and building relationships with others, and sharing and expanding upon their strength, power, beauty, and majesty. I want to dream in gold in this new and most important phase of my journey through life and volleyball.

# Acknowledgments

This book would not have been possible without the wisdom, insights, memories, inspiration, dedication, commitment, love, support, patience, and sense of humor of a team of people.

There are no misfits in this bunch, just an enormous, devoted crew of family, friends, and colleagues who were as determined as we were to produce a book of which we all could be proud.

Our thanks to Misty's agent Dan Levy of Wasserman Media Group and his assistant Marissa Nilon, who brought us together, always had our best interests at heart, and never stopped offering to lend helping hands. Thanks, too, to Farley Chase of the Waxman Literary Agency, who buttoned up our collaboration agreement and helped us navigate the publishing waters. A big thank-you as well to Brant Rumble and Anna deVries of Scribner, who provided direction and guidance every step of the way. We appreciate your passion, and especially your vision, for the project, one and all.

When it comes to dreaming in gold, Misty wouldn't have been able to attempt to do that if not for the love and commitment of so many people—in the gym, on the sand, in the operating and treatment rooms, on the bench, in the living room, in the classroom—and for that, she is, and always will be, extremely grateful. Misty's life has been blessed, and her time on earth has been truly golden. As her father Butch always says, "It takes a small village to raise a child." Misty always has been cognizant of the tremendous effort of all of those people who've nurtured and supported her every step along the way, and she is so happy to have grown up in the village she did. Their strength allows her to soar, and what they've done, and continue to do, for Misty is priceless.

At times, with the dozens and dozens of characters who've touched her life, Misty kiddingly says she feels as if she's living in a circus, and quite honestly, when reaching out for stories, anecdotes, facts, and remembrances for this book project, the number of people who stepped up to the plate to help out was seemingly endless. It certainly resembled that famous circus gag—the steady, nonstop stream of clowns filing out of a Volkswagen Beetle.

Thanks to Misty's family, friends, extended Muscle Beach Family, and of course, Misty's Misfits, who spent hours and hours sharing stories: Butch May, Brack May, Scott May, Jim Steele, Gail Gaydos, Eileen Clancy McClintock, Betty Ann Grubb, Edward Grubb, Gen Vanek, Bonnie Wong, Helen Terleckyj, Stacy Bonomi, E.T., Sandra Golden, Mina Dods, Bobby Barber, Ernie Suwara, Jim Oppliger, Toni Bowermaster, and Ann Davenport.

Thanks to Misty's teammates and coaches, who recounted hours and hours of anecdotes: Kerri Walsh, Holly McPeak, Dane Selznick, Troy Tanner, Nicole Branagh, Elaine Youngs, Mike Rangel, Debbie Green, Brian Gimmillaro, Jessica Alvarado-Brannan, Brandy Barratt Kosty, Kristy Kierulff, Robert Puscus, Tom Pestolesi, Mollie Kavanagh, Roger Goodwin, Lee Maes, Jen Hecker, Jen Pavley, Christi Phillips, Dan Glenn, Melissa Schutz, Elsa Binder, Alice Chambers Sanchez, and Maks Chmerkovskiy.

Thanks to Misty's healers and personal trainers for working so hard to make her the best she can be, then taking the time to put their magic into words: Dr. Bill Schobert, Gail Wetzler, Paige and Dan Rawson, Matt Stresak, Kelly Woods, David Bradley, Eddie Winslow, Miriam Richter, and Anya Tronson.

We appreciate the time volleyball icons Karch Kiraly and Kathy Gregory spent on this project, and the care they took in speaking about Misty, her growth and development as a player, her impact on the game, and her place in history. Thank you for all you have given to volleyball and all you gave to this book. You continue to inspire Misty every single day.

We relied on Misty's NBC Olympics "historians" David Neal, Rob Hyland, and Lyndsay Iorio for being our behind-the-scenes eyes and ears at the 2004 Athens and 2008 Beijing Games. Thank you for your personal remembrances, as well as the piles of DVDs of all of Misty's Olympic matches. Hopefully, you, and your cameras, finally have dried out from Beijing's monsoon-drenched, gold medal final.

We appreciated those who helped in researching the book: Doug Beal and Takuya (Tak) Naito of USA Volleyball, Roger Kirk of Long Beach State, Bruce Smith of Santa Monica College, Kay Crooks of the All England Lawn Tennis and Croquet Club, and Tommy Thall and Guy Hansen of the Myrtle Beach Pelicans. We are indebted to those who transcribed so many digital interviews that we've lost count: Kay Rowland of Word Power and her assistants Cheryl Robertson and Gretchen Rapp Sakkinen. Our computer guru, Steve Cole, and our digital recording expert, Curt Warren, were lifesavers as well.

We are eternally grateful to Misty's Olympic Gold Medal Gifts: Diane and Amber Peters, Christy and Nicholas Rydzynski, and Jenna Pilipovich. We also want to thank Mario Cicchinelli, who helps facilitate my annual get-togethers with Special Olympics athletes at the Mason, Ohio AVP event. You've taught us so much about faith, fortitude, perseverance, selflessness, and grace.

A very special thanks to Jill's dear friend Julie Ward, our relentless managing editor on the project, who went above and beyond, both personally and professionally. She always was game, from the first read to the last. Not to mention up for attending three Broadway shows in twenty-four hours to add some much-needed distraction before crunch time!

Also, thanks to Jill's dear friend Lisa Fryman, whose moral support was as vital to the project as her early read of the manuscript. She's a Swimming Mom in Lexington, Kentucky, but she dug deep down to her Southern California roots and got enormously energized about Misty and beach volleyball. Jill's dear friends Denelle Smalley and her mother Linda, who have lived and breathed volleyball in Manhattan Beach, California, and knew many of Misty's cast of characters, also were kind enough to give the book early reads and provide important feedback. Denelle, thank you for arming Jill with a library of volleyball books, teaching her about the game (especially the role of a libero), and most of all, sharing her love for Fenway and presenting her with an unexpected gift named Lexi. (Thanks to you, she dreams in golden retriever and German shepherd.)

A big shout-out to Jill's Team, especially Cara Regas Haughey, Anna Renderer, Debbie See, Bill Lieber, and Bob Green. You always listened, and without fail, you always provided comic and stress relief.

Above all, the authors would like to thank our husbands, Matt Treanor and Jim Steeg, who are the wind beneath our wings. You were forced to do without us on countless days and nights, forced to share us for a year and a half with this book project, but you never once complained, you only encouraged, which enabled us to remain focused, fresh, passionate, and pointed forward. Your undying love and support provided constant inspiration. We also wish to give pats to the tummies of our beloved dogs, Gruden and Boogie, and Fenway and Lexi, who patiently slept at our feet during our writing, editing, and interview sessions. Their loyalty and unconditional love also kept us going! And last, but certainly not least, a very special thank-you to our parents, Butch and Barbara, and Bill and Paula, for always believing in us, for always driving us to be our best, for always encouraging us to be pioneers in our fields, for always inspiring us to dream in gold, in each and every aspect of our lives.

Thank you all from the bottom of our hearts!

Love,
Misty and Jill